Legislative Politics In New York State

Alan G. Hevesi

The Praeger Special Studies program—utilizing the most modern and efficient book production techniques and a selective worldwide distribution network—makes available to the academic, government, and business communities significant, timely research in U.S. and international economic, social, and political development.

Legislative Politics In New York State
A Comparative Analysis

PRAEGER SPECIAL STUDIES IN U.S. ECONOMIC, SOCIAL, AND POLITICAL ISSUES

Praeger Publishers   New York   Washington   London

Library of Congress Cataloging in Publication Data

Hevesi, Alan G
    Legislative politics in New York State.

    (Praeger special studies in U.S. economic, social,
and political issues)
    Bibliography: p.
    Includes index.
    1. New York (State). Legislature.   2. New York
(State)—Politics and government—1951-   I. Title.
JK3467 1975.H48   328.747   74-6864
ISBN 0-275-05520-5

PRAEGER PUBLISHERS
111 Fourth Avenue, New York, N.Y. 10003, U.S.A.
5, Cromwell Place, London SW7 2JL, England

Published in the United States of America in 1975
by Praeger Publishers, Inc.

Printed in the United States of America

Page

v

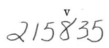

One of the most vital congressional battles of the early 1970s centered around President Richard Nixon's proposals to share federal revenues with America's state and local governments. His original suggestion was that some $16 billion be turned over to these governments, although only about one-third of that total would have represented new money to the recipients. Although modified, revenue sharing was passed into law by the Congress in late 1972. The president was, in this manner, responding to the escalating series of fiscal crises that were facing not only major urban centers but also many local and state governments. The president intended that the funds in question be entrusted to the governments of the states for distribution by them according to needs as they, the states, determined.

Clearly, these revenue-sharing proposals were predicated on the assumption that the states were sufficiently well-organized, experienced, and wise to spend the new revenues in a responsible and effective manner. However, many observers of state government do not share this view. This opposite attitude was clearly reflected in the decision made in 1971 by Congressman Wilbur Mills, chairman of the House Ways and Means Committee, to block the president's plan and substitute for it one of his own which would have bypassed state governments and would have fed federal funds directly to the crisis-ridden major cities. Apparently, Mills had reservations about the ability or the willingness of the state governments to apply the new funds toward the most severe of the problem areas—the large cities. The final legislation reflected Mills's concern.

The question of the ability of the states to govern effectively has been open to debate throughout our history, but most particularly during the last generation, a period in which our municipalities have, for fiscal reasons primarily, become increasingly unable to provide adequate services to their residents. The Citizens Conference on State Legislatures, a foundation-funded private research organization which studied American state legislatures, issued a preliminary report in February 1971, ranking in numerical order the legislatures of the 50 states, based on an assessment by the Citizens Conference of the quality of their performance (New York ranked second behind California). The authors of the report noted:

> State legislatures are heavily involved in making state policy. It seems fairly obvious that, by and large, they have not been doing their job satisfactorily. The

evidence is in the many crises that beset American society. The fact that few people think of the state as a real source of answers to their problems presents further evidence that the state government is a gray area in the minds of most Americans.[1]

Writing in The New York Times, Piers Von Simson, a British attorney who spent a year studying the American political system at the Center for the Study of Democratic Institutions at Santa Barbara, California, went considerably further:

> The states, as presently constituted, are inefficient and corrupt, have long outlived their original purpose, do not correspond to any actual economic or social interest, and no longer inspire either public involvement or public confidence. The continued validity of the states as units of organization and representation is open to serious challenge.
> The states suffer from weak executives, fragmented and obsolete fiscal procedures, badly staffed and malapportioned legislatures, poorly administered and politically selected judiciaries, and constitutions which severely restrict their ability to meet and respond to the demands made on modern government.[2]

While Von Simson's observations regarding the widespread lack of public confidence in the governmental institutions of our states and in the functional adequacy of our current forms of local government are substantially accurate, they fail to take into account that our constitutional system endows both enormous responsibilities and great power upon our states to determine for better or worse the quality of life in our nation.

According to the Citizens Conference on State Legislatures: "Federal policies succeed or fail largely on the basis of state action or inaction. In fact, there is hardly an issue of public life that is not affected by what the states do or don't do."[3]

Herbert Jacob and Kenneth Vines, authors of one of the standard texts on state politics, have noted:

> In most other countries, political affairs are concentrated at the national capital. In the United States, most political decisions are made outside of Washington—in the Albanys, Columbias, and Sacramentos which house their state's government.
> The fate of most domestic programs and policies is settled in state capitals. Most of them are supervised in

whole or in part by state governments. Even when the program is a national one, states must often decide whether to participate or what local policies to adopt for administering the program. Education, public health, regulation of businesses and professions, and policing are functions that are primarily under the control of state governments and their subdivisions. Most decisions with respect to such programs are made in the states.[4]

Commenting on what the states are empowered to do in our federal system, Harvey Mansfield has written:

They can raise and spend their own funds, though they are no longer self-sufficient financially. Subject to the Fourteenth Amendment, the Federal Voting Rights Act of 1965, and similar restraints, they conduct both federal and state elections and provide most of the legal controls over parties and elections. They enact and en-force the main bodies of civil and criminal law. Subject to desegregation requirements, they control the public education systems. They license occupations, charter corporations, and regulate utilities, insurance, and other businesses. They establish, help, support, and regulate the counties, municipalities, and other political subdivi-sions. . . .

Every local unit traces its legal existence and powers to state enactments. State constitutions, laws, and regulations not only establish local governments, but also place limits, furnish aid, and provide super-vision in a great variety of forms. Municipal charters and local taxing and borrowing powers tend to be even more specific and limited. Many local administrative actions are subject to state approval or audit. State legislatures intervene in county and municipal affairs by means of special enactments or restraining acts. When local officials complain of overcentralization as they have for the past half century, they have their state capitals in mind.[5]

The question of what goes on in the states and whether or not state governments are capable of properly governing in the public interest is of crucial importance to those who are concerned with the growingly troublesome problems confronting America. While it would be natural to expect that the interest of political scientists should be focused on the institutions of national government, recently it has become increasingly necessary for them to concentrate their efforts upon the assessment of the nature of the state politics in order to determine whether answers may be found to our critical needs. Since the offices of the governor and the state legislature are the two centers of power that exert the greatest influence upon the destinies of society in each state, it makes good sense to devote special attention to the study of these important institutions.

Accordingly, the present study will focus upon one of these institutions, the New York State legislature, with a view toward determining whether or not it can answer the challenges thrust at it by the demands of the people of New York. The primary aim is to ascertain the distribution and proportional weight of decision-making power. Consequently, this study will focus upon the New York legislative system itself and the participants in that system who influence its character and who hope to control it for their own purposes. The leading participants are the governor, the elected lawmakers, and most particularly the legislative leaders (those legislators elected by their peers to serve as party leaders in the Assembly and the Senate). Additionally, the impact of such other participants in the legislative process as lobby groups, the political party organizations, the judiciary, and the press will be evaluated.

In its scope, the study will be limited to the period of the last 20 years (1954-74). The year 1954 was a pivotal year in which a Democratic governor was elected, replacing a Republican, and a new Senate Majority Leader was chosen. During this 20-year period, both major political parties controlled the governorship and each house of the legislature, at different times, although, for reasons to be discussed subsequently, the Democrat's control of each of these institutions was relatively shortlived.

The following examination of the lawmaking process of the governmental entity that, until the late 1960s, was the most populous state in the nation, should permit the development of certain findings of general validity regarding the ability of states, as constituted today, to cope with their relentlessly growing new responsibilities. If New York State, certainly one of the richest and most powerful in the nation, cannot deal adequately with the tremendous problems of urban and suburban life, then the question may arise whether any other state can adequately face up to its responsibilities. Few states have been as richly endowed as New York with natural resources, a diversified and informed population, and a quality of leadership that has produced many of the great men of the American past. Indeed, New York has led the way for the nation as a whole with some of the most far-reaching innovations in government and in progressive legislation and has seen many of these innovations adopted by other states and by the national government for national implementation.

Notwithstanding these achievements, it is still an open question whether New York's institutions will be capable of creatively and satisfactorily resolving the overwhelming problems that now plague its society. Even if the existing institutions are, in technical terms, of sufficient durability and strength to confront these new responsibilities, it is still possible that the political system of the state of New York has failed to develop leaders with the ability, or at least the inclination, to reach out for new and adequate answers. If either possibility turns out to be the case, incisive reforms will be required in the structure of the political system or of the governmental institutions or of both. If such reforms prove unattainable, then maybe Von Simson's radical demand for entirely new forms of regional government and the abolishment of state governments will become the long-sought method of resolving America's domestic crises.

This study is divided into two parts. Part I deals with the internal decision-making process in the New York legislature. Emphasis is placed on the centers of power in each house, the elected majority party leaders (the Assembly Speaker and the Senate Majority Leader or President Pro Tempore). These two officials are granted enormous powers by the formal rules, by the unwritten expectations of the members of the legislature, and by tradition, to control most legislative and political decisions in their respective houses.

Chapters 1 and 2 detail the formal rules that govern the legislature, the distribution of power, the political skills of the leaders who have served since 1954, and the general atmosphere in which power is used.

Chapter 3 then defines the relationship between the two predominant leaders and among other influential lawmakers (Minority Leaders, Assembly Majority Leader, committee chairmen) whose decisions can dramatically influence the legislation that governs most of the activities of the residents of New York State.

Part II of the study deals with the outside pressures on the legislature that affect legislative decisions. The role of the governor as a participating and sometimes leading lawmaker is examined in Chapter 4. Subsequent chapters detail the influence of the courts, political party organizations, and lobby groups on legislative decisions. Chapter 8 offers a set of conclusions regarding the nature of power in New York State and in that state's ability to cope with the enormous problems of the 1970s.

NOTES

1. Report of the Citizens Conference on State Legislatures, quoted in The New York Times, February 4, 1971, pp. 1, 70.

xiii

2. Piers Von Simson, "Do We Need the States?," The New York Times, May 1, 1971, p. 26.

3. Citizens Conference on State Legislatures, op. cit.

4. Herbert Jacob, "State Political Systems," in Politics in the American States by Herbert Jacob and Kenneth Vines (Boston: Little, Brown and Company, 1965), p. 3.

5. Harvey Mansfield, "Functions of State and Local Governments," in The 50 States and Their Local Governments, James Fisher, ed. (New York: Alfred A. Knopf, Inc., 1967), pp. 106-108.

LEGISLATIVE LEADERS IN NEW YORK
STATE SINCE 1955

Governor

Averell Harriman (D) 1955-58
Nelson Rockefeller (R) 1959-73
Malcolm Wilson (R) 1974
Hugh Cary (D) 1975-

Assembly Speaker

Oswald Heck (R) 1937-59
Joseph Carlino (R) 1959-64
Anthony Travia (D) 1965-68
Perry Duryea (R) 1969-

Majority Leader

Assembly:
Lee Mailler (R) 1947-54
Joseph Carlino (R) 1955-59
Charles Schoeneck (R) 1959-60
George Ingalls (R) 1961-64
Moses Weinstein (D) 1965-68
John Kingston (R) 1969-

Senate:
Walter Mahoney (R) 1954-64
Joseph Zaretzki (D) 1965
Earl Brydges (R) 1966-72
Warren Anderson (R) 1973-

Minority Leader

Assembly:
Eugene Bannigan (D) 1953-58
Anthony Travia (D) 1959-64
George Ingalls (R) 1965
Perry Duryea (R) 1966-68
Stanley Steingut (D) 1969-

Senate:
Francis Mahoney (D) 1953-56
Joseph Zaretzki (D) 1957-64
Earl Brydges (R) 1965
Joseph Zaretzki (D) 1966-74

Note: The Assembly Speaker, Assembly Minority Leader, Senate Majority Leader, and Senate Minority Leader are elected to their posts by their legislative colleagues. The Assembly Majority Leader is appointed to his post by the Speaker.

I

THE LEGISLATURE: INTERNAL POLITICS AND LEGISLATIVE LEADERSHIP

1

POWER AND LEADERSHIP:
THE FORMAL RULES

The general institutional structures of the 50 American state legislatures are rather similar. All legislatures have presiding officers, party organizations, and committee systems. However, similarity in general form does not necessarily mean similarity in the distribution of power. Closer examination is required to establish which actors in the legislative subsystem are most influential in determining legislative outcomes.

As a matter of fact, there are several patterns of power in the American state legislatures. Individuals with the same titles may have significantly different resources of power and even different responsibilities. John Wahlke, one of the foremost experts on legislative politics, has noted "a bewildering variety of leadership structures among the fifty states."[1]

The fact is that political party organization in an American legislative body is a crucial element in the operation of that institution. Therefore, one must focus upon party life in the legislatures to come to an understanding of how they work. What has not been given sufficient attention by scholars in the field—and what is the focus of Part I of this study of the New York legislature—is the position of elected party leaders. The fact that the elected head of the majority party in every lower house of every American state legislature almost automatically becomes the Speaker of the House, and that the President Pro Tempore of every Senate is chosen by the majority party membership in the upper house, indicates the significance of party leadership in legislative decision making.

Since, in most states, the Speaker and President Pro Tempore (or Majority Leader) are granted very substantial and sometimes extraordinary powers to dominate the legislative process in their respective houses, greater scrutiny into the nature of party leadership in the states is required.

3

LEADERSHIP POWERS
IN AMERICAN STATE LEGISLATURES

The formal rules of a legislative body provide the basic regulations regarding the distribution of power. The roots of the power of party leaders and other legislative officers lie in these rules. In assessing the formal rules (found in constitutional provisions, statutes, or rules adopted by legislatures), however, scholars have disagreed about their significance.

For example, William Keefe and Morris Ogul believe that the position of the majority party leaders in the state houses is, in general, very strong because ". . . there has been no counterpart in the states to the 1910 revolution in the House of Representatives. Ties between the Speaker and the committee system . . . are firm in the states—thus helping to centralize decision making."[2]

Examining the role of Speakers in the lower house of the state legislatures, Keefe and Ogul have found that in all but a few states, the Speaker controls appointments of committee members and chairmen, appoints all special committees, is an ex officio member of all committees, is a member of the Rules Committee which generally serves to screen and regulate the flow of legislation to the floor, assigns bills to committee, and so on. These are substantial powers, and Keefe and Ogul make a strong case for the notion that the formal rules thus grant legislative leaders quite substantial, and sometimes enormous, resources to control legislative results.

Malcolm Jewell, in his important study of American state legislatures The State Legislature: Politics and Practice, makes the same argument:

> The Speaker of the lower branch is clearly the most powerful figure in that branch. . . .
> In the thirteen states where the members of the Senate elect their own presiding officer, he usually has power comparable to those of the Speaker of the House. Where the lieutenant governor presides, he frequently must share power with an elected President Pro Tempore with a committee of Senate leaders. . . .
> In states with a strong two-party system, the choice of minority members is normally delegated to the minority leadership. . . . In most states the legislative leaders who choose committee members have much greater authority than is true in the Congress. Seniority is likely to have some influence over the choice, but it is much less important than in the Congress. . . .

The importance of leadership control over committee assignments is magnified by the fact that the Speaker in forty-five states and the presiding officer of the Senate in forty-two states assign bills to committee, and in many cases can assign bills arbitrarily, unbound by jurisdictional rules.

The presiding officer of a state legislature has greater opportunity for arbitrary action than would be possible in Congress because his actions are less publicized, because his party or faction has complete dominance, and because rank and file members are usually ignorant of the rules.[3]

While agreeing that significant formal powers are granted to party leaders in state legislatures, Wahlke refuses to accept the conclusion that this circumstance automatically grants to these leaders greater influence over legislative decisions than is enjoyed, for example, by congressional party leaders who are granted fewer powers by the formal rules of Congress.

But few Speakers in any of these cases wield the kind of unfettered influence that led some Speakers of the United States House of Representatives to be called "boss" and "czar." Few really make appointments to committees except within the traditional bounds of members' rights and titles to assignments; in only a few houses do they have significant discretion to assign bills arbitrarily to one committee instead of another; they can use the power of recognition to steer debates in directions they wish, only in the fashion generally tolerated by their members [emphasis added]. . . .

Whereas in Congress the informal structure of party leadership provides much of the animating force behind legislative decisions made by formal leadership, party leadership in most state legislatures tends to be much more fluid and less influential.[4]

Examination of the New York legislature seems to indicate that the degree of discretion in the wielding of the leaders' formal powers is, indeed, greatly dependent on the general atmosphere of the legislature and upon the tolerance of the membership. The formal powers granted by law and rules form only the framework of the actual power relations. In practice, the leaders know very well how far they can go in the exercise of their formal powers and usually stop on the threshold of conflict with the majority of members.

The essential difference between the views of Jewell and Wahlke does not center around the question of whether the leaders in the Congress or the leaders of statehouses exercise greater power over their respective legislative systems. The meaningful difference is that Jewell attributes greater significance to the weight of the formal powers of leaders, Wahlke to the restraining influence of the limits of "toleration" on the part of the membership as a whole. The realities of life in the New York legislature appear to indicate that the two opinions, which appear contradictory, are not mutually exclusive and that, in practice, the two factors can be mutually reinforcing. This is true because most New York legislators generally "tolerate" and even expect the application of strong leadership, and these expectations thus reinforce the assertion of leadership prerogatives. This chapter will examine the formal powers vested in the legislative leaders in New York and the reaction of some legislators to the employment of the these powers. A more systematic examination of the memberhsip reaction to, and encouragement of, strong leadership is offered in the next chapter.

LEADERSHIP CONTROL OF PROCEDURES
IN THE NEW YORK LEGISLATURE

The formal constitutional and statutory powers vested in the party leaders in New York grant these leaders significant control over the procedures of their respective houses. These procedural powers given the leaders are, in general, means in their hands to influence the passage, modification, or defeat of pending bills.

The New York State Constitution is remarkably restrained in the specification of the powers of legislative offices, with the probable intent of granting autonomy in the matter to the legislature itself. Thus Article 3, Section 9, states only:

> A majority of each house shall constitute a quorum
> to do business. Each house shall determine the rules of
> its own proceedings, and be judge of the elections, returns,
> and qualifications of its own members; shall choose its
> own officers, and the Senate shall choose a temporary
> president and the Assembly shall choose a Speaker.[5]

No single word about the powers of these officers is offered. These powers are, therefore, established through rules adopted by the two houses of the legislature. Pursuant to Section 15 of the legislative law, each session must readopt (or modify) these rules every year.

Under the rules of the Assembly, the Speaker is the presiding officer of that house. He controls proceedings on the floor and rules on points of order and on all questions of procedure. He determines the order of speakers and controls the order and decorum of the proceedings. His signature is required to certify the passage of all bills and resolutions.

The Speaker also controls the administrative machinery of the Assembly, even though the clerk of the Assembly (the chief administrative officer) is elected by the members. Actually, the clerk is the designee of the Speaker and serves as his right-hand man. All other members of the Assembly staff responsible for the preparation of legislation or for the housekeeping of the entire operation are the Speaker's appointees, although most of them are permanent career people who are not replaced when the speakership changes hands.

Rule No. 1, paragraph 4b, is particularly important because it authorizes the Speaker to appoint a Majority Leader (floor leader) who directs the party strategy in floor debates and who is also a member of the Rules Committee and of all other legislative committees ex officio. (The relationship between Speakers and their Majority Leaders is discussed in Chapter 4).

The Speaker's police authority is spelled out in paragraph 7:

> He shall have general control, except as provided
> by rule or law, of the Assembly chamber, lobbies and
> rooms, and of the corridors and passages in that part
> of the Capitol assigned to the use of the Assembly. In
> case of any disturbance or disorderly conduct in the
> galleries, corridors, or passages, he shall have the power
> to order the same to be cleared and may cause any per-
> son guilty of such disturbance or disorderly conduct to
> be brought before the bar of the House. In all such cases,
> the members present may take such measures as they
> shall deem necessary to prevent a repetition of such mis-
> conduct, either by the infliction of censure or pecuniary
> penalty, as they may deem best, on the parties thus of-
> fedning.

The Speaker appoints a sergeant-at-arms and a corps of assistant sergeants-at-arms who patrol the chamber and the immediate vicinity. They are directly responsible to the Speaker. They are patronage appointees.

Since the Senate President Pro Tempore or Majority Leader is not the presiding officer of the Senate, he is given fewer procedural responsibilities than the Speaker. The sessions of the Senate are presided over by the lieutenant governor of the state. Rule V, of Section

II, of the Senate Rules details the powers of the President Pro Tempore in the following manner: "The temporary president, when acting as president, or the senator presiding upon designation of the temporary president during any such period, shall be vested with all the powers and duties conferred by these rules, and by Section 40 of the legislative law upon the president." By tradition, the Senate Majority Leader or President Pro Tempore never presides over the Senate. The honor is usually given to a senator designated by the Majority Leader both in case of the absence of the lieutenant governor and whenever the Senate is sitting as the Committee of the Whole, on which occasions the lieutenant governor may not preside.

Rule XIV, Section II, states:

> When any bill, resolution, or motion is under consideration and it appears that no senator desires to be heard further, the president shall put forth the question: Does any senator wish to be heard further? If no senator shall arise to debate, the president may declare the debate closed, except that thereafter the Minority Leader may speak once . . . and the Majority Leader may speak . . .

The party leaders in the Senate thus frequently do take part in debate, and they have the right to close debate for their own party. However, even after the debate is closed in this matter, the members still have a chance to speak. There is a provision which permits a member to rise for two minutes during the roll call to "explain his vote," and this right is often used by members to answer a point made in the closing debate by a party leader. The provisions of debate in the Senate differ from those of the Assembly mainly because the Speaker, as presiding officer of the latter house, rarely leaves the podium to join the debate on the floor.

On the surface, it may appear that the Speaker of the Assembly is in a better position to control the procedures of his house than the Senate Majority Leader. In reality, the powers of the two offices are about equal. This is because parliamentary decisions by the lieutenant governor as president of the Senate are subject to appeal, and such appeals are decided by majority vote. The President Pro Tempore, in his capacity as Majority Leader, usually can control the votes of the majority. Consequently, both officers try their best to avoid conflict and to settle their differences before it comes to an appeal. As a matter of fact, there is a telephone hookup between the president's rostrum and the Majority Leader's desk so that they may promptly discuss matters of urgency. There is, likewise, a hookup between the Speaker's rostrum and the Assembly Majority Leader's desk, but apparently these discussions revolve more around tactics than parliamentary procedure.

8

Other provisions of the Rules of Procedure specify two different methods of voting on bills and resolutions in both houses. The most frequently used method is the "short roll call." In order to save time, the presiding officer in each house has the right to order a short roll call, asking the clerk in the Assembly or the secretary of the Senate to call the roll. The official then first calls the name of the member whose name is first in the alphabet, then the names of the Majority Leader, the Minority Leader, and finally the last name in the alphabetical listing. All those members present at the opening of the session are recorded as having voted "aye" with the exception of those who raise their hands to be recorded "nay." Thus, members absent from the chamber are recorded in the affirmative. In the procedure named the "slow roll call," the name of every member is called, and each must rise in his place and vote. Slow roll calls are mandatory only in the case of formal request by legislators themselves. In 1967, electronic voting machines were installed in each house as a gesture toward "good-government" groups whose leaders felt that the machines would expedite matters. They were rarely used and were removed in 1971. Another form, the voice vote, is employed in cases of certain procedural motions, but not on matters of substantive legislation.

The removal of the voting machines resulted from a leadership determination that speed and efficiency would have to be sacrificed to the need for ensuring favorable results. A quick vote on a controversial measure (short roll call votes on noncontroversial items are relatively swift) has a certain inherent value, but not, as frequently happens, when there are not quite enough votes to pass the measure. Since a majority of the entire membership is needed in both New York houses, as it is in about two-thirds of the states, an absence is effectively a negative vote. It is not rare for the Speaker or President Pro Tempore to delay the final announcement of a roll call for 10 or 15 minutes—or even longer if necessary—while party staff scour the legislative offices, hallways, cafeteria, and rest rooms to round up needed votes. Electronic voting, an obvious reform, thwarts such practices.

Despite retreat in New York, voting machines are spreading. Already, 36 lower houses and 12 Senates have adopted them.[6] Nevertheless, many states, including the gargantuan lower house of the New Hampshire legislature with 400 members, refuse to adopt the method.

Former senator Clinton Dominick described the potentialities of these procedural powers and of the fact that the Majority Leader is also chairman of the Rules Committee in his house in these terms:

> The Majority Leader controls the calendar; he can
> st ar a bill (the placement of a star on a bill already on the

9

calendar means that it cannot be acted upon unless and until the star is removed; starring a bill is the exclusive prerogative of its sponsor and of the leader). He can also "lay aside" a bill, which means temporary postponement of action. Thus he can determine when controversial bills will come up for debate. He also decides whether unanimous consent motions are, or are not, in order. (Such motions are usually aimed at the interruption of the debate for the purpose of raising a subject matter that is not strictly related to the business pending before the House.) He can even hold secret Saturday and Sunday meetings to "age" bills he supports. (Under the Constitution, a bill must age, that is, sit on the desk of the legislators for three days before it can come up for a final vote.)[7]

An assemblyman who wished not to be identified recalled, for example, that on the last night of the 1967 session a bill to outlaw topless waitresses was due for debate on the floor. The last days of a session are often chaotic in the attempt to finish a mass of legislative work. Sometimes a mimeographed list of bills received from the Rules Committee guides the action rather than the normal printed calendar. On the evening in question, the Speaker instructed his Majority Leader to call a 15-minute recess so that the two leaders might take care of certain "technical matters." The two men then used the recess to put the topless-waitress bill on the list of legislation adopted by the Assembly. Since there was no calendar, no one knew until much later that the two leaders had usurped the power of the Assembly to pass a bill which they wanted to see enacted without delay and without lengthy debate. Even after the trick became known, there was no protest, and some oldtimers smilingly dismissed the occurrence as a matter within the "prerogatives" of the Speaker.

The bold and public assertion of leadership sometimes becomes necessary. In a profile of Speaker Anthony Travia, Richard Reeves of The New York Times recalls this scene:

> Occasionally Travia displays his power in a shout. In the rush for adjournment after a six-month session last year, he wanted Assemblyman Joseph St. Lawrence recommit a bill to committee, instead of opening a floor debate. Assemblyman St. Lawrence stood and began to speak about his bill. Travia interrupted him with a shout: "I only want to hear one word from you!"
> "Recommit," St. Lawrence said.
> "That's the word," Travia said, banging his gavel lustily.[8]

A former Democratic assemblyman tells of another kind of "prerogative" of the Speaker. This prerogative consists of a slight manipulation of the vote in order to see a bill passed. He recalls that once, after a bitter debate, a slow roll call was taken, and the final result announced was 76 ayes, 49 nays. Since 76 votes are needed for passage (a majority of the entire membership regardless of the number present), the vote was just enough for passage. When the clerk read the names of those who had voted in the negative, as is the custom, the assemblyman noticed that his name was not listed, although he had voted in the negative. He rose and said, "Mr. Speaker, I voted in the negative, but my name is not listed. Would you please have my vote recorded in the negative?" The Speaker answered, "Certainly, Mr.—Your vote is ordered recorded in the negative. The clerk will announce the final results." The clerk looked up at the Speaker and nodded. Then he read the final results: "Ayes, 76; nays, 50." The assemblyman's vote had been added to the negative tally, but not substracted from the aye vote, since this would have resulted in the bill's defeat. The assemblyman did not protest this fact.

On another occasion, again on the last day of a session, a bill passed with 76 votes, although all Democrats voted no and only 75 Republicans were in the chamber. When minority members challenged the results, Majority Leader Irving Ives told Democratic Leader Irwin Steingut that one Republican had left for home a little early, anticipating that the session would soon end. Ives told Steingut that he could object to the vote, in which case it would be invalidated, but in that case Speaker Heck would have to order the state police to track down the absent Republican somewhere in upstate New York and bring him back to the Assembly for the vote. This, of course, might take many hours, but of course the Speaker would have to keep the Assembly in session as long as necessary to pass the bill. Steingut withdrew his objection in a hurry, and the Assembly adjourned for the year without delay.[9]

In recent times, such "prerogatives" are no longer employed very often, but sometimes, in cases of very close votes, they still are. Another assemblyman told this writer that one Speaker once had the votes of four assemblymen recorded in the affirmative, although they were absent, engaged in a public hearing elsewhere. The Minority Leader did not object, realizing that the four assemblymen could have been brought into the chamber within a short time.

These examples of questionable leadership interference in the destinies of some legislation constitute a little semilegal "extra" thrown in with the very effective legitimate powers of the leaders to influence the business of lawmaking. It stands to reason that the use of such questionable methods would not be possible if the general mores prevailing in the legislative body would resist in their application. The fact is that the legislative leaders in the state of New York avail themselves only on infrequent occasions of such methods.

THE ORGANIZATION OF THE
STANDING COMMITTEES

Unlike the Congress where the rule of seniority with respect to committee chairmanships is binding (despite some recent rule changes which have the potential of watering down the absolute nature of the rule), the New York legislative leaders appoint all committee chairmen and all members of committees. This situation is not atypical, however, in the American states.

In most states, the Speaker of the lower house of the legislature is empowered to make such appointments. It is rare for formal rules to inhibit this power. There are a few cases, however, where the discretion is shared. A committee on committees in New Mexico is required to advise the Speaker. A similar committee in Alaska recommends the makeup of standing committees to the entire Assembly. In Nebraska, a committee on committees is empowered to select other committees without reference to any other institution or person. These are exceptions. New York follows the traditional model.

In American state senates, there are three methods employed for organizing committees. Half the states grant this power to the lieutenant governor in his role as Senate president. Another 10 states employ a committee on committees. Most of the rest vest the power in the President Pro Tempore or Majority Leader, and New York follows this pattern.

A crucial question is one that inquires as to the standards utilized in the choice of committee chairmen. Seniority, it seems, is simply one among several. The New Mexico Senate does have a rule stipulating that seniority be the primary factor in the choice of chairmen, and the California Senate rules provide that seniority, preference, and experience should be the bases for decisions. But these requirements are rare exceptions. Only these few states list preconditions, and most legislative rules are silent as to qualifications, leaving discretion entirely with the appointing officer.[10]

As a result, seniority must take its place along such other variables as party identification, factional loyalties, individual expertise, geographical balance, and personal relationships in the determination of who will be appointed to what. Thus, for example, rural domination of the Florida legislature dramatically minimizes opportunities for lawmakers from urban areas. Additionally, there

12

are some states in which pressure from outside the legislature influences appointments. This has been the case in California where interest groups have a very strong say in the makeup of certain committees and in Alabama where the governor has actually selected committee chairmen of committees in which he was particularly interested.

In New York, the appointment power is clearly located in the hands of the Speaker of the Assembly and the Senate Majority Leader. Rule V, Section III, of the Senate Rules states very simply and very explicitly that "he [the Majority Leader] shall appoint the chairmen and members of all committees and shall be chairman of the Committee on Rules, except when the president shall otherwise order." Rule I, paragraph 3, of the Assembly Rules applies the same procedure to the appointment of committees by the Speaker:

> After the November election and before the convening of a new Assembly, the Speaker brings out a wooden board that measures about three feet long. On it the names of the 38 standing committees are posted and the names of the old committee members are fastened with pins. The pins are easily removed. Each new member gets his own pin, but only the Speaker can move it. Occasionally an old committee name is removed and a new one pasted on. The committees are established by resolution; the appointments to them are made by the Speaker, minority members on recommendation of the Minority Leader.
>
> In both parties, the new members indicate their preferences to the leader, and he usually tries to match their interests and experiences with the vacancies created by the election. The returning members usually keep the committee assignments they held in the previous session, but not always.[11]

In the choice of the committee chairmen and members, the leader is entirely free to follow his personal preferences. He may be assumed to consider the candidates' qualifications and competence, but loyalty to the leader is, of course, a decisive consideration. Now and then, for reasons of political expediency, a candidate of less than perfect loyalty may receive some important assignment, but such appointments constitute the exception to the rule. Seniority, too, enters consideration (without obligation, but sometimes it also serves as an excuse to explain a decision made in the filling of some highly desired position). In general, the great and frequent turnover in the legislature's membership tends to reduce the importance of seniority as a criterion. The candidates' stature and popularity among the membership are other factors that the Speaker often finds worthwhile to take into consideration.

In 1965, the Democrats won control of both houses of the legislature. It took five weeks of a bitter factional fight to elect party leaders. The victors, Speaker Anthony Travia and Senate Majority Leader Joseph Zaretzki, appointed their supporters to key posts. "It should be noted that while Travia in the leadership fight received the votes of only 40 percent of his party, 67 percent of the eighteen most important committees (measured in terms of the 1966 workload) were given to his supporters, and 67 percent of the eighteen least important committees went to Steingut supporters."[12] Assemblyman Stanley Steingut was Travia's rival in the leadership fight. The supporters of the Steingut faction expected to be bypassed but, as it turned out, they had no cause for real complaint. It could have been a lot worse. For example, Travia appointed John Satriale of the Bronx as chairman of the Ways and Means Committee and Max Turshen of Brooklyn as chairman of the Judiciary Committee. Besides the Rules Committee, these committees are the most highly desired ones. Both Satriale and Turshen had supported Steingut. But Travia, attempting to unify the party, decided to recognize the seniority of both men on their respective committees, where both had served as ranking minority members under the Republicans.[13]

Senator Zaretzki followed the same pattern. In general, he paid heed to the rule of seniority, but in cases where seats were contested, he rewarded those who had voted for him. For example, three men had equal tenure on the Public Health Committee: Senators Ohrenstein, Kraf, and Thaler. Only the last had backed Zaretzki, and so he was appointed chairman.[14] Ohrenstein, however, had a special interest in problems of mental health, and he applied pressure on Zaretzki to create a separate Committee on Mental Hygiene. He prevailed upon a number of psychiatrists and psychologists to write to Zaretzki, clamoring for recognition of their specialty as a separate area of concern. Since he was concerned with a variety of other important health matters, Senator Thaler did not object, and so Zaretzki established the new committee.[15]

Speaker Travia used the appointment power to maximize his control over the Assembly. When Assemblyman Satriale was defeated in the 1965 primary election, Travia appointed his very close friend Harvey Lifset of Albany chairman of the Ways and Means Committee. He knew that Lifset would stand by him in any difficulty. On the other hand, Assemblyman Daniel Kelly of Manhattan, an independent, with the reputation of a maverick and the inclination to play the role of the "conscience of the legislature," was appointed chairman of the Committee on Taxation. When the matter of assigning budgets to the committees was settled by the Speaker, it turned out

14

that Lifset's committee received a budget of $275,000. Kelly, six years senior to Lifset, had to put up with a budget of $5,000.[16] "A chairman has to vote with Tony if he wants to be sure he's going to stay chairman," said one upstate legislator during a floor fight.[17]

Chairmanship appointments can be powerful weapons in a leader's arsenal. Richard Reeves of The New York Times has pointed out that 78 of 79 Democrats voted with Travia to recommit a bill to committee, thereby killing it for the 1967 session. The bill would have prohibited the forced bussing of schoolchildren for the purpose of racial integration, a method rejected by Travia. The overwhelming vote was obtained by Travia with the arduous help of most committee chairmen, despite the fact that 80 percent of the Democrats were certain that the rejection of this bill would hurt them politically. The only maverick to vote against recommitment was Frederick Schmidt of Queens, the only Democrat to run with Conservative party endorsement, who felt that he would be defeated if he stuck with his party in the killing of the measure. "Remember what happened to Schmidt," was the warning that Travia's counsel, Harold Fisher, delivered to wavering assemblymen before the bussing vote.[18] What he had in mind was the fact that ever since Schmidt had defied Travia for the first time on a tax bill in 1965, only one single bill sponsored by him managed to get out of committee (a bill that would have permitted retired policemen and firemen to serve as school-crossing guards).

On another occasion Travia's readiness to use his political muscle to maintain discipline within the membership manifested itself in this manner: Word had spread in 1966 that Travia fired Assemblyman Albert Blumenthal, a Manhattan Reform Democrat, from the chairmanship of a recently created "Democratic Advisory Committee." Travia actually never wanted to see such a committee reach the functioning state because he knew that sooner or later it would interfere with his freedom of action as Assembly leader. At first, he acquiesced in the establishment of the group, mainly because The New York Times and The New York Post strongly advocated its creation as a step toward the desired decentralization of the Democratic party. However, as soon as some of the senior members of the new committee objected to Blumenthal's appointment, Travia decided right away that the committee must be made harmless. He never fired Blumenthal nor dissolved the committee formally and officially, but as a first step he simply used his prerogative as Speaker to preside himself over the committee's meetings. Blumenthal knew what this slap in the face meant. Next day, Travia received a note from Blumenthal saying in effect, "I quit." Thereafter, little was heard of the Advisory Committee; it met less and less frequently and hardly ever produced any "advice" that may have affected the work of the Assembly.[19]

In 1963, Walter Mahoney, Senate Majority Leader, was faced with the task of appointing a new chairman to the Senate Finance Committee upon the death of Senator Austin Erwin. The leading contenders were the senior members of the committee, Earl Brydges of Niagara County and Warren Anderson of Binghamton. Mahoney chose Elisha Barrett of Suffolk County, bypassing both chief candidates. Barrett was far behind them in seniority. Mahoney was probably motivated in part by the desire to balance the distribution of influence among Republicans representing different areas of the state. Mahoney himself represented a Buffalo suburb. More important may have been, however, his desire to avoid building up the stature of a rival spokesman on behalf of western New York in the person of Senator Brydges. When Brydges succeeded Mahoney to the majority leadership in 1966, he immediately fired Barrett as finance chairman and appointed Anderson in his place. As a sop, Barrett was named vice chairman of finance, a new position, but the intention of Brydges was clear—to obtain revenge and to place, in the person of Anderson, a trusted friend into the chair of one of the most important committees of the Senate. In 1973, Anderson succeeded to the majority leadership upon Brydge's retirement.

The power to appoint committee chairmen and members greatly helps the leaders in making their own legislative desires respected and followed. Having created a committee, the leader is, more often than not, in a position to predict the legislative action the committee is likely to take. A parallel power invested in him, that of the referral of bills to committees of his choice, further strengthens his ability to determine the destinies of any given piece of proposed legislation. This is so because the leader can often choose from among two or more pertinent committees the one committee that is most likely to follow his personal desires. A classic example of the calculated use of the powers of referral was the treatment of the proposed abortion law. Assemblyman Blumenthal had been in the forefront of repeated yearly attempts to change the state's abortion law which legalized abortions only in case the life of the mother was threatened by the birth. Blumenthal's bill created a storm session after session until 1970 when a sweeping abortion repeal bill was finally passed.

When it was first introduced in 1966, Speaker Travia chose to refer the bill not to the Public Health Committee chaired by Blumenthal which was competent in terms of the bill's subject matter but to the Codes Committee, 12 of whose 15 members were Catholic. Travia himself opposed the bill personally and wished it to die in committee, which it did in 1966 and 1967. He was also motivated by the desire to spare the members of the Assembly the embarrassment and political consequences of taking sides on such a controversial measure. Travia also knew that the bill did not have the required votes anyway.

By 1968, however, liberal forces had mobilized sufficient public support for the bill to compel the holding of hearings throughout the state. Most New York newspapers blasted Travia for having bottled up the legislation, so under pressure he had to instruct the Codes chairman, Thomas LaFauci of Queens, to release the bill to the floor. After bitter debate, the roll call was to begin. However, when Blumenthal saw that the number of hands raised in opposition to the bill was overwhelming, he himself moved that the bill be recommitted to the Codes Committee. The membership was once again saved from unpleasant consequences.

In 1969, the bill was again debated on the floor and defeated in a slow roll call. By then, the oft-redrafted bill contained a number of important new grounds for legal abortion. These included situations in which the physical and mental health of the mother was substantially threatened, where pregnancy was caused by rape or incest, where the mother-to-be was under 15 years old, and where there was substantial evidence to the effect that the fetus would be physically or mentally deformed.

Until 1970, the battle had been fought each year in the Assembly. In that year it shifted to the Senate where, in March, Majority Leader Brydges announced that he would release from the Rules Committee for a vote on the floor an entirely new abortion bill, prepared and sponsored by Senator Clinton Dominick of Rockland County. This bill turned out to be much simpler and much more liberal than the Blumenthal measure. It simply provided that all abortions could be legally performed upon the consent of a doctor within the first 24 weeks of pregnancy. All previously stipulated "grounds" were swept aside.

Personally, Senator Brydges was opposed to this bill. It appears, therefore, that his idea was merely to appease and silence the supporters of the legislation, which seemed to be so sweepingly radical as to be totally unacceptable to most legislators, even to supporters of the Blumenthal bill. In fact, however, the Dominick bill was passed after bitter debate on March 18, 1970, by a vote of 31 to 26 by the Senate. Two weeks later, after an initial defeat, the bill passed the Assembly with the minimum 76 votes in favor.

For the purposes of this study, the important fact that emerges from the case history of the New York abortion law is that the individual volition of one man in a key position within the existing legislative setup can delay, over several years, the consideration and enactment of legislation desired by millions, while later the tactical maneuvering of another man in the same position of power can lead to relatively quick action on a much more radical version of the same, highly controversial measure.

THE JOINT LEGISLATIVE COMMITTEES

Both the Speaker and the Majority Leader of the Senate are authorized by the rules of each house to appoint members of their respective houses to joint legislative committees (JLCs) and to other statutory commissions (Senate Rule 5, Section 3, and Assembly Rule 1, paragraph 3). Statutory commissions, generally called temporary state commissions, are created to study specific problems, and their members are appointed by the governor from among people outside the legislature and the two leaders from among members of their houses. Their existence is limited to a certain period, at the end of which they must report and then go out of business.

The JLCs are also created for the study of specific subjects. They are composed of legislators alone. Each JLC is made up of a number of senators and a number of assemblymen. Half of the various JLCs are chaired by senators, the other half by assemblymen. They are created annually by resolution and exist from April 1 of each session to March 31 of the following year. Although composed of legislators, they have no power of decision regarding passage of legislation. They can only submit recommendations, and their proposals, put into the form of bills, must be referred to standing committees and go through the normal legislative process to be passed.

The JLCs are meant to function between sessions and, on one level, to serve as instruments through which the legislature can vie with the executive branch in the development of specialized expertise required for the preparation of important legislation. Thus, some of the JLCs have been instrumental in conducting major research projects, which greatly helped in the drafting of bills of importance such as those dealing with divorce reform, abortion, and Medicaid.

On another level, however, the JLCs are intended to serve as political vehicles at the disposal of the leadership and the JLC chairmen, through which a rather significant amount of patronage may be channeled. For example, in 1968, a total of 27 JLCs were created, and they provided jobs for at least 200 people. The quality of staff work depends on the attitudes of the JLC chairman. Some of the chairmen have recruited full-time, hard-working staffs who produce valuable research documents and legislative proposals. Other chairmen pay little attention to these staffs who, therefore, do little work, produce padded reports, and keep idlers on the payroll. Almost all of the staff appointments are political, in the sense that the employees had either worked for the chairman or one of the ranking JLC members, or else worked on other committees or on legislators' personal staffs, or are appointed in response to recommendation by political party leaders outside the legislature. This does not mean, however, that they are incompetent. Some are extremely able veteran staff people whose impact on legislation has been significant. Some of the ambitious JLC chairmen additionally call in nonpolitical technical experts to help with the work of the regular staff.

Most appointments are made by the chairman, but they must be certified by the Speaker or the President Pro Tempore. Thus, the leaders' influence extends beyond the appointment of legislators themselves and even extends over the choice of their staff members. This is another means by which the leaders can exact loyalty and discipline from the members. "The Assemblyman (or senator) interested in a joint legislative committee chairmanship is not going to do too much to alienate the appointing officer during the session."[20]

In 1965, Speaker Travia appointed Assemblyman Albert Hausbeck of Buffalo chairman of the Temporary State Commission on Water Resources Planning. In the great intraparty battle of 1965, Hausbeck's county leader, Joseph Crangle, supported Steingut against Travia. A staff person of the aforementioned commission told this writer that Crangle and Hausbeck used some of the Temporary State Commission money to hire staff in the Buffalo area and thus reward a number of party workers loyal to them. However, they failed to clear the appointments with Travia. Thereupon, Travia simply decided to let the commission die by refusing to reappoint it for the year of 1966. Its mandate and funds were transferred to the Joint Legislative Committee on Conservation chaired by Assemblyman Charles Stockmeister of Rochester, and Hausbeck was deprived of any JLC or Temporary State Commission chairmanship in 1966.

LEADERSHIP CONTROL OF MONEY

The control of funds by the leaders is another power by which they can solidify their control over the legislature. All expenditures in each house must be approved by the leader, although he may delegate this function to some legislator or staff person. This control extends over the payroll for the staff estimated to cost some $2 million a year (approximately 900 legislative posts in each house) and over all housekeeping expenses as well.[21] The latter includes the printing of bills, calendars, and all other legislative documents, the maintenance of the Capitol offices and chambers, and the purchase of equipment such as typewriters, rugs, lamps, and office materials. Most housekeeping chores are supervised by the secretary of the Senate and the clerk of the Assembly, who run large administrative operations with the help of dozens of employees.

The leaders have considerable discretion in the distribution of certain types of funds. While every legislator may receive a flat grant for the pay of clerical staff (in 1973, all senators received

$11,500 and all assemblymen received $7,500), the leaders may reward certain members with additional staff grants. These grants are in addition to the "lulus" (monies given to legislators "in lieu of expenses" for their personal costs of traveling and maintaining residence in Albany). Today each member receives a minimum lulu of $5,000, although the leaders, committee chairmen, and certain ranking minority members get additional lulus.

Staff grants, however, are distributed by the leaders in widely differing amounts to senior legislators. These are often political rewards. A committee chairman's request for additional funds may be satisfied if he proves a need and notably if he has been loyal.[22] JLC funds vary from committee to committee, and the determination of who gets what rests with the leaders. Even minority staff appointments are indirectly controlled by the Majority Leaders. The Minority Leaders usually get a lump sum to be distributed according to need. When, however, a Minority Leader needs more money for the staff of one or another senior legislator, he must approach the Majority Leader of the Speaker for help. If the help is granted, a kind of moral indebtedness arises which may compel the Minority Leader to secure some minority votes for the passage of a critical bill in which the Majority Leader or the Speaker is interested.

The leader who can dispense rewards in exchange for voting support can also withhold them in punishment of disloyalty or insufficient performance. Such punishment can cross party lines. For example, Speaker Travia, who could use a heavy hand whenever the occasion called for it, once was angry at the new Minority Leader Perry Duryea for the latter's refusal to cooperate on a governor's program bill that Travia also wanted adopted. One day during the session of 1966, Travia announced from the rostrum that from then on all members of the Assembly would receive the same supplemental flat grant of $2,500 for office and staff needs. Thus, by naming the exact amount due to each member, Travia destroyed Duryea's freedom to decide which member should receive more or less money. In this manner, the Speaker neutralized a good part of the Minority Leader's ability to influence his membership's voting proclivities.[23]

THE RULES COMMITTEES

A critical power in the legislative process is the control of the calendar. The determination as to which bill will be taken up at what point in a legislative timetable, and whether a bill will be taken up at all, is a crucial power resource. Calendar control is a function of the majority party leadership in most state legislatures. That means the majority party leaders themselves control the calendar in about three quarters of the statehouses. However, in about one quarter, the party conference or caucus (the regular meeting of the entire membership of a party in a house of the legislature) controls the flow of legislation. In Connecticut, for example, the majority party members in the Senate meet every day in caucus and discuss every bill on the calendar. Joint action is decided.

Most state legislatures employ Rules Committees to control the flow of bills, to decide which should take priority, and to generally control the legislative process. There are some modifications of this practice. The Pennsylvania House Rules Committee shapes the majority party program and drafts bills as well as controls the calendar. The California Senate Rules Committee appoints standing committees, refers bills to standing committees, appoints interim committees that are important in that state, and determines committee budgets. In the California lower house, the Rules Committee is an essential part of the patronage dispensing process.

In general, state legislative Rules Committees serve to screen bills during the hectic close of the sessions. At this most critical time, they become all powerful, deciding on the life or death of legislation. It is at this time that the majority party leaders have their greatest influence over legislation if, as is the case in New York, they control their respective Rules Committees.

In New York the rules of both houses specify that the majority party leader must serve as chairman of the Rules Committee (Senate Rule V, Section III, and Assembly Rule 1, paragraph 8).

The Rules Committee in each house is the most powerful of all legislative committees. At the beginning of a session, the presiding officer refers bills to the standing committees. No bills are referred to the Rules Committee directly, but the Majority Leader or the Speaker has the right to transfer any bill under its jurisdiction. Additionally, there is a deadline in the Assembly for the introduction of bills by individual members in unlimited numbers. After that date each member can introduce only a total of 10 more bills within the following two weeks. Thereafter, no further bills may be introduced except through the Rules Committee. Another week later the standing committees stop functioning, and all pending legislation must pass through the Rules Committee. From then on until the end of the session, the Rules Committees completely dominate the legislative work of both houses. Since relatively few bills have been finally passed or defeated at the time the standing committees cease to function, the majority of bills are processed by the Rules Committees. For example, in 1966, when the session lasted to July 5, the Assembly had passed only 24 percent of its bills and 12 percent of the Senate bills it was eventually to pass at the time the standing committees ended their work.[24]

21

Since the membership of the Rules Committees is chosen by the top leaders, the latter can completely dominate its work. Speaker Travia was proud to say, "I've never lost a vote in the Rules Committee."[25] The Assembly Rules Committee will have about 19 or 20 members in a given year, some 15 of whom are majority party members. The Senate Rules Committee will have eight or nine members, three of whom may represent the minority party. The leaders choose the members on the basis of the latter's reliability, and many chairmen of important standing committees are among them. The crucial fact is, however, that whatever the Rules Committees' composition may be, everybody knows that they are tools in the leaders' hands, used by them at will. For these committees important decisions are often made by the leader alone, even without consultation with the representatives of the majority party on the committee. During certain sessions, minority party members have never been called to meetings of the Rules Committees. Here we are again confronted with great lassitude on the part of the rank and file of legislators that permits the leaders to enhance their powers far beyond the legal limits.

As to the authority of the Rules Committees themselves, not only do they control all bills after a certain date in the session, they may also suspend the rules, limit debate, and of course control the calendar of bills. Although suspension of the rules is a rarity, it is a reserve power of significance.[26]

The Rules Committees' control over legislation covers not only major program bills, but also many hundreds of minor bills introduced by individual legislators. Over the latter category of bills, the Rules Committees and, through them, the leaders have total control. No local or private bill gets out of committee without the leader's approval. Members in good standing with the leader get their private bills reported out with great regularity by the committee; those who have been troublesome often pay the price of waiting in vain for the passage of their bills.[27] According to former Speaker Joseph Carlino, "The control of the Rules Committee over local bills is absolute; no such bill passes without the okay of Rules."[28]

THE MINORITY LEADERS

The Minority Leaders are chosen by their party conferences; they serve as the recognized spokesmen for their parties' program. They conduct the debate for their side and have the right to be heard next to the last speaker in any debate. The majority party floor leader has the last word. The Minority Leaders are ex officio members of all standing committees, JLCs, and statutory commissions.

The power and influence of the Minority Leader is based on the tradition that both the Speaker and the President Pro Tempore of the Senate appoint minority members to standing committees, JLCs and commissions alike on recommendation of the Minority Leader. The same applies to the hiring of staff. The Minority Leader receives a lump sum totaling about 15 percent of the total legislative budget allocated for staff and office costs which he distributes at his discretion.

This control of positions and of the purse strings enables the Minority Leader to exercise some measure of leadership and disciplinary authority over his party. But the means of reward or punishment at his disposal are much less significant than that of the Majority Leader. Actually the Minority Leader is faced with a more difficult task in preserving party unity and, in his case, force of personality is a more important factor than in the case of a Majority Leader.

CONCLUSIONS

The formal rules governing the operation of the New York State legislature provide the Speaker of the Assembly and the Majority Leader or President Pro Tempore of the Senate with weighty powers that enable them to dominate and control the operation of their respective houses and the outcome of legislation. Even advocates of legislative reform often come out in favor of the kind of centralization of power and responsibility in the hands of the party leaders, of which New York has become a model. A study of state legislatures by the American Political Science Association has, for example, this to say on the subject: "Equally important [as getting the fiscal committees into a pattern of behavior in which they would recognize the oversight of the executive branch as an important function] is the focusing of responsibility for legislative affairs in the temporary president of the Senate and the Speaker of the House, as has been done in New York State."[29]

In New York the leaders have formal authority to determine the composition of the entire committee system and to govern the two Rules Committees which, in turn, control both matters of procedure and the flow of legislation to the floor. They also possess the power to determine the makeup and functioning of special committees and to allocate all available financial resources. The consistent exploitation of all these instrumentalities of power usually enables these leaders to effectively influence the outcome of most legislative action in which they are interested.

In the present chapter we have dealt with only one aspect of the total picture: the apparently unfettered power of the legislative leaders. However, as has been previously indicated, the total picture has two sides, and that second side shows clearly that the extent of the leaders' ability to dominate the processes of legislation directly depends on a rather complex but very important countervailing factor, namely, the general response of the membership as a whole to the ways in which the leadership uses its powers. This overall response is, most of the time, agreeable to or at least tolerant of the quality of the existing pattern of dominance. However, no leader can long stay leader if he offends the sensibilities of the membership at least of his own party or of important segments of it.

In fact, the rank and file majority can and occasionally does criticize, defy and even reject the authority of the leaders and thereby restrains the undesired total exercise of their powers. Revolts against the behavior or actions of the leaders do occur. Occasionally these rebellions are reactions to leadership behavior. More often, however, they are aimed at particular legislative outcomes that the leaders support.

The following chapter deals with the general manifestations of membership attitudes toward the position and prerogatives of the leaders. It also looks into those characteristics of personal conduct and style that may help the leaders to improve the quality of their relationship with the members, and thereby strengthen their own position and the discipline of their parties.

NOTES

1. John C. Wahlke, "Organization and Procedure," in State Legislatures in American Politics, Alexander Heard, ed. (Englewood Cliffs, N.J.: Prentice-Hall, Inc.), p. 139.

2. William Keefe and Morris Ogul, The American Legislative Process (Englewood Cliffs, N.J.: Prentice-Hall, Inc., 1968), p. 293.

3. Malcolm Jewell, The State Legislature: Politics and Practice (New York: Random House, 1962), pp. 77, 78, 81, 82, 83.

4. Wahlke, op. cit., pp. 140-141.

5. Manual for the Use of the Legislature, prepared by John P. Lomenzo, Secretary of State (Albany, 1968), p. 38.

6. Malcolm Jewell and Samuel Paterson, The Legislative Process in the United States (New York: Random House, 1973), p. 293.

7. Former Senator Clinton Dominick, interview, February 10, 1970.

8. Richard Reeves, "The Other Half of State Government," The New York Times Magazine, April 2, 1967, p. 86.

9. Warren Moscow, Politics in the Empire State (New York: Alfred A. Knopf, Inc., 1948), p. 177.

10. For a good summary of committee appointment practices, see Keefe and Ogul, op. cit., pp. 187-188 and 196-198.

11. Stuart K. Witt, "The Legislative-Local Party Linkage in New York State," unpublished dissertation, Syracuse University, 1967, p. 155.

12. Ibid., p. 159.

13. Former Speaker Anthony Travia, interview, December 23, 1969.

14. Senator Manfred Ohrenstein, interview, December 8, 1969.

15. Ibid.

16. Reeves, op. cit., p. 88.

17. Ibid.

18. Ibid. p. 90.

19. Travia, op. cit.

20. Witt, op. cit., p. 150.

21. Reeves, op. cit., p. 88.

22. Former senator Thomas LaVerne, interview, February 2, 1970.

23. Travia, op. cit.

24. Witt, op. cit., p. 121.

25. Travia, op. cit.

26. Former senator Seymour Thaler, interview, December 13, 1969.

27. Richard A. Brown, former associate counsel to the Speaker, interview, December 3, 1969.

28. Former Speaker Joseph Carlino, interview, January 12, 1970.

29. Belle Zeller, ed., American State Legislatures, American Assembly report (New York: Thomas Crowell, Inc., 1954), p. 183.

2

**POWER AND LEADERSHIP:
THE INTANGIBILES**

In their efforts to influence legislative outcomes, some of the leaders have been markedly more successful than others, even though all of them were granted the same formal powers. This chapter attempts to identify some of the less tangible variables which can affect the ability of leaders to lead. It will examine the nature of such environmental influences on the legislative process as the aspirations and expectations of members and the resultant atmosphere in which the leader must operate. Differences in the personality traits of leaders and their skill in dealing with members of the legislature will be considered as well as the significance of leadership staffs.

MEMBERSHIP EXPECTATIONS OF THE LEADERS' BEHAVIOR

John Wahlke, Heinz Eulau, William Buchanan, and LeRoy Ferguson have studied in great detail the perceptions and attitudes of legislators in four states (California, Ohio, New Jersey, and Tennessee).[1] One important chapter of their study deals with membership expectations regarding the behavior of the officers of legislative bodies. According to Wahlke and his coauthors:

> The law and the rules tell an officer what he may or should do; for example, they tell the presiding officer of a chamber to preside, to appoint committees, to refer bills to them, and so on. They do not tell him how to do it: whom to recognize, when to brook delaying tactics and when to curb them, which of two aspirants to appoint to a committee or chairmanship, where to refer a bill if two committees' jurisdictions overlap. These are likely to be the crucial decisions.[2]

After developing categories of responses to the questions asked of members of the four legislatures and after analyzing and interpreting these responses, the authors reached this conclusion about the character of power in state legislatures:

> These expectations with regard to officers, as we shall see, are rather consistent and well structured, and they may be as much a boundary on what officers are allowed to do as are the formal rules. If so, the "power" of particular officers—chairmen, Speakers, Rules Committees—cannot be appraised apart from the system in which they find themselves. The evidence already is that legislative officers are far from free agents, that they are hedged about by commandments from the membership as to what they should and should not do if they are to perform effectively. There is substantial consensus as to how each officer shall act, which is expressed in these appraisals of their roles. The consensus determines, in Bentley's phrase, whether the Speaker is "Moses the law giver" or "Moses the registration clerk." Whether a particular speaker, or an average speaker, is more powerful, or less powerful, than the Speaker of the national House of Representatives depends upon how the respective memberships intend for this power to be exerted upon them.[3]

In the preparation of the present study, no attempt has been made systematically to question all members of the New York legislature regarding membership expectations of leadership behavior, but a sufficient number of discussions with legislators and staff experts has been conducted to produce at least an estimate of the prevailing pattern of membership views on what the leaders ought to do, and how they ought to behave to maximize the effectiveness of their leadership.

There is general consensus among those interviewed that strong centralized party leadership is a positive and desirable characteristic of the New York legislature. Members, for example, expect that the leader be judicious and restrained in his use of the available means of punishment, but in case a member is really troublesome without good cause, he definitely should be chastised. Very often an attack on the leader is felt by most members to be an attack on the leader's party or faction, and so they are likely to join in a call for punishment. A clever leader often waits for such opinions to coalesce before imposing sanctions.

In 1969, for example, Governor Rockefeller attempted to obtain the support of some Democratic assemblymen for his bill to increase the state sales tax. He was faced with a united Democratic minority led in the Assembly by Minority Leader Stanley Steingut. It was claimed that to win their votes, Rockefeller offered certain administrative appointments to two Democratic assemblymen, Charles Stockmeister of Rochester and Albert Hausbeck of Buffalo. Both men voted for the sales tax in the face of the fact that all the other Democrats held firm against it. When Steingut demanded publicly that as a punishment the two men be dropped from the committees of which they were members, the Republican Speaker refused to comply. The Democrats continued to clamor for punishment, but in vain. Assemblyman Albert Blumenthal pointed out, for example, that the two assemblymen were guilty not only of turning against their own party, apparently in the expectation of material gain, but also of the even more serious impropriety of having broken their pledge given in conference to stand with their party.[4]

In practice, however, actual punishments for disloyal behavior are infrequently imposed. One single instance of punishment by a leader usually has a widely felt deterrent effect. It tells the membership that, if warranted, the leader will be ready to use his power of punishment. Such occurrences remind the lukewarm party member of the possibility that while he may not be directly and formally punished for his lacking or unsatisfactory cooperation, he may easily lose the goodwill of the leadership, become isolated within his party, and in a subtle manner be deprived of the benefits which the leaders and the party can bestow upon him—like the easy passage of his private bills.[5]

According to Assemblyman Blumenthal, many members keep a careful mental tab of their relations with the leaders. If and when they make up their minds that they cannot cooperate with the leaders, they instinctively realize that they have forfeited, or at least weakened, their traditional right to ask favors from the leader. They develop a feeling which tells them: "I have no right to ask; I haven't been on his side."[6]

Assemblyman Charles Henderson, Republican of Steuben County, who has served in the Assembly for 18 years, had this to say about the relationship:

> A leader must have the respect of his men and must reflect the majority sentiment. He also must be tolerant of mavericks where he knows that they can't go along with him for some good reason. But if the leader has real trouble from an obstinate member, he must punish. It depends on who has violated good faith.[7]

Former assemblyman Anthony Savarese, a Queens Republican, said:

> The leaders generally don't act in a high-handed way, or assert their power unnecessarily. They, too, must get reelected, and so they try to reflect what the members of their party want. But we always knew that they would use their power over the distribution of emoluments and over giving members a chance to gain stature whenever it became necessary to get cooperation. That's part of the leader's job.[8]

Assembly Minority Leader Stanley Steingut commented on the subject: "The guts of the Speaker's power is his control of appointments and patronage. But mostly he gets the men to go along with him through his personality and the friendships he develops, not the use of strong-arm techniques."[9]

In general, party members recognize that many of the functions of the leaders devolve to their benefit, or are performed on their behalf. In turn, they also consider the use of power to punish mavericks or to deter potential mavericks fair play, serving the common interest. The fact that such punishments are not applied frequently pleases both the legislators and the leaders.

The fear of punishment thus is only one of the features of the relationship between members of a legislative party and their leaders. For the senior, more independent and powerful members, it is a minor factor indeed. "Fear is no important element," says Senator John Marchi,[10] and his opinion is shared by Mark Welch, former counsel to Senate Majority Leaders Earl Brydges and Walter Mahoney. Says Welch, "The threat to the member's local bills or jobs plays very little part in bolstering the average senator's loyalty to the leader. Rather, it is based on a feeling that 'we have chosen him to represent and lead us. Therefore, we owe our loyalty to him.'"[11]

There is usually less fear of retribution among senior legislators than among junior men. The latter do not have the advantage of years of service and experience, usually conducive to good working relations between legislator and leader. Their loyalty has yet to be proved.

What is important in all this is the fact that the personal relationship between leader and members is the decisive criterion of the leader's ability to cultivate consensus and preserve party unity. Therefore, the effective leader carefully controls his own behavior to make sure that it fosters confidence and respect; he tries to create goodwill and a sense of indebtedness by taking care of the members' needs. Debits of this nature can greatly help him in mobilizing support and resolving crises. In general, the good leader attempts to maintain a clublike atmosphere of togetherness, with its own informal rules of polite and considerate behavior. The following remarks by legislators and staff people reflect the leader's need to create a climate in which he can assert as smoothly and fastidiously as possible his power to mobilize his membership behind the legislative plans he favors:

> The strength of the Speaker is much more than his apparent powers. The members freely chose him and they must have a feeling for him either of friendship or respect. His personality and ability to deal with them is the key. He's got to recognize their little problems, and they'll respond in kind when he needs them. The fear that he'll hurt them may be in the back of their minds, but it's not as important as his friendship and helpfulness toward them.[12]

> The good leader keeps a mental record of the favors he's done for his men. It's not that each favor demands a loyal act in return. Rather, it's a climate of opinion that he creates which says to the men, he'll work for me, I owe it to him to work for him.[13]

> Personal relationships are critical to power, but they mean more than being friendly; they also mean being knowledgeable so as to have respect and, even more importantly, being accessible to the members who have needs to be taken care of.[14]

> I don't recall a senator being outwardly punished. Our unity is based on the commonality of our backgrounds and our independence of local party domination. We Republicans are freer to be loyal to our leader. We were wedded before we arrived, and this was reinforced through the chemistry of personal relations.[15]

> The most significant part of the picture is the personality of the leader. Members elected him and must be assured that he is a right guy. They will give him every opportunity to prove it and if he doesn't, he's probably incompetent. The election is very confidential. No one, other than the members, are allowed in the caucus room. It's quite a club, and the members are faithful to the rules. He's the leader and that's it![16]

There's no tyranny. The maverick gets punished but by the loss of access, by losing his ability to get favors. [Former senator Whitney North] Seymour is an example since he feels he's got to buck Brydges because he comes from a liberal New York City district. Brydges has great affection for him, but Seymour gets few favors done. The leader will constantly adjust himself to his members' needs so that he can call on their support when the time comes.[17]

However, there is general consensus among those interviewed that in the 1960s, the responsiveness of legislators to their leaders had diminished. The turning point, according to some observers, was the 1964 Democratic victory, which resulted in an enormous turnover of legislators. In that year, the Democrats captured control of both legislative houses for the first time in 30 years. Only 47 of 150 assemblymen who served in 1964 were still in the Assembly in 1972. Of these, only 22 were Republicans.[18] The result is that the older men who appreciated and lived by the values of party discipline and personal loyalty to the leader are far fewer in number than before, and they are far less influential. "The tightness is gone; the older men who knew the ball game are gone."[19] "With the changes since 1964, we have newer men, new ideas, members who are more independent of leadership than their predecessors. The new men don't know the rules of the game, and when they learn them, they leave."[20]

Another important change that resulted from the temporary Democratic comeback and from the revisions of the reapportionment system mandated by the federal courts is the small margin of majorities by which the majority parties have recently ruled. This is especially true in the Assembly. Speaker Duryea, for example, took office in 1969 with 78 Republicans, only two more than the 76 votes needed to pass legislation. A total of 6 of the 78 were elected as Conservative party members or won with the help of votes obtained on the Conservative party line. Thus, Duryea had a much more difficult time in his first two years keeping members in line than did most of his predecessors.

The legislature went through the turmoil of drawing new district lines three years in a row (1965, 1966, and 1967). The successive changes in districts led to the retirement or defeat of many veterans. The turnover was further increased by the continuing flow of people from New York City to the suburbs. Since many of the newcomers to suburban counties (like Nassau, Suffolk, Westchester, and Rockland) were Democrats, many former Republican strongholds became marginal districts. As a result, senators and assemblymen had to pay even greater attention to constituency demands. The frequency

31

with which such constituency needs conflicted with leadership demands
for party unity has increased dramatically. As one Republican staff
man put it:

> Senator [William] Condon ran in a safe Westchester
> district, and he could thumb his nose at The New York
> Times editorials which his commuters might read. His
> successor, John Flynn, cannot. The flight to the suburbs
> and the effects of reapportionment have made him very
> much more responsive to his voters, and changes like
> this make the leader's job much tougher.[21]

Another circumstance that measurably contributes to the continuing weakening of party unity is the fact that the activities of the
legislature are becoming much more visible to the voters. Newspapers cover the debates much more frequently and extensively than
in the past, and television cameras regularly record legislative events.
Visibility enhances voter interest and causes the legislator to take
much more careful heed of the wishes and preferences of his constituency. This growing attention to the views of the voter greatly
complicates the task and weakens the position of the legislative leader.
This tendency is further strengthened by the fact that most young legislators, whose numbers are increasing, are themselves less prepared
to accept old norms of behavior and more willing to resist the leadership when its purposes conflict with constituency demands. This does
not mean that the present leaders have become weak partners in the
legislative process. They still have the same strong potential for
influencing decisions. However, to prevail, they must work much
harder and more carefully than their predecessors.

THE LEADER'S PERSONALITY AND APPROACH:
THE SENATE

Walter Mahoney

Senator Walter Mahoney served as Republican President Pro
Tempore for 11 years, between 1954-64. He was one of the most
effective and powerful legislative leaders in past decades. Some
observers consider his tenure as a model for party leaders to follow.
According to legislators, staff members, and reporters who worked
with him, few men have mastered the workings of power in a legislative body as fully as Senate leader Mahoney.

32

It is true that his stewardship started under very favorable auspices. He became Majority Leader at a time when most Republican senators still deeply felt the need for strong party leadership. Accordingly, throughout most of his tenure, he presided over a solid Republican majority whose dominance appeared to be secure. "Power accrued to Mahoney through time, and so history was on his side."[22] According to former Speaker Joseph Carlino, "Mahoney could count on his majority through thick and thin. I couldn't match his control, since the Assembly was so much bigger and the members were not as mature and sophisticated."[23] By maturity and sophistication Carlino clearly meant loyalty to the leadership.

One of Mahoney's other valuable assets as Majority Leader was his warm, outgoing personality. Governor Harriman, with whom Mahoney had fought bitterly, described him as "very charming."[24] Albert Abrams, who served as a senior member of Mahoney's staff and as secretary of the Senate (a position he subsequently held under Senators Brydges and Anderson) had this to say:

> Mahoney was not science oriented, or staff oriented, or even issue oriented. He was simply people oriented, with an inborn talent for getting to people, for appreciating their problems with sympathy, and for placing living human interests ahead of theory or philosophy. He possessed the touch of the ward leader who knows everyone on the block and cares for the problems of everyone, and whom people love because they know that he alone would help in times of trouble.[25]

Mahoney methodically used every means and technique that would help him develop a spirit of camaraderie and fellow feeling among the senators. He hardly ever punished anyone for disloyalty but, at the same time, created the impression that he could be ruthless whenever necessary. He was a master in developing cordial personal relations with all senators by continuous intimate conversations with each, learning their needs, desires, and ambitions, inquiring about their families, and creating through all these amenities growing dispositions to cooperate.[26] What is more important, Mahoney was always eager to help and to "service" his colleagues. With the exception of the most hostile and recalcitrant Democrats, no senator would be denied his assistance. He would help get local bills passed, obtain favors for constituents, patch up quarrels, or intervene on behalf of a member with the governor or with other executive officials. If an important bill came up for a vote, he would expect his members to support it. However, even here, he showed considerable flexibility. If a senator wished to be "let off the hook" to vote against a bill supported by Mahoney, he would understand and look the other way. If more than a few wanted to be released, he would even revise the bill to satisfy them. In this manner, intraparty tensions were reduced, and the membership conditioned to rank together behind the leader whenever he had to insist on united action.

Mahoney's ability to obtain cooperation even from Democrats was extraordinary. His techniques were very interesting. For example, in 1959, freshman Democratic senator Seymour Thaler placed a bill of his own on the calendar. Mahoney "starred" the bill, which meant that the bill would remain on the calendar, but action on it would be suspended until further notice by Mahoney. As a novice, Thaler did not know how to react. Some time later, he made up his mind to approach the Majority Leader and ask him whether some amendment would be needed to make the bill acceptable to him. Mahoney said, "Do you want this bill to pass?" Thaler said, "Yes." Mahoney said simply, "Then you've got it." And then he turned to the presiding officer: "Mr. President, please remove the star on Senate Bill No.—."[27] All Mahoney wanted was for Thaler to come to him and ask directly for the passage of the bill, thereby placing himself in a position of indebtedness to Mahoney.

A Republican senator recalls that he needed more money for the committee that he chaired. He called Mahoney's counsel and was told that he would have to see the Majority Leader in person. The senator then visited Mahoney and received the amount requested, but only because he applied directly to the leader himself for the favor.

In addition to accruing debts, Mahoney was more than willing to protect his colleagues. In the early 1960s, a Republican senator was at loggerheads with the party leadership in his home county. The county leader was determined to deny the senator reelection to his seat. One night the senator was in a serious automobile accident, and the county leader promptly spread the word that the senator had been drunk while driving and, for this reason, must be eliminated as a candidate for the Senate. Mahoney immediately called a conference of all Republican senators in Albany and secured their unanimous consent to the suggestion that the county leader should be given an ultimatum that if the senator was not renominated, the Republican organization of his county would lose all legislative patronage as well as all bills in which the local party had an interest. He also obtained authorization to secure the governor's agreement to withhold executive patronage, from the county in question. The county leader was, of course, more than impressed, and the senator was renominated. He served for several terms until his death.

By his decisive intervention, Mahoney won much more than the lifelong gratitude and devotion of a single senator. He also obtained the admiration of all senators who saw that he was ready to stand up for them and protect them. The effect, in terms of Mahoney's potential to unify the party, was enormous.

In another instance, Mahoney walked into the Senate chamber one day and confidentially asked a rather vociferous Democratic orator to attack a Republican senator by the name of Henry Wise. Wise, a Southernor by birth, was one of the most conservative members of the New York Senate. He was the only man to vote against the repeal of the poll tax in New York, and so the Democratic debater approached by Mahoney was eager to oblige. His opportunity came in the form of a rather harmless resolution that was sponsored by Wise. The Democrat lashed out at the man, calling him ignorant and irresponsible, his resolution insidious and vicious, and he went on thundering that its adoption would undermine the Senate and American democracy altogether. Thereupon, Senator Mahoney rose on a point of high personal privilege and, in apparent rage, denounced the Democrat for his lack of common courtesy, his insulting manner, and his brazen hostility to Senator Wise, "one of the most distinguished and able men in the legislature." The Democrat, of course, apologized. It seems that Mahoney wanted to patch up a controversy he had with Wise. What better way than to secretly stage an attack against the man and then rise to his defense in public.[28]

On another occasion, Mahoney promised a Democratic lawmaker his help in getting a certain bill passed. Weeks later the bill came up for debate on the floor of the Senate, but Mahoney was out of the chamber, making a phone call. In near panic, the Democrat ran out, searching for Mahoney. He reminded Mahoney of his pledge of support. By then, with Mahoney out of the chamber, the debate had turned against the bill, and the roll call was almost over, with the nays in the majority. Mahoney rushed back into the chamber and asked that his name be called immediately on the basis of his right to "explain his vote." Under the rules, after debate is closed, members are permitted to speak for two minutes during the roll call. Mahoney rose and said, "Gentlemen, several weeks ago I promised to help get this particular bill passed. I gave my word, but I forgot about the whole thing. I always keep my word; it is the only way to operate. But now I'm in a position in which only you can help me to keep my promise by voting for this bill." Thereupon, most Republicans who had already voted nay rose to change their votes (the count becomes official only after the roll call is completed and the secretary has announced its outcome), and the bill passed.[29]

Mahoney took great pains to develop in the members the feeling that the Senate was one of the world's greatest deliberative bodies. He made the members believe, as he did, that no one had the right to challenge any of its prerogatives. He was very successful in developing a very high degree of institutional patriotism, which proved particularly effective in cases where he chose to challenge the governor. The Democratic Harriman administration was to suffer often and considerably from the united stance of the Senate which Mahoney had organized.

One final incident may serve to show the degree of control that Mahoney held over the Senate and the kind of loyalty he could expect. In 1964 Governor Rockefeller, who had spent most of the legislative session campaigning in various statewide primaries for president, returned to New York to demand passage of his program designed to reform the state's liquor laws. The battle over the liquor package became one of the most controversial and heated issues of that session.

At the time, it was alleged that in order to ensure passage of the liquor bills, the governor had made a deal with Congressman Charles Buckley, Bronx Democratic county leader. If the four Bronx Democratic senators loyal to Buckley would vote for the liquor reform bills, Rockefeller would get Republican votes for a certain bill Buckley desired. That bill was called the slate voting bill, and it provided that in the next primary election (June of 1964), political candidates could align themselves in slates on the ballot, so that one faction's entire slate would be listed in one column, with another faction's slate in another column. Without slate voting the ballot would show the office for which the election was being held, and then list all the candidates aspiring to the post with positions determined by the drawing of lots. Buckley was at the time opposed for his congressional seat by reform Democrat Jonathan Bingham, and he desired to be aligned in a column on the ballot with other regular Democratic candidates running for legislative posts or judgeship positions, many of whom were incumbents with large voter followings.30

On the last day of the session, March 26, 1964, the slate voting bill was brought up in the Senate for final debate and vote. Mahoney, out of the chamber during the debate, returned during the roll call to find that the bill was in trouble. He had promised the governor that he would support the bill (probably knowing of Buckley's need). But during the debate, senior Republican senator John Hughes of Syracuse, a bitter enemy of Rockefeller, had attacked the bill as being part of a deal. With Mahoney out of the chamber, many Republicans joined the reform Democrats and the anti-Buckley regular Democrats to defeat the bill by a vote of 27 to 30.

After the roll call, but before the final results were announced, the sponsor of the bill, Senator Robert Brownstein, moved to recommit the bill to committee, a traditional face-saving device, permitting the sponsor of a losing bill to avoid formal defeat. The roll call was withdrawn without objection, and the bill recommitted.

Three hours later, Mahoney moved that the slate voting bill be once more reported out of committee and be debated anew, and he opened the second debate himself. He explained that he had given his word to the governor to help pass the bill, but stressed that he had not been part of any deal. Even so, the charges by Hughes of a deal had the indirect effect of impugning his (Mahoney's) integrity, and he felt obliged to clear the record. He then dramatically pleaded for support. He called on the members to ignore the merits of the bill and vote in the affirmative for the sake of Walter Mahoney. Whenever any senator needed help, he said, he was available, whether it was to get constituents serviced, to pass bills, or to help with personal problems. Now it was he, Mahoney, who had to ask for a return show of goodwill. He needed the help of his colleagues to clear his reputation, and so he was asking each man for his personal assistance. Democratic senator Edward Lentol of Brooklyn was so moved that he rose and urged that the slate voting bill be passed unanimously by acclamation. Thereupon, all senators, the Republicans who had originally voted against the bill, the anti-Buckley regular Democrats, and even the reformers all agreed to follow suit, even Senator Hughes himself. The bill was recorded as having passed 57 to 0.

This special ability of Mahoney to call upon personal friendships on both sides of the aisle to get even very controversial bills passed is testimony to his great command of the Senate throughout the decade of his leadership.

As a postscript, it might be noted that although the slate voting bill was passed, Buckley lost to Bingham anyway. In that session the liquor reform package was defeated in the Assembly, and the legislature adjourned on March 27. However, Rockefeller made some changes in the liquor package and called the legislature back into special session. On April 16, the Bronx Democrats joined a sufficient number of Republicans to pass the liquor bills in the Senate. The same day the bills passed in the Assembly and were signed by the governor to become law.

Earl Brydges

Senator Earl Brydges of Niagara was elected Republican Minority Leader for one year (1965) and then one year later was elected Majority Leader during a time of dramatic changes in the legislature. He served as Majority Leader from 1966 to 1972. Those changes and the impact of the personality of Brydges introduced a somewhat different style of Senate leadership from that of Walter Mahoney.

The Goldwater defeat in 1964 swept into office many new senators, some of whom did not share with their older colleagues the same spirit of loyalty to leadership and of party discipline. The imposition of new apportionment standards led to the creation of new districts and thus to the election of new lawmakers. The flight of the urban middle class to the suburbs caused further political changes in many areas and helped the election of more new men, most of whom were less sure of their chances of reelection.

At the same time, the nature of the issues with which the legislature had to deal began to change. The increasing complexity of social issues required greater technical expertise in the legislature and forced the leaders to bring more people with greater specialized knowledge into the decision-making process.

The most important difference between the Brydges and Mahoney regimes was the fact that during Brydges's first years in the leadership, the decision-making process in the Senate became, for various reasons, rather substantially decentralized. One reason was already mentioned: the arrival of younger, relatively more independent senators who often had to pay greater heed to their constituencies than to the leadership of the Senate. Another reason was that as a leader, Brydges was less secure in terms of membership loyalty than his predecessor. Men like Senators Edward Speno of Nassau and John Hughes of Syracuse had their own measurable power bases within the membership and a marked potential to stand up to the elected leader. To mollify these men, and at the same time to satisfy the growing need for specialized expertise in conducting the various legislative committees, Brydges gave the most competent senior members greater new opportunities to take the lead in the conduct of major committees, each in his own field of special interest and experience. According to Senate secretary Albert Abrams, this almost instinctive decision by Brydges to decentralize and redistribute legislative power in the Senate proved helpful. It gradually built closer personal and working relations between him and the new subleaders and increased their readiness to recognize his overall authority. Thus, in the long run the change did more good for Brydges as a leader than the price he may have paid for it in terms of a more decentralized structure.[31]

Brydges as a man was often described as gracious, gentlemanly, warm, and friendly. He was "an old country lawyer" with all the courtliness and shrewdness that the label implies, according to one senior staff member. His friendliness toward his colleagues, however, while consistent and sincere, was not as energetic and outgoing as was Mahoney's. One senator described the difference as follows:

If a death would occur in a senator's family,
Brydges would send condolences and flowers and provide
all the usual amenities anyone could expect. Mahoney

38

would personally look after the family and find out what he could do for them in any possible way (whether they needed money, for example), thus completely involving himself in the family's problems.

On the other hand, Brydges seems to have been more willing to grant political benefits to his fellow legislators than Mahoney, without making sure a debt has been created. Brydges granted benefits simply because the members desired it. Said one senator, "Brydges has never said no to any legitimate request and will give you what you need, faster than Mahoney. He'll expect you to be thankful but not bound by any obligation. I like that approach, and I'm going to be with him as a result." On the other side of the coin is this statement by a Republican legislator about Brydges: "Brydges would never call in political credits; it's not his personality. He wouldn't say, 'Do it for me' as Mahoney would. He'd rather say, 'The hell with it; it's not worth it.' He's not as personally close to the members as Walter. He'd help anyone on a personal matter, but not as readily or as closely as Walter."

Not all senators liked Brydges. Some Democrats felt that his leadership responsibilities had changed him into a more formal and severe person. One Democratic senator said: "He is a highly moral and ethical person, but too much of this is potentially dangerous in a legislative leader. It can make him orthodox and rigid, too willing to judge the behavior of others, and too intolerant of the needs of others. I think Brydges has shown some of these traits." Another believed that "he has sometimes lost control of his temper, and disagreements have become personal. He is quick to get angry and slow to forgive. He has become very partisan, not in Mahoney's way—for public consumption—but because of personal pique."

Conversely, not all Democrats were unhappy with Brydges either. Former senator Basil Paterson of Harlem enjoyed good relations with the Majority Leader. "He has given a great deal of time to my constituents, when they ask to meet with him, as a favor to me. When Rhody McCoy and David Spencer came to Albany to discuss the school decentralization bill, he spent over one and a half hours with them. On another occasion, a group of black residents came to Albany to protest the welfare cuts; after talking with them, Brydges referred them to me as an expert. When we were negotiating on the school decentralization bill, he had an open mind, although we didn't agree. He's been quite fair with me."32

The fact is that Brydges was very successful in getting Democratic votes on crucial issues. Such occurrences made some of the younger Democratic senators very angry. They desired a strong, unified minority in their house, as they saw it developing in the

Assembly under Stanley Steingut. By the judicious use of patronage and of the control over local bills, Brydges had often been supported by some of the older Democratic senators. Some were very willing to cooperate; others held out for an exchange of favors. It appeared that Senator Joseph Zaretzki, the Senate Democratic leader, was not interested in organizing the minority into a forceful opposition. He was very friendly and cooperative with Brydges and Governors Rockefeller and Wilson. Senator Manfred Ohrenstein of Manhattan, one of the more outspoken reform Democrats, pointed out his frustrations in trying to get Zaretzki to stop playing ball with the Republicans:

> I must be getting old because I've stopped fighting with Joe. The reason is that I need small favors to be effective myself, and why should I hold out with just a few others and continue to get nowhere. Jack Bronston and I led a fight in 1966 to drop Zaretzki as leader. We failed. Now I need staff and JLC assignments to be effective. But then, how can you take from a guy and then spit in his face. So I've been quiet the last few years. But I am ready to join in a move to obtain real leadership.[33]

Brydges and Mahoney have also acted differently in their role as spokesmen for the governor's programs. For most of his years as leader, Mahoney was more independent of the governor than Brydges and more confident of his own powers. Mahoney would sometimes commit his members to an administration program without consulting them. Brydges never did this. If pressure was needed to convince majority party members to vote for such a program, Mahoney did the job himself without asking for the governor's help and considered it a breach of faith and an incursion on his prerogative if the governor considered bypassing him to talk to legislators.[34] Brydges has no such distaste. For example, in February 1968, Rockefeller obtained on his own the support of some upstate conservative lawmakers for his sales tax increase by bargaining with them about a reduction of the cost of the Medicaid program (through the imposition of a 20-percent coinsurance program for all Medicaid patients who were not welfare recipients).[35] Such willingness on the part of the Senate leader to permit executive involvement in negotiations with his membership about legislation expanded the role of the then Lieutenant Governor Malcolm Wilson in that direction. For example, when in 1966 Brydges and Speaker Travia bitterly disagreed over the controversial Medicaid legislation, Wilson was called in as a mediator.[36]

I had to serve as an honest broker in the Medicaid negotiations since the leaders rarely met together. I was also in on the discussions over the sales tax increase of 1968, and since then my role has further expanded in this area, whenever the leaders felt that I could be helpful in dealing with certain legislators. I'm often asked to discuss issues with upstate members, particularly those from Westchester.[37]

Wilson, of course, is from Westchester County.

Brydges, only after several years as Majority Leader, finally began to approach the kind of strong control that Mahoney was able to exercise. However, that level of control was never actually reached, mainly because Brydges was much less ready and willing to use Mahoney's strongest weapon—his insistence that personal indebtedness to him as a leader obligates the party member to loyalty in matters of policy. Brydges could not match Mahoney's toughness when dealing with mavericks, and the changed environmental factors which we have already examined reduced Brydges' freedom of action in this respect.

Joseph Zaretzki

Senator Joseph Zaretzki was the Democratic leader in the Senate from 1957 until his defeat at the polls in 1974. He served as President Pro Tempore for one year, 1965, when the Democrats were in the majority. Most of the following observations relate, therefore, to his tenure as Minority Leader, but they have some relevance to his brief service as Majority Leader as well.

Zaretzki, of immigrant stock, was brought up in New York City. "He was raised in an unfriendly environment and had to prove his toughness to survive. Some of that instinct for survival remains."[38] He has developed skills and techniques of action which have stood him in good stead in the highly competitive world of the legislature and helped him, often in the face of strong opposition, to survive as Democratic leader for 17 years. Zaretzki, over 70 years old in 1974, in his many years in politics "developed a sixth sense for survival; it is made up of a cunning which enables him to debate the most complex technical matters one day, and play the clown the next."[39]

Zaretzki was a loner. He did not socialize very much and kept to himself most of the time. He was a tireless worker and felt duty bound to read every bill on the calendar. Thus, he built up a vast storehouse of knowledge regarding legislation.[40]

41

However, he showed little initiative in proposing legislation and expected from his staff little more than keeping files and memos on bills. No major programs issued from the Senate Minority Leader's office, nor did alternatives to Republican proposals originate there.

Most observers feel that Zaretzki's exaggerated concern with maintaining himself as leader was his greatest shortcoming. This one-sided orientation may have been the factor that prevented him from uniting the Democratic senators into a cohesive force, able to affect the trend of legislation. Quite the reverse, he was more willing to work for Senator Brydges and Governor Rockefeller, by providing them with Democratic votes, than to help develop a creative program for his own party.

One can only guess the reasons for Zaretzki's willingness to play such an accommodating role. First, it is true that his cooperation with the Republicans once saved his career. In the leadership fight of 1965, the Republicans decided to throw their support to Zaretzki, and he certainly must have felt an obligation to them. Second, he was an older man who may have lost the zest for combat. Third, one member of his family had a very serious, long-term and ultimately fatal illness, and his concern may have further diminished his interest in a more assertive type of leadership.

The Republicans were, of course, pleased with their relationship with Zaretzki. Many Democrats deeply resented it, but they were unable to do anything about it. Occasional talk of removing Zaretzki from the leadership always foundered, mainly because it was recognized that it would be very difficult to overcome the influence of forces opposing such a change within the party but outside the legislature. These forces include the bitter, semipermanent party factionalism which resulted in semipermanent division between anti-Zaretzki lawmakers themselves, and so even for them it was better to have Zaretzki than to see someone from another faction take his place.

Particularly galling to some of the Democratic senators who desired a united Senate party under strong leadership was the fact that Assembly Minority Leader Stanley Steingut had, relatively speaking, accomplished just that feat in the Assembly where the Republicans were generally hard put to crack the solidarity of the Democrats.

THE LEADER'S PERSONALITY AND APPROACH: THE ASSEMBLY

Oswald Heck

Assemblyman Oswald Heck served as Speaker for 22 years. He came to power in 1937 at a time when the appreciation of party

42

loyalty and unity was among the most important values in the New York legislature. In such an atmosphere, Heck was able to build up such a large reservoir of goodwill and of personal indebtedness to him as leader that he was able to dominate his house very effectively. He believed in party regularity and orthodoxy and, therefore, in responsiveness to party leadership.

A large, heavyset, and gregarious man, Heck spun his web of relationships quite softly, helping as many members as he could, giving all equal access to him, and listening to them with great patience.[41] He was a pragmatist, not committing himself to any specific philosophy of government, with the one exception that he had a burning desire to be recognized as a liberal on issues of racial and religious discrimination.[42] He is given credit for having been the major force in the passage of such landmark laws as the Ives-Quinn law prohibiting discrimination in employment, the Quinn-Olliffe law prohibiting discrimination in college admissions, the Metcalf-Baker law which prohibited discrimination in the sale and rental of certain types of housing (the first of a series of Metcalf-Baker bills, one of which became the object of enormous controversy after Heck died), the Roman-Wicks law prohibiting discrimination in public accommodations, and the law that abolished the segregated Negro regiment in the State National Guard.[43]

Those members of the Assembly who served with Heck and who were interviewed by this writer credit him with being an outstanding public speaker. Former assemblyman Samuel Berman said, "He was a great speaker, sincere and simple. He spoke rarely but when he did, he was as good as any man I've heard in my 30 years in Albany."[44] According to former Democratic assemblyman William Clancy of Queens:

> He was an outstanding Speaker. I remember when he left the rostrum to debate against the one-year residence bill (barring welfare payments to people who had not lived in the state for one year). He even used the theme "tsedocah," the Hebrew term for charity. It was an extremely powerful speech, and it helped kill the bill. I don't recall a single instance in which Heck did not get what he really wanted.[45]

He rarely spoke on the floor. His ability to persuade was put to more frequent and probably more effective use in conference. Assemblyman Charles Henderson recalls: "He was extremely good at achieving a consensus in a caucus. He would exploit personal relationships and ask the fellows to do it for him as a favor to him."[46] Of course, he also used his great powers as a backup. "His favorites were taken care of. They got better committees, more staff, special assignments, the politically important debates to lead, and local bills passed."[47]

But Heck would try to assist all members, even the Democrats. Assemblyman Berman recalls:

> I represented Bedford-Stuyvesant during the period it became an overwhelmingly black area. When Emmett Till was lynched in the South, I introduced a resolution condemning the lynching. Now Heck hated resolutions because they didn't have any legal meaning, they were often debated at great length, and, he felt, wasted the time of the Assembly. I happened to agree, but I felt I needed the resolution in my district. When he saw that I had introduced it, he said, "Sam, you know how I feel about these things." I answered, "Ossie, I need this resolution for my constituents. It'll be very helpful to me." That's all he needed to hear. The resolution was passed the next day.[48]

But Heck, who has been characterized as "a benevolent dictator,"[49] could be quite partisan and a tough political infighter. With his skills and with the inherent powers of his office, he was rarely a loser.

When the Quinn-Ives bill prohibiting job discrimination was passed in 1945, Heck had to defeat a clever maneuver by members of his own party who opposed the bill. The bill prohibited discrimination in businesses and industries in which there were four or more employees. Upstate conservative Republicans, led by Malcolm Wilson of Westchester, hoping to defeat the bill, offered amendments to make the measure even more liberal. They moved to reduce the number of employees in businesses covered by the bill to two or more, then to one or more. The strategy was aimed at building up the opposition. Heck and Minority Leader Irwin Steingut, hoping to pass the original proposal as a major first step and fearing that the amendments would prevent the passage of the bill, instructed all those supporting the measure to resist the temptation of liberalizing the bill and to vote against the amendments. The amendments were defeated and the bill passed.[50]

On another occasion, in 1949, there was heated debate over the proposed Condon-Wadlin bill prohibiting strikes by public employees. During the debate Heck ordered that the doors to the chamber and to the galleries be locked to prevent disturbance by spectators. Democratic leader Irwin Steingut protested and appealed the decision of the chair. Heck came off the rostrum to remind the members that during a fierce debate in the 1930s, a spectator had gotten so involved in the debate that he fell out of the gallery on top of Speaker McGinnies. Then he said that if he were to lose the vote on Steingut's motion appealing the decision of the chair, he, Heck, would in effect no longer be Speaker. The motion was defeated by a party vote.[51]

On one occasion the chairman of the Committee on Military Affairs, Assemblyman William Doig (who doubled as an upstate county leader), bottled up a bill which would have prohibited racial discrimination in the State National Guard. At the same time, Doig was pleading with Governor Dewey to increase his county's patronage allotment. Dewey refused. In order to embarrass and prod the governor, Doig suddenly reported the National Guard bill out of his committee. The liberal New York City newspaper, PM, picked up the story and gave it wide coverage. Dewey was worried not only over the political impact of the bill, but also by the possibility that its enactment might jeopardize federal funding of the State National Guard. At Dewey's request, Heck told the bill's sponsors that the bill ought to be amended to delay its effective date, so as to give the federal government time to take comparable action prohibiting discrimination. The bill was sent back to the printer and never came back. A few days later the legislature adjourned. Thus, Heck had delivered for Governor Dewey, but he himself felt guilty about it. The next year, through Heck's efforts, the segregated Negro regiment that existed by virtue of state law was dissolved.[52]

When in 1959 Speaker Heck died, his prestige was exceptionally high, and his power and influence exceptionally great within the Assembly.

Joseph Carlino

Joseph Carlino was elected to the Speaker's chair in 1959, vacated by the death of Oswald Heck. He was Heck's Majority Leader and most loyal supporter. From the start, he tried his best to develop with his membership the same kind of effective working relationship maintained by Heck. Soon, however, he had to discover that the effect of the recently emerged changes (described earlier in this chapter) in the relationship between Speaker and membership, continued to prevail in a manner that was bound to make his own leadership performance even more laborious and difficult.

These difficulties may have been augmented by the personal habits of the man. Carlino was a rather aloof and stern person. At least this was the impression he generally made.[53] Some felt that "he was accessible to his friends but basically an arrogant man."[54] However, to those really close to him, he appeared to be a friendly

and charming man, responsive to his members' needs.[55] Possibly
the most intimate available portrayal comes from Henry Paley,
Carlino's public relations officer and close adviser:

> Joe was a compulsive worker who was very loyal to
> Heck. He was liberal regarding basic questions of civil
> rights, didn't view with such horror, as other Republi-
> cans, strikes by public employees. He favored the Dem-
> ocratic position that graduated income taxes are prefer-
> able to sales and user taxes. But he wasn't so liberal on
> questions like the stop and frisk bill. He was, and still
> is, a physical fitness bug who enjoyed 6 a.m. swimming
> and who liked to work late. He had very good rapport
> with staff and would socialize with them, even joining in
> our gin rummy games. He loved to debate with contro-
> versial people like Nick Kisburg and Jesse Gray. He
> also liked hard workers, whether or not they agreed with
> him; fellows like Al Blumenthal and Tom Jones, the black
> assemblyman from Brooklyn who's now a judge. He also
> liked to "finesse" things. I remember him threatening
> the City University of New York with mandated tuition if
> they didn't increase the percentage of nonwhite students
> there.[56]

However, the fact remains that most people consider toughness
as Carlino's outstanding character trait. Said former assemblyman
Anthony Savarese, "Carlino was more direct and tougher than Heck.
Of course, it depended on one's relations with him; I got along well
with Joe, and he needed people to be confident in. So I never got
instructions, not even on patronage. But I knew that had I fought him,
he would have had my legs chopped."[57]

Carlino himself spelled out his attitude toward those who tried
to carve out a reputation for themselves by consistently opposing
the Speaker:

> I never disciplined someone in the sense of taking
> away what he had. It was merely a question of his not
> getting anything from me in the future. You know the
> Speaker can be very helpful to an assemblyman regarding
> legislation, local bills, debate assignments, committee
> and JLC assignments, staff appointments; the whole idea
> of access to the Speaker is involved.[58]

Through most of his six years as Speaker, Carlino enjoyed
close relations with the governor, a fact which measurably helped

him to overcome, or at least reduce, the difficulties in the way of the assertion of his leadership. One breach in this warm relationship between Carlino and Rockefeller came in 1964 when Carlino, after having first sided with the governor, suddenly assumed the leadership of a small Assembly rebellion against the governor's budget. Suburban Republicans demanded increases in state aid to local school districts and, with Carlino's support, succeeded in obtaining from Rockefeller a concession which increased the education budget by $12.5 million (transferred from other parts of the budget).[59]

Carlino liked to circumvent the Democratic leadership of Anthony Travia whenever he discovered a chance to capture the votes of those Democrats who were independent of the Minority Leader or feuding with him. He used Hank Paley, a member of his staff and a former Democrat, in the attempt to obtain Democratic votes in favor of his bills. Occasionally, Paley had success with reform Democrats and sometimes even with Stanley Steingut.[60] Every once in a while, Carlino would try to needle Travia, by granting the floor to Democratic assemblyman Daniel Kelly of Manhattan to lecture his colleagues on proper legislative and personal behavior.[61]

Whatever techniques Speaker Carlino may have used to bind the Republicans to him, to crack down on mavericks, and to annoy or divide the Democrats, the fact remains that he never went beyond the bounds of "proper" behavior or betrayed the expectations of the membership. The recognition by the Assembly as a whole of this correctness of Carlino's conduct as Speaker found its clearest manifestation in 1961-62 when he was faced with a grave personal crisis resulting from charges against him of conflict of interest. The Assembly, with one exception (the man who leveled the charges against him), rallied to Carlino's defense, and no one of either party attempted to take political advantage of the occurrence.

Time magazine summed up the accusation against Carlino as follows:

> Sleek, sonorous Joseph F. Carlino, 44, . . . was fighting for his political life (because of charges) that he had had an interest in an atom shelter firm that stood to profit from a $100 million school and college shelter program that Carlino helped get enacted last year.[62]

About the accuser, Assemblyman Mark Lane of East Harlem and Yorkville, *Time* had this to say:

> "Mark," says a friend, "sees himself as a beplumed knight on a white charger whenever he undertakes a cause." He clearly hopes to make his assault against

Carlino a springboard for a try this year for Congress.[63]

The problem for Carlino began with a trip to Washington by Governor Rockefeller to visit President Kennedy. There the governor spoke with Secretary of Defense Robert McNamara about the need for building bomb shelters. The governor considered this a serious necessity and promised to make New York the first state to develop such a program. When, in October 1961, he called a special session of the legislature to enact the reapportionment of congressional district lines, he added his fallout shelter program bill to the agenda. On November 10, the legislature passed the shelter bill and a bill granting tax relief to GIs, both with relatively little dispute. The fight in that session centered around the reapportionment measure, which the Republicans finally rammed through both houses.

On November 21, 1961, Assemblyman Lane issued a press release in which he accused Carlino of conflict of interest on the ground that Carlino was a member of the board of directors of Lancer Industries, manufacturers of fallout shelters. According to Paley, Carlino was playing golf one day at the Lido County Club near his home. He was approached in the locker room by a businessman who asked him if he would be prepared to fill a vacancy on the Board of Lancer. At the time Lancer manufactured plastic swimming pools. Carlino agreed. He bought no stock in the company and attended only one meeting. Later, says Paley, the company began producing small fallout shelters for family backyards, not the concrete and cement shelters which the 1961 law prescribed for large public buildings. Therefore, says Paley, Carlino could in no way have profited by the passage of the law.[64]

When Carlino joined the Board of Lancer, his law firm went on retainer for the company at $500 per month. When the company shifted to fallout shelters, Carlino said he called to resign from its board. Unfortunately, however, he never put his resignation in writing because, he said, of "the press of business."[65]

Whatever the merits of the case, the incident proved very damaging to Carlino. After a hearing of the Committee on Ethics of the Assembly, at which he testified, Carlino found himself faced with a battery of reporters. One of the newsmen asked if Carlino thought Lane was a Communist, and if his attack on him was part of a plot. Although Carlino had been advised by his staff carefully to avoid any allegation or reference to Lane's ideological preferences,[66] he blurted out, in front of numerous reporters and television cameras, that "the enemies of the United States, those closely connected with the Communist party," were behind the attack. "Their technique is to beat fallout shelters throughout the United States. I don't know if he [Lane] is being used or if he is part and parcel of it!"[67]

In the end, the Ethics Committee issued a report clearing Carlino of all charges and severely criticizing Lane's action. On February 21, 1962, following a series of bitter attacks on Lane from the floor, the Assembly exonerated Carlino by accepting the report, and then the entire membership, with the single exception of Lane, rose to applaud the Speaker.[68]

Anthony Travia

By the time [Anthony] Travia was elevated to the speakership in 1965, the minority tradition of the Democratic party was so firmly established that the transition to majority status was painful. Old habits had to be broken and new ones learned. . . .

Travia had been Minority Leader for six years under the same governor and the same mayor of New York City. His task was essentially to see how much he could get for the city out of the all-Republican state government, to advance the cause of perennial Democratic issues such as minimum wage legislation, and to try to waken the Republicans to his party's presence.[69]

Travia, brought up in the rough and tumble of Brooklyn politics, was, like Carlino, a tough Speaker. Although considered by some to be a mild man in the role of Minority Leader, as Speaker he went after as much power as he could. "He changed from a pussycat into a lion," according to one lobbyist. He was respected for the incredibly long hours he put in, for his complete dedication to the job, and for his solid knowledge of what was going on in his house. He had no other interest than being the Speaker. "His whole life was the legislature, and he worked 18 hours a day at it."[70]

He did not socialize and did not "romance" his members. His relationship with them was strictly business, and they viewed him as a tough, hard Speaker, ready to fight and to punish opponents.[71] He disliked the idea of sharing power with anyone. For example, he considered the existence of the short-lived Democratic Advisory Committee, the appointment of which he agreed to only under considerable pressure, an imposition he rid himself of as fast and as effectively as possible.

Travia had a very interesting relationship with the governor. He was a hard negotiator and always tried to wring concessions from Rockefeller. The relationship will be discussed in greater detail in Chapter 5. In this context, may it suffice to say that Travia felt confident enough of his power to often determine his party's position on gubernatorial program bills. His first step was always to decide whether he himself liked the bill or not. If the substance of the bill satisfied him, he would call a conference to discuss the details with the membership of his party. Then he would sit down with the governor, usually to argue for amendments he considered necessary.

One Rockefeller bill, to which Travia had committed himself, required that both he and the governor use maximum pressure to obtain passage. On April 9, 1968, the Assembly passed the Urban Development Bill, but only after a bitter floor fight. The purpose of the bill was to create a new superagency, the Urban Development Corporation, with broad powers to rebuild slums. But the upstate conservative elements of both parties, who saw in the bill only a large diversion of funds for the benefit of New York City, were stubbornly opposed to the legislation. What is more, some reform and liberal Democrats had joined New York City Mayor John Lindsay in opposition to the bill because it permitted the corporation to ignore certain local preferences. On the evening of April 9, after the bill had easily passed the Senate, it came up for a vote in the Assembly. First it was defeated by a vote of 63 to 69. Several members then asked to change their votes to the negative (since the bill was dead anyway), and the party leaders assented. As a result, the final tally (on the main bill out of a package of several bills) was 48 to 85.

In this apparently irreversible situation, Travia decided to act. He called for a recess, which lasted for three hours. This gave him and his staff time to "rediscuss" the bill with all men who had voted against it. It also gave time to the governor to apply maximum pressure on his own behalf, something he candidly admitted next day at a press conference that followed the ceremonial signing of the bill.

> Governor Rockefeller disclosed today that he had forced the passage of his $6 billion slum rebuilding program in the Assembly last night by threatening to stop doing "personal favors" for the legislators, such as signing their pet bills and appointing their friends to jobs. . . .
>
> Later, in a chat with some reporters, the governor added: "These guys have never seen this side of me before."[72]

Probably to the great relief of Travia, The New York Times article completely failed to refer to the great campaign in which he himself was engaged during that memorable recess. According to a staff man, this included pleas and threats to Democrats and horse trading with the Republicans (about releasing some bills which they wanted to get out of the Rules Committee). It also included the counting of the votes of at least two assemblymen in the affirmative (with their permission over the phone) who were absent from the chamber. On the second roll call, the bill was passed 86 to 45. The governor and the Speaker thus changed the votes of over 40 members.

In general, however, Travia was unable to muster the kind of reliable support based on friendship and loyalty that Mahoney and Heck had enjoyed. This failure must be attributed to the man's personality, his urge to dominate, and his inclination to use a heavy hand. He could use political muscle much more effectively than diplomatic persuasion, and this engendered bitterness instead of harmony. As a result, Travia had his share of setbacks.

On April 2, 1967, the Assembly passed Rockefeller's bill amending the Condon-Wadlin law which prohibited strikes by public employees. The bill, which Travia supported in the face of strong labor opposition, upheld the legal principle that denied public employees the right to strike, but it changed the penalty provisions in a manner penalizing the unions instead of their members.[73] Travia delivered a sufficient number of votes to secure the passage of the bill which most Republicans supported. Before the vote, Travia asked for a discussion of the situation in party conference. His purpose was to secure his colleague's help in mitigating the consequences of his support of legislation deeply resented by the labor movement. He wanted his men to refrain from debating the bill on the floor. But reform Democrats refused to comply. They launched a full-scale debate on the bill.[74]

When in March 1968, Governor Rockefeller settled the sanitation strike in New York City over the objections of Mayor Lindsay, he was severely criticized by an angry public and the press, who felt that he had capitulated before an arrogant and lawless union. When Travia asked the Democratic conference to permit the governor to address a joint session of the legislature for the purpose of explaining his role in the affair, the Democrats rebelled against him. Travia was defeated once again.

In March of 1968, the Republican-controlled Senate passed a bill drastically cutting back the New York State's Medicaid program which, in 1966, was enacted with great fanfare. It was generally expected that under Travia's leadership, the Democratic Assembly would kill the cutback legislation. But the situation had greatly changed. In most communities upstate, there had developed a furious mood of opposition to the high cost of Medicaid, which compelled many local governments to find new revenues to pay the local share of the program. As a result, hardly a single upstate legislator could politically afford to stand by the costly original law. When the new bill aged in the Assembly, Travia called a Democratic conference only to discover that his upstate Democrats would join with the

51

Republican minority to pass the cutback bill. In more normal situations, Travia could have used the powers of his office to prevent the bill from coming up for a vote. But in the face of the upstate revolt and of the fact that by that time it was common knowledge that the Speaker would soon retire to accept a judicial appointment by President Johnson to the federal bench, he was helpless. His own heavy-handed use of the powers of his office had already destroyed his ability to take recourse in the nice, old-fashioned personal appeal that Heck and Mahoney had employed so effectively. Consequently, the lame duck Speaker could not stem the tide of rebellion, and the Medicaid cutback legislation passed.[75] The governor promptly signed the bill into law.

Thus, in following his inherent bent to act as the strong man and dominant force in the Assembly, Speaker Travia went a little too far beyond the bounds, the respect of which would have preserved his popularity and his ability to lead by persuasion. Consequently, he had the respect but not the affection of his members, many of whom he had offended and alienated. When he no longer could effectively use the threat of punishment, he had no resources left for inducing the membership to vote his way. The last few months of his tenure were disturbed by mounting rebellion and backsniping which he had difficulty to control.

Perry Duryea

After having defeated George Ingalls in 1966 for the minority leadership of the Assembly Republicans, Perry Duryea was elected Speaker in 1969. He took the gavel at a difficult time for a new presiding officer. He had only 78 votes on the Republican side. He needed 76 votes to pass bills; so there was very little margin for error what with the hard fact that half a dozen assemblymen in the majority could win only with the help of votes given them on the Conservative party line. A few of them such as Vito Battista of Brooklyn and Rosemary Gunning of Queens were actually members of the Conservative party.

The difficulties of Duryea were compounded by the fact that in 1969 and 1970, for the first time in a long while, the Democrats in the Assembly had obtained a measure of party unity. Their leader, Stanley Steingut of Brooklyn, had forged the party into a fairly solid bloc that was often capable of standing up to the Republicans, Steingut, a cautious, quiet veteran politician, was able to develop a rather high degree of minority consensus on many issues.[76]

Flexibility seemed to be the secret of Steingut's success. He was prepared to consider alternatives to his own viewpoint. He did not mind groups of his colleagues suggesting programs. He established a Democratic Policy Committee in 1969 to draft legislation on behalf of the party. Was this a delegation of authority and a sign of weakness? On the contrary, one observer felt that thereby Steingut strengthened rather than weakened his influence over the directions of his party's program.

> Consensus is built at meetings where lots of people are brought in to give their views, and compromises are reached. The clever consensus-builder chairs the meeting, defines the problem, offers a possible solution, calls on his supporters to speak in favor of the solution, and then waters down opposition by creating an apparent, if not real, atmosphere of agreement on the solution.[77]

Whatever the techniques may be, the results were impressive. Assemblyman Albert Blumenthal, a reformer and Deputy Minority Leader (a post created for him by Steingut to unite the party's two major factions) said:

> The result of Stanley's willingness to bring lots of people into policy making has created a good feeling among the members for him. The consensus we reach is considered binding, and the fellows go along with it. We have, for example, been united on many vitally important issues such as the deficiency budget, the Taylor Law revisions, welfare cuts (we opposed them despite the desire by many of our men to support them), and the Medicaid cuts.[78]

The consequence of this working unity of the Democratic opposition was that Duryea had to walk a thin line during 1969 and 1970. As Speaker, he did set the directions for the work of the Assembly, but in the process he had to watch every step he took. He was easier to deal with than his predecessor, Travia. He delegated responsibilities to his subordinates and allowed them greater decision-making discretion than did the Democratic Speaker.

The limitations imposed on him, the unity of the Democrats, the small margin of his majority, and the tenuous loyalty of those who owed their election to the Conservative party certainly disturbed and irritated him. But he did not show it. He proved to be a nimble tactician in a delicate situation, and the results, in terms of Republican unity, were substantial.

By 1971 and through the 1972 session, Duryea began to change. Although the Republican majority of 79 votes was only slightly above the crucial 76-vote plateau necessary for legislative control, the Speaker acted more confidently and forcefully. He seemed more securely in power. Part of the reason had to be the seasoning he acquired during his first term as Speaker. He had command of the various resources of office. Additionally, the membership expectations regarding the assertion of power by the Speaker acted to motivate him. Finally, he had had the time to develop the kinds of relationships with the Republican membership that reinforced his hold over the Assembly. Debts were now owed to him for services he had rendered. His apprenticeship as party leader was over, and most of his colleagues were pleased with his leadership. By 1972 the confident, dominant figure that the lower house lawmakers had come to expect had finally emerged, shedding whatever inhibitions regarding the use of power that had existed during the first term.

The one incident that best exemplifies Duryea's willingness to dominate the Assembly occurred in early 1972. Governor Rockefeller had announced the need for increased taxes. In order to obtain some Democratic votes, he submitted tax legislation that incorporated some long-term Democratic proposals—adding new income tax brackets for persons earning over $25,000 per year and increasing capital gains levies.

A number of conservative Republican legislators opposed the taxes, although Duryea, with minimal enthusiasm, committed his support to the program. One upstate conservative, Assemblyman Edwyn Mason, a 20-year veteran of the legislature, was particularly outspoken and vocal in opposition. His continuous assaults on the program being submitted by his own party's leadership became a source of embarrassment, not only for Rockefeller and Duryea, but also for those Republican Assemblymen who were planning to vote for the new taxes in support of their leaders but who did not wish to be highly visible while doing so.

Mason apparently ignored the entreaties of his colleagues to tone down his opposition. As a result, some Republicans felt he had to be punished. At the end of January 1972, Duryea announced his appointments for committee chairmen. Almost all the 1971 chairmen were reappointed in pro forma fashion. The one exception was Mason, who was not reappointed chairman of the powerful Agriculture Committee, a cherished post for a rural representative. He was, additionally, cut off from the center of influence. Few Mason bills were taken up by the Assembly, and he spent the remainder of the 1972 session in isolation. Later that year, he resigned his Assembly seat to run (successfully) for state senate.

Some Republican lawmakers claim that Duryea was only following the lead of the Republican conference in punishing Mason. This is possible. What is more probable, however, is that the Speaker, operating within the legislative value system, felt that Mason was far out of line and had to be dealt with. Mason's actions had to be interpreted by Duryea as a challenge to the Speaker's leadership. Therefore, he probably waited for the general antagonism toward Mason to grow before he acted. It may be that a Duryea ally proposed the punishment in the conference so that the Speaker could appear to be acceding to a consensus. However, it is unlikely that such a proposal would have been made without Duryea's knowledge and consent.

During the 1973-74 sessions, Duryea's hold tightened even further. In spite of Democrat unity in opposition to major Republican program bills such as Governor Rockefeller's 1974 drug law, the Republicans maintained a high level of party cohesion.

Occasionally, Duryea reached across the aisle to obtain a Democratic vote, and occasionally a Republican refused to cooperate (Queens assemblyman John LoPresto changed his mind and opposed legislation restructuring the Board of Higher Education which governs the City University of New York when he discovered his senator had voted against the bill in the upper house). But Duryea's control remained firm.

As a matter of fact, he had tremendous confidence that his party would support him in almost every circumstance. In a fierce procedural battle with the Democrats during the 1974 session, he was constrained to rule that Brooklyn assemblyman Stanley Fink's motion to adjourn was out of order. It is unlikely that a motion to adjourn is out of order in any American legislature. In New York, the rules specify that a motion to adjourn takes precedence over all other business. When this writer rose on a point of order to read the rule to the Assembly, the Speaker listened politely, nodded, repeated his ruling, banged his gavel, called for a voice vote on the ruling, and was upheld with a roar by the entire Republican majority. At this point, Democratic leader Stanley Steingut called for an immediate Democratic conference, and the entire minority party began to head for the doors as a protest against the Speaker's behavior. Duryea immediately ordered the doors locked and instructed the sergeant-at-arms to seat all the members. The session then proceeded to the next order of business.

The respect and affection felt for Duryea by his Republican colleagues were manifested most dramatically during the 1974 session. Duryea, Majority Leader John Kingston, another assemblyman, and three Republican staff people were indicted for allegedly conspiring to siphon votes from Democrats in Nassau County. The defendants were subsequently found not guilty by a court decision stating that the statute they had been accused of violating was unconstitutional.

There was a strong belief on the part of Republican lawmakers that the information given to the Manhattan grand jury that led to the indictment had originated in Governor Rockefeller's office, or at least in Attorney General Lefkowitz's office with the latter acting on behalf of the former. The feeling was that Rockefeller, wishing to guarantee Lieutenant Governor Malcolm Wilson an unopposed accesion to the governorship upon Rockefeller's resignation in late 1973 and wishing to prevent a primary for the office in 1974, leaked the information in order to nip Duryea's possible candidacy in the bud. At this, he was successful since Wilson ran for a full term without a Republican primary opponent.

There was substantial bitterness in the legislature over the alleged ploy. The affection for Duryea increased significantly during the session. He received a tumultuous round of applause as he took the podium on the first day of the session. The Republican conference refused, through most of the session, to approve legislation granting the attorney general a pay increase (the bill ultimately passed as part of a larger package at the end of the session). When the then Governor Wilson committed himself to a major pro-tenants bill in an alliance with Democrats, the Assembly Republican conference refused to approve the measure despite the fact that many suburban legislators favored it (since it helped tenants in their communities) and despite the fact that only a dozen or so Republican affirmative votes were needed. A bill opposed by tenant groups was finally passed. His failure to deliver on the liberal bill was a blow to Wilson since he could be portrayed as indecisive and unable to control even his own party. It was the belief of many Democrats that the merits of the legislation had substantially less to do with the defeat of the tenants bill than the residual bitterness felt by many Republican lawmakers.

Thus, within the Assembly, the Speaker Duryea of 1974 was a much more secure and therefore influential officer than the Speaker Duryea of 1969. His ability to affect legislative decisions and to control most of what transpired in the Assembly was not destroyed by the indictment, although his ambitions for accession to the governorship may have been. Quite the reverse, Duryea's influence on legislation and control over the operation of the Assembly were at peak during the 1974 session.

LEADERSHIP STAFFS

One of the glaring weaknesses of American state legislatures is the consistently inadequate supply of professional staff services available to legislators.

Most states have a legislative reference service of some kind, and many have legislative councils that provide research reports on issues, but there are few states that provide anything like adequate research assistance readily available to the member when he needs it. . . . By not providing desperately needed help, the legislature is assuredly undermining its own foundation. Legislators, as a result, are dominated by governors, bureaucracies, and lobbyists, in part because they cannot provide any alternative sources of information for substantiating their independent judgment.[79]

In many states, lawmakers have no staffs at all, or share secretaries or else obtain occasional help from stenographic pools. Central research staffs, if any, are often controlled by the party leaders for partisan purposes. The quality of legislative performance is thus grievously affected.[80]

In New York State, the picture is somewhat better than in most other states. But the availability of staff depends on one's position in the legislative body. A freshman, in the minority, will receive only a small amount of money to hire a secretary and possibly a clerk, and that for the length of the legislative session only. A senior man may get a better deal. A ranking minority member of a committee can negotiate for additional staff for himself. The chairman has a sizable appropriation for hiring a number of professionals above and beyond the secretarial help he himself needs.

On top of the pile, the party leaders have large staffs, about which the following observations seem to be in order. The character of the staff operations of a leader bears, to a large extent, the imprint of the personality and background of the leader himself. Since most of these men are experienced at administering small law offices with a handful of personnel, they approach the administration of their leadership staffs in much the same way. They operate fairly informally, permitting their staff people to share or exchange functions or maintain overlapping jurisdictions. "The administrative talents of the leaders are set by the time they reach Albany and are circumscribed by their small office and law office backgrounds; they instinctively stay away from administration and stick to policy."[81]

The leader's strengths depend mainly on his skill in handling personal relations. He is generally friendly with people, skillful at negotiating, building coalitions, and planning action. He is geared to influencing people and to deciding policy, not to the bureaucratic business of carrying out decisions once made.

Of the three aspects of his functioning—
government, politics, and office administration—the

57

third is the lowest priority. A well-run leadership office is assumed. It can't reinforce his functioning in the other two areas of government and politics. But a poorly or corruptly run leadership office can seriously damage the leader's functioning in the other two areas.82

A significant improvement in leadership staffs has taken place in the last six or seven years. In the Senate, under the influence of Senate secretary Albert Abrams, an increasing number of specialized researchers has been brought in. People competent in public administration, the social sciences, and subject area experts have been employed in growing numbers. Senator Brydges was particularly receptive to Abrams's idea of professionalizing the staff, partly in recognition of the increasing complexity of legislative problems and partly with a view to his own rapidly growing need for information of every description.

The most complete professionalization in the last 10 years has taken place in the area of budget analysis. Under Senator Austin Erwin, chairman of the Senate Finance Committee during Mahoney's early years as leader, there was no systematic review of the executive budget. Legislative reaction to the budget was motivated solely by political considerations. Politics is, of course, still there, but the Finance Committee is now tooled up to do an effective job of scrutinizing all budget requests and of assessing their impact on public policy. There are now 35 to 40 people serving full time as committee staff. About a dozen are budget analysts assigned to review various executive departments. Another six people evaluate the financial implications of every bill introduced into the Senate. The budget analysts now review budget requests line by line and prepare reports on them for mandated public hearings and for the guidance of the senators themselves. These analysts work under the authority of the secretary of the Finance Committee. He is an appointee of the Majority Leader, not of the chairman of the committee. Therefore, with the leader controlling the appointment not only of the chairman but also of the ranking staff man, he can rely on the Finance Committee as the source of the competent fiscal information he needs.

Changes similar to those in the Senate have taken place in the Assembly and for similar reasons. The growing complexity of problems to be solved, the steady increase in the volume of legislation, and the resultant need for speedier action all have increased the need for the professionalization of leadership staffs.83 Since, in the Assembly, a much larger number of members has to be serviced, the pressure in that house for change has been even greater than in the Senate. As a result, the Speaker's and the Minority Leader's staffs are today more competent than a decade ago, better trained and specialized, and more inclined to consider their work in Albany semipermanent. Many key staff people stay on from one leader to the next.

As in the Senate, the Assembly Ways and Means Committee is the focal point for the professionalization of staff. It is also a major source of power for the Speaker who has authority over it and its staff. Today, for example, the chairman of Ways and Means is Assemblyman Willis Stephens, the Speaker's appointee (whose father incidentally was Heck's appointee to the same job). But the key staff man is the committee secretary, Albert Roberts, also an appointee of Speaker Duryea. Roberts runs one of four units in the committee, but that unit is really important to the Speaker. It is the budget section with eight budget analysts, each in charge of reviewing the budget requests of several departments. These analysts are authorized to make recommendations regarding budget requests and legislation with fiscal implications relating to their departments. Said one of them, William Lithgow, only two years on the job, "I have a good batting average regarding recommendations, particularly on bills, since they assume I'm the expert. If I tell the counsel to star (permanently postpone action) on a bill, he'll usually do it. I must give my reasons; though last year, they didn't even ask reasons."[84] The other units of the committee are the Tax and Fiscal Policy Section dealing with revenue legislation, the counsel's office reviewing all bills submitted to the Assembly that have fiscal implications, and the Public Information Section consisting of the press relations man and Chairman Stephens's personal aides who deal with his bills and problems in his home district and write his speeches.

According to Lithgow, Speaker Duryea does not interfere with the day-to-day internal operations of the committee, but he definitely does determine the policy guidelines of its work, the results of which are then at his disposal as sources of his influences over the membership.

One of the innovations that may place the Assembly a step ahead of the Senate in the effort to professionalize its staff work is the creation in 1970 of a so-called Central Staff Office. While recognizing that 4 of the 21 committees (Rules, Ways and Means, Judiciary, and Codes), on the average, handle some 70 percent of the Assembly bills, the leadership came to the conclusion that not only these four central committees but all committees needed good staff. The central staff idea, now in effect, creates teams of research experts to be assigned to each committee chairman as supplements to their staffs. They are hired by the Central Staff director, Mrs. June Martin, who has been research director for several legislative leaders and also for Governor Rockefeller. She is directly responsible to the Speaker.

The teams help prepare legislation and do research or other work assigned to them by the chairman. The idea originated with Ways and Means secretary Roberts and was carried into effect by Duryea.

The Way the Ways and Means Committee operated and the creation of the Central Staff Office both indicate that by 1970 there was greater understanding of the need to institutionalize staff arrangements if the Assembly was to attain a high degree of working efficiency. Most observers feel that the trend is there, but they know that the future depends on the personal inclinations of the two top leaders of the legislature. Mrs. Martin, for example, believes that a Speaker with the power-retaining and centralizing bent of Anthony Travia would be an obstacle in the way of the further strengthening, institutionalization, and professionalization of staff structures, notwithstanding the fact that, for example, the professionalization of the Ways and Means Committee has enhanced the Speaker's power by deepening his knowledge and competence.85

CONCLUSIONS

The formal rules grant substantial powers to the Speaker of the Assembly and the Senate Majority Leader. However, such powers are only part of a broader set of resources available to the leaders.

One of these important resources emanates from the membership. It consists of the expectation of the members of the legislature with regard to the authority of the leaders and the manner in which it ought to be exercised. In the New York legislature, such expectations generally serve to reinforce the acceptance by most lawmakers of the strong assertion of leadership prerogatives and of a value system based upon strong centralized leadership.

The leaders themselves cultivate personal relations with their members, continually trying to service their needs in order to consolidate their hold over their colleagues. Some leaders are, of course, more effective than others in developing the required spirit of camaraderie, good feeling, and unity that can be translated into greater support for leadership initiatives. A variety of techniques have been employed by different leaders, such as the development of a clublike atmosphere, the exchange of amenities, assistance to lawmakers in their nonpolitical problems, and the building of personal relationships based on shared experiences. The most important techniques are, however, of a political character, such as assistance to members in legislative matters (such as passing local and private bills), giving members meaningful debate assignments, granting them extra lulus or staff allotments, interceding with the executive branch on behalf of members or their constituents, and so on. The occasional use of available punishments for the member who is consistently un-cooperative adds dimension to the character of the relationship, al-though such punishment, more often than not, takes only the form of lost access for the maverick to the rewards that the leader has avail-able for distribution.

Another important leadership resource is the potential monopoly of knowledge that the control of the distribution of staff facilities provides for the leader. Staff expertise is a power resource that gives to those with larger and more effective staffs a significant advantage in the advocacy of legislation. In New York, the distribution of legislative staffs depends overwhelmingly on the will of the Assembly Speaker and the Senate Majority Leader, although certain traditional staff allotments to important committees and senior members do have the effect of limiting leadership choices to some extent.

The full employment of these factors grant the leaders of the New York legislature considerable decision-influencing power. It must be asserted again, however, that under certain circumstances even the fullest possible employment of all these resources will be of no avail. Regardless of the extremely strong feelings and efforts of the Senate Majority Leader, a very liberal abortion law was passed in 1970. The totality of leadership power failed to contain a rebellion in 1968 on a different major and controversial piece of legislation. Defying not only the Speaker and the Majority Leader but also the governor, the revolt severely cut back the two-year-old Medicaid program. All three leaders had to acquiesce in the will of the major-ity in both houses of the legislature.

Cases of this nature do not occur frequently. However, the cases that do occur are usually of great significance and lead to the conclusion that the dominance of the legislative leadership is by no means absolute. In matters of legislation over which society and, consequently, the legislature are sharply divided, moral and political pressures may force the leadership either to retreat or to suffer defeat.

NOTES

1. John C. Wahlke, Heinz Eulau, William Buchanan, and LeRoy Ferguson, The Legislative System (New York: John Wiley and Sons, Inc., 1962).

2. Ibid., p. 171.

3. Ibid., p. 175.

4. Assemblyman Albert Blumenthal, interview, December 8, 1969.

5. Victor Condello, general counsel, New York State Associa-tion of Railroads, interview, January 16, 1970.

6. Blumenthal, op. cit.

7. Assemblyman Charles Henderson, interview, February 9, 1970.

8. Former assemblyman Anthony Savarese, interview, February 18, 1970.

9. Assembly Minority Leader Stanley Steingut, interview, February 2, 1970.

10. Senator John Marchi, interview, February 9, 1970.

11. Mark Welch, counsel to Senator Brydges, interview, January 27, 1970.

12. Phillip Bisceglia, counsel to the Speaker, interview, February 23, 1970.

13. Blumenthal, op. cit.

14. Condello, op. cit.

15. Marchi, op. cit.

16. Welch, op. cit.

17. Anonymous Senate staff member.

18. Bisceglia, op. cit.

19. Ibid.

20. Welch, op. cit.

21. Anonymous Republican staff member.

22. Albert J. Abrams, secretary, N.Y. Senate, interview, January 21, 1970.

23. Former Speaker Joseph Carlino, interview, January 12, 1970.

24. Governor Averell Harriman, interview, January 30, 1970.

25. Abrams, op. cit.

26. Former senator Seymour R. Thaler, interview, December 13, 1969.

27. Ibid.

28. Ibid.

29. Former Senate Majority Leader Walter Mahoney, interview, December 18, 1969.

30. The New York Times, March 27, 1964.

31. Abrams, op. cit.

32. Former senator Basil Paterson, interview, December 8, 1969.

33. Senator Manfred Ohrenstein, interview, December 8, 1969.

34. Mahoney, interview, op. cit.

35. Thaler, op. cit.

36. Ibid.

37. Governor Malcolm Wilson, interview, March 4, 1970.

38. Abrams, op. cit.

39. Thaler, op. cit.

40. Joel Cohen, former associate counsel to the Senate Minority Leader, interview, December 12, 1969.

41. Former assemblyman William Clancy, interview, January 20, 1970.

42. Former assemblyman Samuel Roman, interview, January 21, 1970.

43. Ibid.

44. Former assemblyman Samuel Berman, interview, February 2, 1970.

45. Clancy, op. cit.

46. Henderson, op. cit.

47. Roman, op. cit.

48. Berman, op. cit.

49. Former assemblyman James McNamara, interview, January 20, 1970.

50. Clancy, op. cit.

51. Roman, op. cit.

52. Ibid.

53. Henderson, op. cit.

54. Condello, op. cit.

55. Nicholas Kisburg, legislative representative, Joint Council 16, Teamsters, interview, December 10, 1969.

56. Henry Paley, former director of information to the Speaker, interview, December 18, 1969.

57. Savarese, op. cit.

58. Carlino, op. cit.

59. The New York Times, March 20, 1964.

60. Paley, op. cit.

61. Ibid.

62. Time 79 (February 16, 1962): 22,23.

63. Ibid.

64. Paley, op. cit.

65. Time, op. cit., p. 23.

66. Paley, op. cit.

67. Time, op. cit.

68. The New York Times, February 22, 1962.

69. Stuart K. Witt, "The Legislative—Local Party Linkage in New York State," unpublished doctoral dissertation, Syracuse University, 1967, p. 116.

70. Cohen, op. cit.

71. Richard A. Brown, legislative representative for the city of New York, former associate counsel to the Speaker, interview, December 3, 1969.

72. The New York Times, April 11, 1968, p. 1.

73. Ibid., April 3, 1967, p. 1.

74. Kisburg, op. cit.

75. The New York Times, March 5, 1968, p. 1.

76. Arvis Chalmers, "Mark of Steingut: 'Consensus Politics,'" in The Albany Knickerbocker News, April 25, 1969, p. 4.

77. Condello, op. cit.

78. Blumenthal, op. cit.

79. Duane Lockard, "The State Legislator," in State Legislatures in American Politics, Alexander Heard, ed. (Englewood Cliffs, N.J.: Prentice-Hall, Inc., 1966), p. 114.

80. See Wahlke, op. cit.

81. Abrams, op. cit.

82. Ibid.

83. Bisceglia, op. cit.

84. William Lithgow, budget analyst, Assembly Ways and Means Committee, interview, February 16, 1970.

85. June Martin, director, Assembly Central Staff, interview, February 26, 1970.

64

3

INTERNAL
POWER RELATIONSHIPS

THE SENATE MAJORITY LEADER AND
THE ASSEMBLY SPEAKER

The relationship between the Speaker and the Majority Leader of the Senate is a complex one, due to the fact that there is an inherent rivalry between the two, while, on the other hand, they need each other so much.

More often than not, they are natural competitors. Thus, they compete automatically for legislative and political power no matter whether they are of the same or of different parties. The passage of some important piece of legislation not only means redistribution of political power among the interests concerned with the bill, but it also means political rewards for those responsible. The legislative accomplishments of one leader automatically lessen the prestige of the other, unless they share the spotlight.

On the other hand, there is a fundamental mutuality of interests. Both houses must pass bills, and each leader needs the cooperation of the other in this respect. Almost as important is the fact that neither of the two leaders alone can consistently stand up to the governor's power and influence, while together they sometimes can prevail against him. In legislative controversies, it depends on the circumstances whether the lack of cooperation between the two leaders and parties hurts one side more than the other. But if one house passes some controversial bill while the other house refuses to comply, usually both leaders are hurt.

In most cases, the relationship finds practical expression in a curious interplay of agreements and bickering, with attempts to work together alternating with attempts to get the better of the rival. These paradoxical elements are inherent in the job of the leader, so that each man must find, again and again, ways of reconciling the need to cooperate with the need to compete.

For quite some time, the relationship between Speaker Oswald Heck and Senator Mahoney appeared to be an exception to the observed rule: The two men cooperated quite closely in the establishment of their party's program. Both dominated their respective houses, and there was little ideological difference between them. However, toward the end of Heck's career, the relationship returned to pattern, and the two leaders started to fight each other in earnest.

The controversy started in the course of a special session in June of 1957 when Heck and Democratic governor Harriman joined in support of a bill to reduce a $55,500,000 rate increase granted to the N.Y. Telephone Company. In the Assembly, Heck saw to the passage of this consumer-oriented measure in 1956, but it died in Senate committee. The Senate Finance Committee killed it by a 13 to 7 vote (all 13 were Republicans). A week later Mahoney devised a strategy in the Republican conference whereby the Finance Committee would report the bill out for floor debate and vote, but then the Republican majority would kill the bill by a party vote, all Republicans voting in the negative.[1] Despite the defeat in the Senate, Heck decided to have the bill passed in the Assembly anyway to get at least some political mileage for the Assembly Republicans and to put the onus for the higher rate increase directly on the shoulders of the Senate.[2]

By late 1957, both Heck and Mahoney had an eye on the governorship, and this circumstance cooled their friendship even further. In December 1957, Heck came forward with a broad legislative program of reform proposals which included a number of popular measures such as the creation of a special antirackets prosecutor as a response to the Mafia meeting at Apalachin, New York, and, as the result of the Soviet Union's Sputnik flight, a plan to aid science education in the state. This was supposed to become the Republican legislative program for the 1958 session, but for the first time in their entire relationship Heck omitted showing it to Senate leader Mahoney.[3]

Soon thereafter, Heck and his Assembly Majority Leader, Joseph Carlino, issued a series of joint statements to publicize their own positions on a variety of proposed measures, again without consultation with their counterparts in the Senate.[4] What is more, during the 1958 session, Heck took the floor to urge the Assembly to defeat Mahoney's pet project—the imposition of one year's residence as a condition of welfare payments. The Assembly defeated the bill. Heck also killed a Mahoney plan to set up a legislative watchdog committee on crime.[5] The conclusion is that the dual but conflicting ambitions of the two leaders resulted in a series of public disputes, disputes which were natural to their rivalry, but which could, under different circumstances, have been avoided.

Walter Mahoney was a champion of the independence of the legislature and its defender against encroachments on the part of the governor. He made this an article of faith which united the Senate under his leadership in a most effective way. When later he was faced with a more liberal governor, in the person of Rockefeller, and with a more liberal Speaker, Joseph Carlino, he used this unity as an armor protecting his own personal independence from the other two. In March 1960, for example, he introduced legislation to grant a $10 tax rebate to married couples, knowing fully well that Rockefeller and Carlino would object.[6] Later in the year, the governor called for a 10-percent tax reduction, which Mahoney supported but Carlino opposed.[7] A year later, Rockefeller wanted the 10-percent tax rebate eliminated and the revenue restored. Now Mahoney stood alone (although he finally gave in).[8] The 1962 session saw more fighting between Mahoney and Carlino. For example, a bill to permit the city of New York to take over the Fifth Avenue Bus Line was stalled by Mahoney in the Senate because, he said, he had not been consulted on the measure, and it did not pass until he was mollified.[9] Then Mahoney introduced a bill to reapportion the state legislature. The result would have been an increase in Republican seats at the expense of the representation from the city of New York. Carlino and the Assembly opposed the measure and voted not to reapportion, a serious defeat for Mahoney.[10]

The relationship between Senate Majority Leader Earl Brydges and Assembly Speaker Anthony Travia was one of continuous dispute since each led different parties. In addition, the two men were ideological opponents with Brydges the upstate conservative and Travia the New York City liberal. To the top man in the state's leadership triumvirate, Governor Rockefeller, the contentions between the two men offered frequent openings for changing partners, in pursuit of his own objectives. He knew that he could obtain, if needed, Travia's cooperation only through tangible concessions in matters of legislation. Travia never made any bones about the pleasure he got out of extracting his occasional pound of flesh from the governor.[11] So they haggled and bargained as would industry and labor in hour-and-wage negotiations, but always in a friendly and relaxed manner.

Gradually the friendly give and take between Rockefeller and Travia led to Senator Brydges's growing alienation and isolation from the governor. No longer did the three leaders meet together to agree on policy. Rockefeller preferred, for good reason, to meet the two legislators separately. In this manner he could make liberal gestures toward Travia and then tell Brydges that the liberalization of programs was extorted from him by the Speaker. Thus, he could get along with the Democratic Speaker, while Brydges was forced to stick with the governor as the lesser of two liberal evils and as head of his own party.

The result was, of course, growing tension and diminishing cooperation between the two leaders of the legislature. With the two houses divided, it was generally Travia who, as leader of the opposition, took the offensive.

The leadership competition between Brydges and Perry Duryea, Republican Speaker who took on January 1, 1969, has a rather more subdued tone. However, even though both men were leaders of the same party, conflict between them was frequent.

For example, on the three most important issues of the 1970 session, the two leaders were unable to come to terms for months. In connection with the proposed constitutional amendment to lower the voting age to 18, Brydges wanted to lower the voting age at once in 1972. Duryea's idea was to do this in slow stages: to 20 in four years with a referendum needed to approve the move, to 19 four years later, and finally to 18 in another four years, also with voter approval needed. A Federal constitutional amendment has, of course, made both approaches moot. On the issue of repealing the so-called Blaine amendment, the state constitutional provision prohibiting state aid to private and parochial schools, Brydges in the Senate permitted the passage of the repeal bill without amendments. Duryea permitted its passage in the Assembly with an amendment proposed originally by Democratic senator Manfred Ohrenstein, which allowed taxpayer suits to determine whether public funds had been properly granted to nonpublic schools. Finally, Brydges decided to release the long-pending abortion reform bill to the Senate floor, with the result that a sweepingly liberal law, allowing abortion with the approval of the mother and her doctor, was enacted. Duryea on his part arranged for the introduction in the Assembly of two in themselves unimportant technical amendments for the sole purpose of forcing the Senate into another debate and vote on the bill.

Why the lack of cooperation between two leaders of the same party on what were really minor differences of approach? Why this straining between them for advantage? To some extent, competition is inherent in their jobs. However, it appears that a major contributing factor was Duryea's inclination to assert independence for its own sake and to establish for himself an image of independence which would be useful in his subsequent pursuit of the governorship.

In sum, the bicameral nature of the New York legislature seems to breed competition between the two majority party leaders. In the interest of party unity or of satisfactory legislative action, the leaders often try to patch up their differences and avoid conflict, but the basic inherent characteristic of the relationship is reciprocal desire to surpass each other in stature and power. The incidence of variables such as ideological differences, competition for higher office, and of course party conflict between the two houses can only exacerbate the duel for preeminence.

THE SENATE MAJORITY LEADER AND THE
SENATE MINORITY LEADER

In the main, two factors exert influence upon the character of the relationship between the Senate Majority and Minority Leaders. One is the size of the majority enjoyed by the President Pro Tempore's party. If the majority is small, a few defections from the majority party can defeat a bill by joining the minority party united in opposition. There are always a few mavericks or legislators whom constituency pressures compel to vote against their party on some particular measure. In such cases, the Majority Leader must either deal with the Minority Leader or try to secure votes of members of the minority party.

The second variable factor is the approach of the Minority Leader to the task of mustering his forces. Usually the Minority Leader tries his best to organize his party into a cohesive entity, demonstrating unity in debate and standing united when the issue comes up for a vote, or else he uses every possible parliamentary maneuver to delay or prevent action by dramatizing alternatives, offering amendments, and so on. This approach calls for readiness to fight the majority party leader, as well as the governor, if he is of the other party. But there have been Minority Leaders who followed an entirely different approach: Instead of trying to unite the minority as a force of opposition, they have allowed each party member to map out his own role by cooperating with the majority or swapping votes, often in exchange for such benefits as the passage of some nonpolitical minor bills and job patronage. In such a case, the leaders of the majority and of the minority will have no reason to be anything but friends.

From 1954 to 1956, the leader of the Democratic minority in the Senate was Francis Mahoney. He had little opportunity to choose any of these two approaches. The Republicans under his namesake, Walter Mahoney, had a large enough majority to dispense most of the time with Democratic votes. Whenever they needed a few minority votes, Walter Mahoney could easily get them, behind the back of the Democratic leader. Frank Mahoney recognized that it was impossible to unify the Democrats in the Senate into a force capable of influencing legislation.

Joseph Zaretzki reached the office of Democratic leader through the same route and with a similar political background as Frank Mahoney. Carmine DeSapio played a decisive role in Zaretzki's selection.

Zaretzki was a weak leader. He was subservient to the Republicans, although for purposes of public consumption he has publicly berated them on the Senate floor. He was easily cowed by the more vocal among his fellow Democrats. As one Democratic senator said, "The more I threaten him, the nicer he'll be to me." One incident is instructive. During the 1970 session, Zaretzki almost never called his party into legislative conference. By late March, a group of his more dedicated colleagues had enough of the chronic inertia, and they decided to hold a conference, if necessary, without Zaretzki. The meeting was held during a 10-minute recess of a Senate meeting, and Zaretzki was present. After a while, Majority Leader Brydges knocked on the door of the meeting to announce that the 10 minutes were up. Thereupon, to everybody's surprise, Zaretzki invited Brydges to come in and take part in the Democratic conference. Enraged, one of the senior Democrats asked Brydges to leave, at the risk of his own personal relationship with the Majority Leader.

THE ASSEMBLY SPEAKER AND THE ASSEMBLY MAJORITY LEADER

The Assembly Majority Leader is a completely dependent creature of the Speaker. He is responsible for leading the majority party in debate in a technical sense only, since he speaks and acts for the Speaker rather than for himself. He is a member ex officio of the Rules Committee and of other standing committees and has sufficient funds for keeping a sizable staff, but he serves merely as an executor of the Speaker's will.

In the Assembly there is almost complete consensus on the role of the Majority Leader. John Kingston, Nassau Republican and current Majority Leader under Speaker Duryea, said, "My job is simply to sum up the viewpoint of the Republicans in the Assembly and do it well."[12]

During his service as Majority Leader under Speaker Heck, Joseph Carlino knew that he was merely as instrument in the Speaker's hands. By persisting loyally in the modest interpretation of his role, he secured for himself Heck's appreciation and friendship. This factor was at least as helpful to him in his effort to succeed Heck in the Speaker's chair as his personal competence.

Only slightly different was the relationship between Speaker Travia and his Majority Leader, Moses Weinstein, Democratic county leader of Queens. During the bitter leadership struggle of 1965, Weinstein had loyally served Travia in the role of floor leader. His appointment as Majority Leader was his reward. A staff member of the Speaker who wished not to be identified summed up the relationship:

Moe was as effective as Tony allowed him to be, but Tony felt he had one job, to debate. Moe attended few meetings and was ignored when he did. Tony bypassed him completely in much the same way as Duryea bypasses Kingston today. Moe was Tony's cherry bomb to be set off once in a while. And he was very good blasting the Republicans.

Another Democratic staff veteran described the relationship this way: "Travia never asked Moe about major decisions and Moe greatly resented this. Moe was handled poorly. They could have invited him to the key meetings and then ignored his suggestions."

The final word on the role of the Majority Leader under Speaker Travia is Travia's own:

> I reluctantly chose Weinstein when Lifset refused to serve. I was pressured to dump him later on, but he was loyal to me, so I didn't. But it was not the role of the Majority Leader to share power, only to be the Speaker's mouthpiece.[13]

Assemblyman Harvey Lifset of Albany was the Speaker's original candidate for the post of Majority Leader, but he declined under pressure from his county leader, Daniel O'Connel, who felt Lifset's appointment might mean the loss of considerable minor patronage which the Albany Democratic organization had traditionally received.

THE ASSEMBLY SPEAKER AND THE ASSEMBLY MINORITY LEADER

The same variables that influence the relationship between the Senate Majority and Minority Leaders apply as well to the relationship between Assembly Speaker and Minority Leader. The crucial factor is the size of the majority party margin in the House, and the perception of the Minority Leader of his own role is second.

Eugene Bannigan, who served as Democratic Minority Leader from 1953 to 1958, had a very warm, close, and friendly relationship with Speaker Heck. Heck, however, did not need the votes of the Democrats very often because most of the time his own party was strong and united. Since the relationship was close, Bannigan occasionally helped to bail Heck out, but these instances were infrequent. From 1955-58, when Democratic governor Harriman himself initiated much of the major legislation dealt with, chances to cooperate with the Speaker diminished for Bannigan. The legislative program of the

Assembly was determined by give and take between Heck, Harriman, and the Republican conference. The Democratic members and their leader had very little to say.

Anthony Travia, Minority Leader for most of his career under Republican Speaker Carlino, was relatively ineffective as well. He, too, was faced with the unchangeable problem of the absence of enough votes to make an impact. However, whereas Bannigan was an excellent public speaker and could at least effectively articulate the Democrat viewpoint, Travia was a poor debater, unsure of himself, and consequently he seldom acted even in the limited role of party spokesman. He rarely went on radio or television and usually left the task of floor debate to others.[14] Carlino felt it quite easy to bypass Travia when once in a while he needed the votes of a few Democrats.[15]

Under these circumstances, unity among the Democrats became more and more tenuous with the result that those minority lawmakers who desired to see a working opposition develop felt the situation increasingly hopeless. The extraordinary improvement in Travia's performance when he became Speaker can be explained in part by the great powers that are at the Speaker's disposal.

Stanley Steingut was elected Democratic Minority Leader in the Assembly in 1969. As we have seen, his election brought about a truly remarkable change in the spirit, cohesiveness, and effectiveness of the Assembly minority. The fact is, however, that no matter how purposeful Steingut's leadership may have been, the marked improvement in the performance of the Assembly Democrats could not have come about at all if they would have been confronted with an adequate Republican majority. In this case, again the size of the margin proved decisive: In 1969, there were only 78 Republicans to 72 Democrats in the Assembly, a majority of only two votes above the minimum necessary to pass a bill. In 1970, a seventy-ninth Republican was elected in Rochester in place of Democrat Charles Stockmeister whom the governor had appointed to a high administrative post. Even so, the margin was still quite tenuous because several Republican assemblymen were elected with the help of their candidacies on the Conservative party line, and thus their votes could have occasionally gone astray. This was the situation that enabled Steingut to forge the Assembly Democrats into a cohesive and effective minority bloc, but as the initiator and promoter of the process of consolidation, Steingut himself performed an effective leadership job, which had changed a badly splintered group of legislators into an effectively operating instrumentality of legislative activity.

THE LEADERS AND THE STANDING COMMITTEES

In the tradition of American legislatures, the New York legislature is organized on the basis of a standing committee system with each committee given jurisdiction over different subject areas. The number of standing committees had been fairly consistent in the last 15 years: The Senate had between 26 and 34 standing committees; the Assembly, 30 to 38. In 1969, however, the Assembly reduced the number to 20.

In both houses committee members are appointed by the party leader. On the average, assemblymen serve on three committees each, while majority senators serve on seven, eight, or even nine committees; minority senators on five or six. The proportion of Democrats to Republicans is determined by the approximate percentage of Democrats to Republicans in the House as a whole. Then a couple of extra seats on each committee are assigned to members of the majority party to assure majority control. All chairmen are members of the majority party, appointed by the Speaker in the Assembly and the Majority Leader in the Senate. The standards for appointment are generally, but not exclusively, seniority and of course loyalty to the leader. Ability to perform well and to the credit of the party as well as expertise in the relevant subject area are other important factors taken into consideration.

Today the committees report out to the floor of their respective houses approximately the same number of bills as they did 30 years ago. In 1941, Assembly committees reported out 1,538 bills; in 1966, they reported out 1,579. [16] However, the number of bills introduced in the Assembly has almost tripled in the past 25 years, from 2,735 in 1945 to 6,091 in 1967. [17] This shows that the committees are screening out an increasing number of bills.

These figures include the product of the Assembly's Rules Committee, and it must be noted that the Rules Committees and Fiscal Committees of each house handle a large percentage of the total number of bills. In 1967, of 6,091 bills introduced in the Assembly, 1,887 were referred to Rules and 1,697 to Ways and Means. Their performance with respect to major bills is comparable. Of 127 bills listed by the Speaker as "significant" in 1965, a total of 36 were reported out of Rules and 41 out of Ways and Means. [18] No figures are available about the share of these committees in the Senate, but the likelihood is that they are similar.

The party leaders derive some part of their leadership power from their control over the committee system. Since they appoint all members and all chairmen, they can count on a measure of loyalty and support. The membership knows that the leaders use appointments to committees as rewards for or inducements to loyalty. We have already discussed the powers of the Rules Committees in channeling the flow of legislation and determining the ultimate shape of legislative programs and noted that these committees are dominated by the leaders. It should be added here that over and above the advantages of title and greater power, committee chairmen and ranking minority members also obtain tangible benefits for holding those positions, in the form of larger offices, better equipment, and larger staffs. They also receive bonus "lulus," allowances "in lieu of expenses," of the kind that in earlier years had accrued only to party leaders. Thus, their stake in remaining chairmen, appointed by the leaders, is quite high.

Currently all members of the legislature receive a salary of $15,000 plus a $5,000 "in lieu" payment. The Speaker and the Senate Majority Leader each get $21,000 lulu, and the Minority Leaders $18,000. The Assembly Majority Leader gets an additional $18,500; the chairman of the Senate Finance and Assembly Ways and Means Committees, $18,000; and the ranking minority members, $9,500. All other committee chairmen get additional lulus running from $5,000 to $7,000, depending on the importance of the committee (with ranking minority members getting $2,500 to $4,000). In the Assembly, in recent years, a number of other party positions have been created with minimal responsibilities but with certain added benefits, such as title, prestige, and more lulus. Thus, each party has today a deputy floor leader, a whip, a conference chairman, conference vice chairmen, and a conference secretary. The additional allotments vary from $7,500 to $1,500.19

All these additional disposables further enhance the power of the party leaders to prevent breaches of loyalty by increasing the losses that might result from members becoming too independent.

Within the context of these formal arrangements, there are other factors that intrude upon the character of the Speaker's and the Senate Majority Leader's relations with, and control over, the standing committees. These factors relate primarily to the security with which the leader holds power. It is almost axiomatic that a new leader will permit much greater freedom to his members and, therefore, to the committees since he is insecure about his power. Additionally the post-1966 leader is faced with the fact that there has been a great turnover in the membership, and new legislators with fewer ties to the older values of centralized leadership have been elected. The impact of reapportionment on this turnover and the insecurity regarding reelection of some lawmakers make them more responsive to home district needs and, therefore, more willing to fight for control over their areas of legislative specialization and their committees to develop a record on which they could get reelected. These factors have been discussed before, but they are again relevant.

Accordingly, Oswald Heck and Walter Mahoney gave their committee chairmen little discretion in determining policy. Everything remained centralized, and decisions of any significance had to be cleared through their offices.[20] Speaker Carlino and Speaker Travia applied the same strict control, although the latter for the first time was confronted with opposition and public protests on this score. On the other hand, Joseph Zaretzki, with only one year's service as Senate Majority Leader, and Earl Brydges, in his first years as leader, did not seek this kind of full domination over their committees. Instead, Brydges's policy was to foster the loyalty of committee chairmen by relatively decentralizing his leadership power and giving greater authority to these men. Speaker Duryea appears to be following the same approach.

This relaxation of central controls does not apply, however, to the treatment of the Assembly Rules Committee and Ways and Means Committee, nor to the handling of the Rules Committee and the Finance Committee of the Senate. The Rules Committees remain the exclusive power preserves of the leader. The record shows no attempt on the part of members of these committees to stand up against this state of affairs. The control of the leaders over the fiscal committees is somewhat more indirect, but through the appointment of the chairmen and the chief staff personnel (the secretaries) their influence is still decisive.

CONCLUSIONS

By comparing the potential influence of the leaders of the majority party with that of other legislative leaders and lawmakers, we have seen that the Assembly Speaker and the Majority Leader of the Senate stand indeed on the top of the pyramid of decision-making power within the legislature of New York.

While their joint power is unrivaled by any other factor within the legislature, the position of these leaders is strongly exposed to rivalry—that of each other. The chief rival for authority within the legislature of one of these leaders is the majority party leader of the other house. The President Pro Tempore of the Senate and the Assembly Speaker are automatic rivals in terms of legislative influence because, in the bicameral structure, they share power. But rivalry leading to confrontation is often muted by the need for cooperation, where the leaders perceive that on a particular issue failure to reach an accommodation will hurt them both.

Such accommodation is, of course, more difficult on the occasions where the two majority party leaders represent different parties, or subscribe to differing ideologies, or have competitive ambitions.

However, even in such situations, only a degree of mutual goodwill can lead to the compromise needed for the passage of mutually desirable legislation.

Since the two majority party leaders occupy a position of dominance over all other legislators including the minority leaders, the latters' ability to successfully oppose majority-sponsored legislation is limited indeed. They may cause difficulties. They may embarrass the leader of the majority. However, they can actually influence important decisions only in cases where a few mavericks from the majority party are ready to vote with the minority to change the outcome of a ballot. This circumstance makes the role of the minority leader as a partisan fighter difficult indeed and may have caused some of these leaders to neglect this important aspect of their office.

Despite the present trend toward decentralization of authority, the leaders still maintain considerable influence over the standing committees and their chairmen. Circumstances might make it good strategy for them to let committee chairmen develop their own areas of authority, but since such chairmen, as well as all committee members, are direct appointees of the leaders, and since their budgets are subject to ultimate leadership approval, the final power over important decisions rests with the leaders themselves.

Therefore, internally at least, the position of the majority party leaders is one of unquestionable authority over all other potential rivals for influence within the legislature. The question whether that authority can extend beyond the boundaries of the legislature itself and into the prerogatives of that other leading participant in the legislative subsystem, the governor, will be examined in the following chapter.

NOTES

1. Newsday, June 5, 1957; June 11, 1957.
2. Ibid., June 13, 1957.
3. Ibid., December 12, 1957.
4. Ibid., October 24, 1957; November 11, 1957; December 4, 1957; October 2, 1958.
5. Ibid., April 3, 1958.
6. The New York Times, March 20, 1960.
7. Ibid., November 23, 1960.
8. Ibid., January 11, 1962.
9. Ibid., March 15, 1962.
10. Ibid., March 21, 1962; March 22, 1962.
11. Anthony Travia, former Assembly Speaker, interview, December 23, 1969.

12. Assembly Majority Leader John Kingston, interview, December 9, 1969.

13. Travia, op. cit.

14. Senator Seymour Thaler, interview, April 6, 1970.

15. Henry Paley, former director of information to the Speaker, interview, December 18, 1969.

16. Stuart K. Witt, Reorganization of a State Legislative Committee System, N.Y. Assembly report, Albany, August 1969, p. 10.

17. Ibid., p. 22.

18. Ibid., p. 21.

19. Ibid., p. 19.

20. Albert Abrams, secretary, New York Senate, interview, January 21, 1970.

4

THE GOVERNOR
AS LAWMAKER

THE GOVERNOR IN THE UNITED STATES

No study of American legislatures can ignore the dominant role played in most legislative systems by the governor of the state. He has become the most visible and prominent of the participants in the system and is the focal point for a great deal of the pressure from interest groups and from the people generally. Where discontent exists, and it is definitely growing in many states, the office of the governor is the main target of criticism and the center of conflict. The ratio of governors who fail in getting reelected is fairly high. Between 1958 and 1962, a total of 26 incumbent governors, representing 44 percent of those running for reelection, were defeated.[1]

The high visibility of the governor's office adds considerable fuel to the public feeling that he must be held primarily responsible for solving major problems. Governors in almost every state are expected to take the lead in the development of legislative programs that may resolve problems of major public concern.

This was not always the case. The powers and responsibilities of early American governors were considerably less extensive. They were elected to short terms, were not expected to introduce legislation, rarely had veto powers, and often had to compete for public esteem with other elected executive officials.[2] The situation changed only after implementation of the democratic reforms imposed during the Jacksonian period, which granted gubernatorial veto powers, expanded the franchise, and extended the terms of service of governors. Toward the end of the 1800s, the item veto was added in many states. However, at the same time, the system of direct election of other administrative officials was adopted by more and more of the states, with the result that many governors began to lose much of the control they might have had over the executive branch.[3]

By the early twentieth century, the complexity of public issues, growing popular demand for social reform and welfare programs, and the increasing public distrust of many legislatures (resulting from evident corruption) gradually led to a new and significant expansion of gubernatorial powers. Reformers clamored for constitutional changes to enhance the powers of the executive, and the record of such creative governors as Theodore Roosevelt, LaFollette, Wilson, Lowden, and Smith gave great impetus to the movement. As a result, in many states the terms of governors were extended to four years; governors were permitted to run for reelection; the item veto was extended; and governors were increasingly expected to initiate major legislative programs.

When, in 1921, Governor Frank Lowden of Illinois successfully reorganized his executive branch by making state agencies responsible to him and by limiting the number of independent boards and commissions, and when Governor Al Smith of New York established in 1927 an executive budget system, they set precedents followed by most of the states. The resultant changes allowed governors greater opportunities for mobilizing administrative resources, and these resources became invaluable reservoirs of expertise in the development of social programs.[4]

As a result of the constitutional and legislative changes, the present scope of gubernatorial powers is much broader in the area of legislation than in the past. In most states, the governor today has the right and, by tradition, the responsibility to submit messages to the legislature to outline his own legislative wishes. According to Keefe and Ogul, "political environments are rare where executive recommendations are not the principal items on the legislature's agenda."[5] The governor may also submit draft legislation of his own making to accompany the messages. Most governors are also responsible for submitting an executive budget which, in actual effect, is the fiscal determinant of policy priorities preferred by the governor. In general, the budget is the most difficult and important piece of legislation facing lawmakers in any given year since, in budgetary matters, knowledge and expertise are usually greater on the executive than on the legislative side. The governor often has great advantages over the lawmakers when the bargaining over the final scope and form of the budget begins.

However, the American governor's greatest constitutionally granted power over the legislative process in the veto. Many state governors also have the power to use the item veto (some restricted to appropriations bills), and in some states they can reduce appropriations items. Governors in 49 of the 50 states (North Carolina excepted) have enjoyed the veto power throughout the twentieth century with 80 percent of them also empowered to employ an item veto. The veto is a very effective weapon in the hands of the governors because, in practice, it can only very rarely be overridden. This is so because the governor is rarely in command of less than one-third or two-fifths of the membership in one house, and such a bloc of votes is usually sufficient to defeat the motion to override. Additionally, most legislatures pass most of their bills toward the end of the session, and the governor has the option of signing or vetoing most bills after adjournment of the legislature. Finally, the mere threat of a veto can greatly influence the formulation of a bill before it comes out for a vote on the floor of a legislative body.

Many governors enjoy the further prerogative of calling special sessions and limiting their agendas. In three-fifths of the states, the call of a special session is an exclusive power of the governor. In one-third of the states, the governor has sole discretion over the agenda of the special session. Thus, the pet programs of the governor, disregarded or even rejected in the regular session, can be revived in a special session (New York governor Nelson Rockefeller saw his so-called liquor reform program defeated in the regular session of the 1964 legislature, but called a special session at which a modified version was adopted).

Constitutions can enlarge gubernatorial powers, but they can also reduce them. Many states restrict their governors to one term in office, and a few to two terms. Many mandate the independent election of other executive officials who have their own patronage to dispense, platforms from which to capture public support, and freedom to court the legislature. They are, therefore, potential rivals of the governor. However, some reformers have begun to pressure for changes in these limitations as they successfully ended other limitations in previous years.[6]

In addition to constitutional powers, governors have increasingly added to their practical power base by asserting their prerogatives as party leaders. This is especially true where two-party competition is strong and where the governor is the acknowledged party leader. The unity that the existence of a strong minority party often imposes upon a majority party is a great help to the governor because it makes breaches of party loyalty much more consequential and risky.

The governor has significant rewards at his personal disposal to grant or to withhold according to his political interest, and these rewards can greatly help him maintain legislative loyalty. He distributes a great deal of patronage among county and local party officials because in most strong two-party states, these officials sometimes have great influence over the nomination of legislators. Even as a threat, the withdrawal of job patronage is strong medicine against party disloyalty. What is even more significant, the governor has veto power over local legislation that can influence the chances of reelection of legislators and over the electoral choices of important local groups clamoring for governmental benefits. All these added powers of the governor as party leader can often make the price of disloyalty prohibitive indeed.

In one-party states, party loyalty is, of course, much less important for the legislator. There is no common enemy. In such states all the greater is the importance of patronage as an instrument of gubernatorial control. Patronage by the governor covers, of course, in addition to jobs, such items as contracts with business or public works, road building, purchasing of supplies, and so on. Many legislators are only part-time politicians, and some have important outside business interests. Rewards can extend (or be withheld from) one's business contacts as well as from the legislator himself and his immediate political family.[7]

Finally, there is a very important factor that can greatly help the governor in any attempt to influence the work of the legislature. This factor is his visibility, the result of his position at the center of the stage of public attention. Most citizens expect him to do what there is to be done; the mass media give him tremendous exposure, exposure far greater than that enjoyed by any single legislator or by the legislature itself. All in all, the governor has become the primary legislator in most states.

Simultaneously with this growth of gubernatorial influence over the destinies of lawmaking, there has been a negative decline in the ability of state legislatures to compete with the governor. Division of legislative labor has led to division of power within many legislatures, with committees and party leaders each controlling only parts of the total process. Even where strong centralized leadership exists, there are always at least two centers of power within the legislative body—the party leaders in each house. The effect of this division is strengthened by the fact that most legislatures are part-time operations conducted by part-time workers who cannot hope to command the mass of technical detail needed for the development of major programs of their preference in the way the governor and his permanent staff handle their own legislative proposals. Many legislators are further distracted from purposeful legislative effort not only by private business or professional careers, but also by attempts to advance to higher office or to service their local constituents and interest groups.

The large turnover within the ranks of state legislators further diminishes the ability of the legislatures to compete with the governor for predominance in their own specific field of competence and responsibility—the field of devising the laws meant to govern the lives of the people of their state. The initiative in these matters has been largely lost to the governor.

In many legislatures the change has already seriously affected the very nature of lawmaking. Realizing their growing inability to initiate really important new programs of their own choice, these legislatures are increasingly prepared to put up with the lesser fare of receiving the governor's proposals and of revising them to fit their political and local needs. Thus, the legislature in most states has reluctantly become a reacting agent to executive leadership, although occasionally it still may display enough institutional pride to resist some of the governor's initiatives.

THE CONSTITUTIONAL POWERS OF THE GOVERNOR OF NEW YORK

Joseph A. Schlesinger has attempted to quantify the formal powers of governors throughout the United States, for the purpose of comparing these powers in different states. Thus, he ascribes a certain value to such aspects of the governor's authority as his tenure potential, appointment power, control over the budget, and veto power. For example, if the governor has full responsibility for the preparation and submission of the budget, he gets five points. If the governor shares such power with another appointed officer, he is granted only four points. If he shares this power with a committee appointed from some restricted list, his power is worth three points, and so on. "To arrive at a general rating of the governors' formal powers, we have combined the measures of each governor's strength already presented: his tenure potential, and his appointive, budgetary, and veto powers. The maximum possible rating is 19, found only in New York."[8]

On any scale, the formal powers granted to the governor of New York are considerable, and he is, as a result, a powerful legislative leader. The state constitution grants, very clearly and concisely, quite formidable legislative powers to him. These are specified in Article IV, Section 3, which requires him, among other things, "to take care that the laws be faithfully executed." The same section grants him the right to recommend legislation to the legislature by stating that "he shall communicate by message to the legislature at every session the condition of the state, and recommend such matters to it as he shall deem expedient."

The same section provides further that the governor "shall have power to convene the legislature, or the Senate only, on extraordinary occasions. At extraordinary sessions no subject shall be acted upon, except such as the governor may recommend for consideration." This power produced an interesting side problem as described by Colemar Ransone:

The fact that the governor has authority in many
states to limit the subjects to be considered at a special
session has brought up the interesting problem of whether
the governor may be impeached at a special session which
was called for another purpose. This situation actually
occurred in New York where the impeachment of Governor
Sulzer took place during a special session, which the governor called for the transaction of other business. [The
state courts upheld the impeachment on the grounds that
it was judicial in nature and not legislative and therefore
extended beyond the requirement that the legislature deal
only with those legislative matters specified by the governor.][9]

Article IV, Section 7, defines the role of the governor in the
treatment of bills passed by the legislature. He has the power to sign
the bill into law or to veto it, in which case it is returned to the House
in which it originated for reconsideration. His veto can be overriden
by a two-thirds vote of the members elected in each house. He can
let a bill sit on his desk for 10 days without signing or vetoing. After
the passage of 10 days (except Sundays), the bill becomes law. If,
however, the legislature adjourns for the year before the 10 days are
over, the bill is automatically defeated. The same section gives the
governor 30 days after the adjournment of the legislature to act on
bills. Of course, any bill vetoed in that 30-day period is automatically
killed since the legislature is not in session to override. The governor's influence as party leader can also prevent override attempts,
since it is unlikely that a New York governor would not have at least
one-third of the members of one house supporting his veto.
    Article IV, Section 7, further empowers the governor to veto
specific provisions in appropriations bills (subject also to the two-
thirds vote to override the veto by the legislature), while approving
the rest of the bill.
    One of the most important constitutional requirements is that
the governor prepare and submit to the legislature an executive budget. Article VII, Sections 1, 2, and 3, detail these requirements.
    There are some other provisions regulating the formal relation-
ship of the governor with the legislature, among them his power to
issue "messages of necessity." The Constitution requires that bills
sit on the desks of the legislators for three full calendar legislative
days (a legislative day is a day that the legislature is in session,
although some legislative days are called for weekends when no member is present except the local member from Albany, who comes into
the chamber, moves that the session begin and then moves that the
session adjourn for the day, so that bills may age one day longer).

Article III, Section 14, provides that the governor may, if he feels that the situation warrants it, certify in writing that there is a need for waiving the three-day rule, and it is thereby waived. This happens with some regularity when less than three days remain before the end of a session.

In sum, the legislative powers of the governor in New York are as broad as that of any chief executive in the country. They offer a governor ample means and opportunities to make his will prevail over the legislature. Warren Moscow described the legislative activity of the governor a long time ago (his book was published in 1948); his description is still substantially accurate for today.

There are about six months a year when the governor can relax, providing his department heads are any good, and there are another six months when he must work hard. The work really starts in the winter, directly preceding the opening of the legislative session in January. Then the governor must map his spending program for the year, as contained in his budget, and all the policies that will lead to future state expenses and activities. During the session he must be in frequent conferences with the legislators of his own party to drive for the enactment of his program. He must also confer with all of the leaders of the legislature, including those of the opposite party. There will always be a dozen proposals, emanating from the legislature, the department heads, or the citizenry, for the spending of every dollar the state has, and many of the conflicting needs will be pressing. The governor decides. While the legislature can refuse to spend money he has asked for, it can spend nothing without his approval, in practice if not in theory. . . .

During the 90 to 125 days of the normal legislative session, changes in laws can be made, and money voted; so the heat is on from all quarters for policy decisions by the governor. And after the session, there is a 30-day period of the most intense work. Under the Constitution, any bill passed before the last 10 days of the session must be signed or vetoed by the governor in 10 days. The governor may take 30 days to make up his mind on any bill passed in the last 10 days. Most bills fall into the latter category, for two reasons. One is that the legislature is naturally as dilatory as most lawmaking groups and stalls during the early part of the session, then embarks on a mad rush before adjournment. The second is that the governor frequently requests that bills be held up so that he can act after the legislators have gone home. Whatever the reason, the executive has close to a thousand measures he must sign or veto in the 30-day period. If the governor fails to sign or veto a bill in the 10-day category, it becomes law regardless, but failure to sign in the 30-day period acts as a veto. In practice this pocket veto is not used.

Once the 30-day period for signing or vetoing bills is out of the way, the governor can be relatively footloose and lighthearted for months to come. He may take a vacation; he may even take time out to campaign for the presidency. He will spend time on patronage matters and party leadership and the problem of law enforcement. [10]

THE GOVERNOR'S LEGISLATIVE PROGRAM

The preparation of the legislative program and of the budget is the most important and critical task of the executive office of the governor. It is a big job, and it requires discreet handling. The contents of the legislative program are usually kept secret, whenever the governor and the majority in the legislature belong to different parties, for the governor does not wish to be upstaged by his rivals. If the governor and the legislative majority are of the same party, however, the governor usually permits parts of his plans to "leak" to the press before the formal announcement of the budget and the publication of the state of the state speech. [11]

The preparation of Governor Harriman's legislative program was almost completely the function of secretary to the governor, Jonathan Bingham. He was responsible for working out the basic ideas and for their organization into a systematic program, as well as for the drafting of the contents of the governor's annual message and his special messages to the legislature. During Harriman's first year, 1955, the development of the program was rather hasty and haphazard. Bingham worked with Thomas K. Finletter on the first annual message, but the two men had to depend greatly on the assistance of the staffs of the Democratic minority leaders. [12]

By 1955, Bingham was able to set up a better system for program development and he also had the assistance of some specialists in functional areas, people like Daniel Gutman, counsel to the governor, who worked on the problems of crime, the waterfront, the judiciary, and narcotics; Persia Campbell, a Queens College professor and expert on consumer affairs; and Phillip Kaiser on problems of the aged. Bingham also arranged for the exchange of ideas with leading interest groups, like the Citizens Union, the Federation of

Jewish Philanthropies, and other "good-government" groups. The general tone of the various recommendations of these groups was distinctly liberal.

It is interesting to note that Bingham had received very few ideas from Democratic legislators. It seems that they either did not feel the need to assist Harriman in the development of legislation, or were afraid that their own projects, if made part of the governor's program, would be credited to him.

The process of developing the program began on about July 1 of each year. Bingham requested that the Departments report their budgetary and legislative needs by October 1 so that by that date he could begin drafting the annual message. After obtaining the governor's and his counsel's approval of both the annual message and his list of program priorities, Bingham would begin the preparation of special messages on major proposals. The budget experts would be brought in to examine the fiscal implications of programs, and then Bingham would receive the go-ahead to preceed with the final drafts. The Democratic leaders in the legislature would be asked to participate in meetings dealing with these matters, but the governor himself decided, with Bingham's help, the final outline of the program and the priorities to be applied in its presentation.

It must be remembered that at this stage, no bills had as yet been drafted. This task was left to a collaborative effort by the Democratic leaders, department personnel, and lobby groups. Little was drafted by the governor's counsel. [13]

Governor Harriman discussed his program with a relatively small group of people, and depended overwhelmingly on one man, Bingham, for its development. Said the governor, "Bingham had the primary responsibility for organizing the ideas, and since he was a very fluent and fast drafter, he prepared the messages. I, of course, touched them up, but he did the bulk of the work."[14]

Nelson Rockefeller had a large campaign staff in 1958, tooled up for making program recommendations. The group, headed by William Ronan, recruited by Rockefeller from the New York University School of Public Administration, prepared over 80 research papers for the campaign, and many of the ideas suggested became part of the governor's first program in 1959. Most of these ideas originated from a variety of sources, including the departments, interest groups, and the legislature itself since the governor and the majority of legislators were Republicans. Ronan organized over 40 task forces of experts, and they generated new ideas.

However, Ronan and Rockefeller agree that the governor himself was his own number one brain truster. Says Rockefeller:

I generate a lot of ideas myself, and we often work
from top down. My Pure Waters Program resulted from

my presidential primary campaign in California where I
saw them spending $2 billion to bring in water to parts of
the state, and I figured why not spend $1 billion in New
York to clean up water? Ronan then worked up a plan with
federal aid, prefinancing, and local contributions. The
Bundy plan for aid to private colleges and the bond issue
for transportation were also my ideas, although I asked
only $1 billion for the latter and Hurd told me it wouldn't
do the job. Also my political people said it was crazy for
me to propose so big a bond issue the year before election,
but I insisted and campaigned for it as I would have for reelection.[15]

Ronan prepared the ideas for discussion at a number of staff
meetings at which the counsel, press staff, budget people, and others,
would advise the governor. Contributing to these discussions were
memos on various subjects submitted by officials like the lieutenant
governor and the attorney general.

The transition from idea to legislation is a lengthy process.
The governor's counsel prepares a large loose-leaf notebook in which
the subjects, proposed solutions, and arguments for and against are
summarized. Copies are circulated among the governor's staff,
department people, budget experts, and other elected officials. Most
priority determinations are based on fiscal considerations: Should
the idea be pursued, or else dropped, for lack of money? In December
closed meetings are held with the governor, lieutenant governor,
attorney general, secretary to the governor, counsel, and budget
director. The counsel is in charge of drafting the annual message
and the special messages, including subjects that were left out of
the annual message. The first drafts are rather long and are revised
and tightened several times. Each member of the core group submits
his last-minute recommendations, and then a final draft is composed,
only the language of which can be changed by press relations people.
At this point the legislative leaders are brought in for the first time,
and their comments and recommendations are sought. Their remarks
deal primarily with the feasibility of getting the program passed in
the form outlined in the annual message. The counsel and his staff
then draft the actual bills, usually getting done with the job early in
the session so that the bills can be sent over to the leaders for the
choice of sponsors.[16]

THE BUDGET

Perhaps the most telling symptom of the increase of executive
influence over the legislative process is the fact that, in most states,

the governor is responsible for the preparation, presentation to the legislature, and enactment of an annual executive budget. The budget serves as the legal and fiscal framework that governs the implementation of public policy. It is a blueprint for the executive's decisions regarding what ought to be accomplished by the state government in a given year.

Today the governor is responsible for the preparation of the budget in 44 states. In five others, budgets are prepared by boards manned by executive officials. In one state (Arkansas), a legislative council has responsibility for budget preparation.[17] A number of state constitutions and laws go even further: They provide the governor with powers that enable him to determine the final version of the budget. Examples of such consitutional or statutory provisions are the item veto, the time limits within which the legislature must react to the budget, and the restrictions placed on the ability of some legislatures to amend the budget (for example, permitting the lawmakers only to reduce or eliminate budget items). The governor's power is also strengthened by the fact that he has a monopoly of knowledge regarding the budget and has access to executive officials with expertise in this area. Such access is not as readily available to the legislature.

Legislators are at a real disadvantage not only because of their own lack of expertise, but also because they have very little qualified staff assistance (although in some of the larger states, legislatures are expanding staffs in order to compete more effectively with the executive). State legislators are part-time people, whose knowledge of state affairs is, in some areas, not sufficiently specialized. All this makes the executive branch the much stronger side in any budgetary battle, the side that keeps the initiative firmly in hand.

This does not mean that the budget is swept through our legislatures without debate, difficulty, or change. This chapter will relate instances in which governors of New York State had enormous difficulty in getting their budget proposals adopted in the face of powerful opposition from within both parties. But, on balance, the chief executive has sufficient resources to get what he wants most of the time.

On the pattern outlined above, the Constitution of the state of New York gives the governor significant advantages in determining final outcomes regarding the budget. Article VII, Section 1, specifies that the governor may require department heads to submit to him departmental money requests in such form and at such time as he feels necessary. Copies of the requests must be sent to the fiscal committees of the legislature. The governor then must hold hearings at which he may require the attendance of executive department heads, and at which representatives of the legislative fiscal committees attend.

91

These rules do not apply to the treatment of the budgets for the legislature and for the judiciary that are sent to the governor for inclusion in the overall budget before December 1 of each year, after certification by the presiding officer of each house for the legislative budget and by the state comptroller for the judiciary.

Section 2 of the same article requires the governor to submit the budget to the legislature by February 1 in the year following his election, or in other years, within two weeks after the opening of the legislative session in January. The document must include requests for money by all agencies of government, explanations of the requests, and statements estimating revenue. Section 3 provides that the governor also submit bills to regulate the implementation of his proposals contained in the budget. Within 30 days after its presentation, he still has the right to amend his budget bills on his own. Later on he can amend them only with the consent of the legislature. The governor has the right and the department heads have the duty to appear before the legislature during consideration of the budget.

Section 4 rules that the legislature may not alter an appropriation bill submitted by the governor in support of his budget, except to the extent of eliminating or reducing single budget items. It may add money to items proposed in the budget, but only through the enactment of separate bills dealing with the single item in question. The same section then declares that the governor's appropriations bills, once passed by the legislature, are the law and do not need further approval on his part. Bills on appropriations to the legislature and the judiciary, as well as separate bills passed for the purpose of increasing the amount expendable under specific budget items, do need executive approval, and it is here that the governor may use his veto or item veto.

Section 5 of Article VII places a further restriction on the appropriations process, by enjoining the legislature from passing any appropriations bill of its own, until the governor's bills have been acted upon (unless the governor himself certifies that an emergency requires the immediate passage of such an appropriations bill.)

These provisions have one very significant effect upon the position and political influence of the legislature in New York. With the erosion of its ability to systematically scrutinize the policy implications of the executive budget, it has lost much of its influence upon the actual use of state moneys. As Albert Roberts, secretary to the Assembly Ways and Means Committee, wrote in a report on legislative fiscal problems in 1969:

> All too often, state legislatures are the weak links in the American governmental process. Many state constitutions have recently been modified to strengthen the

executive branch. The introduction of new budget systems and reorganization of the executive structure—to mention a few innovations—have all added to the power of the executive. State legislatures, on the other hand, have often been sleeping giants—possessing an appropriate constitutional authority to balance that of the executive, but not realizing in practice the full potentials of a power rightfully their own . . . .

State legislatures have lost the initiative in program creation and review, not because they are no longer viable institutions in the federal system of American government, but to a significant degree because their informational systems have not kept pace with the responsibilities these groups face. As a result, the legislature's ability to control resource allocation has become severely curtailed.[18]

The result in New York, according to Lennis Knighton, a legislative budget consultant, is that "over the past 30 years, legislators have more and more limited their debate and detailed scrutiny of budget and program proposals to the incremental changes that are proposed each year, and seldom are full programs reviewed and discussed in depth."[19]

The shift of power over program and budget decisions began in earnest after the voters in a referendum held in 1927 approved a series of recommendations by Governor Al Smith, which were directed at the broad constitutional restructuring of the state government's executive branch. The following year a Division of the Budget was established as a branch of the governor's Executive Department. Since then it has served as the central workshop for the preparation of the budget and for the control of the implementation of the budget law.

The first executive budget was submitted by Governor Franklin Roosevelt on January 28, 1929. By the time Governor Harriman took office, the Division of the Budget and about 100 professional career experts at work.[20] Professor Frederick Mosher of the Maxwell School of Public Affairs at Syracuse University, and a budget consultant, wrote in 1952 that the Division of the Budget had become one of the most important centers of decision making in the government of New York State. Said Mosher:

It has gradually built itself up in size, scope, and power in its 25-year history, in part as a result of the strength and ability of the budget directors and the backing given them by the governors. These officers have assumed

the role of business managers of the state . . . . Few
major administrative decisions escape the notice of the
budget director, and a great many require his approval.[21]

During the summer months of June, July, and August, departmental budget requests are called in and studied by the Division of
the Budget. In August and September, the Division personnel meet
informally with department personnel. In October and November,
formal hearings are held at which members and staff of the fiscal
committees of the legislature are present. From November to January, the budget document and related bills are drafted and submitted
to the legislature. Through February and March, Budget Division
personnel meet with key legislators and department people. Negotiations continue through March, and the budget is hopefully passed
before the new fiscal year which begins on April 1.[22]

The significance of this timetable for the legislature is that
even in nonelection years when the budget must be submitted by the
middle of January, the legislature has, at most, only 10 or 11 weeks
to review the massive document. The early start of the fiscal year
resulted from a gimmick employed in 1942 to obtain more money for
that year. Prior to 1942 the state had a fiscal year running from
July 1 to June 30. In order to pick up $38 million in additional tax
revenue, the fiscal year was moved up. To return to a July 1-June
30 fiscal year today would cost the state about $800 million.[23]

The constitutional requirement that the departments submit
their requests to the governor before the session begins also calls
for the submission of those requests to the fiscal committees of the
legislature so that there is a little additional time for the committees
to study budget items. The fiscal committees hold closed hearings
on the budget at which the relevant department officers appear to
justify their requests. This involvement of the fiscal committees in
budget preparation before the budget is submitted to the legislature
is the only potentially significant incursion into the strong prerogatives
of the executive branch. The practical effect of the incursion is mini-
mized, however, by the existing restrictions on the legislature's
ability to thoroughly review the budget.

After the budget is submitted, the two fiscal committees hold
joint hearings that last for two days. One day is devoted to questions
of state aid, and the other to the examination of the responsibilities
of the government under the proposed budget. Albert Roberts feels
that these hearings are important because "they form a public record
of administrative intent that is nowhere else available . . . and . . .
they provide a direct legislative access to the departments without
the filtering effects of the budget division or other executive control
agencies."[24] However, their relative merit appears to be reduced
by their abbreviated length.

The personal influence of the legislative leaders themselves on the entire process is not institutionalized or formalized. But in an informal manner it is ever present. At some point of his preparation of the budget and of his legislative program which, to a large extent, flows from the budget, the governor does discuss these matters with the Speaker and the Senate Majority Leader. Additionally, the two legislative leaders obtain information on the proposed budget through the early involvement of their respective fiscal committees in the presession scrutiny of the document. As has been noted earlier, the fiscal committees are fully controlled by the party leaders who appoint the chairmen and membership of these committees, as well as their chief administrative officials—the secretaries; they also control their budgets. On this basis the Assembly Speaker and the Senate Majority Leader are almost automatically in a position to inspire the reactions of the Finance Committees and of the legislature as a whole to the executive budget. In the following, the case histories of the legislative treatment of three annual budgetary programs will be briefly told to show the impact of the leaders' initiative and their relationships with the governor.

In the first case, Democratic governor Harriman was faced with a hostile Republican legislature; in the second, Republican governor Rockefeller had difficulty with what he thought would be a friendly Republican legislature; and in the third case, Rockefeller dealt with what he thought would be a hostile Democratic legislature.

CASE STUDY: THE HARRIMAN BUDGET OF 1956-57

Late in December 1955, the Republican legislative leaders, Senator Walter Mahoney and Speaker Oswald Heck, launched an attack on Governor Harriman, claiming that while in the past fiscal year the state had collected over $100 million more in taxes than the budget required (the Democrats admitted to $70 million), the governor had vetoed a Republican plan for an across-the-board tax cut. At the same time, Mahoney and Heck also accused Harriman of being concerned only with his presidential ambitions and of playing the role of a "spoils politician." They also announced that they would press for a tax cut of about $50 million.[25]

On February 1, 1956, Harriman submitted a budget asking for $1,494,700,000, which is $173.6 million more than the previous budget. Of this difference, $65 million represented mandatory expenditures, and the rest was earmarked for increases in aid to education, in salaries, and in capital construction. The Republicans attacked the plan as both extravagant and as an indication of the fact that the previous year Harriman had misled the public by claiming a financial crisis. It was an election year, and a substantial reduction of the budget seemed inevitable.

During the month of February, the staffs of the fiscal committees of each house reviewed the proposals with a view to cutting them back as far as possible. It should be noted that under Governor Dewey, no executive budget had been cut for 12 years (although a 1949 rebellion led by Senator Mahoney had resulted in the reduction of requested tax increases). However, now everyone knew that under Harriman, political considerations would make a sizable tax cut inevitable. Not only was Harriman interested in national office, but all legislators were themselves up for reelection that November.[26] What was the result of the Republican insistence on tax cuts?

> Despite the fierce cries of the "economy-minded" legislators, very little was cut. Well over 90 percent of the governor's expenditure budget was assured adoption because it represented such legislatively endorsed programs as local assistance, or salaries for state service . . . .
> The legislature usually worked quietly on its budget-cutting operations; sometimes the majority worked so quietly that a minority member of the fiscal committee could not learn what cuts would be made. Normally the legislature held one day of public hearings on the budget in mid-February. In 1956 the hearing started in the afternoon and ended at 10:00 p.m. Very few legislators attended. No record was kept . . .[27]

On February 28, the Republican leaders announced cuts of $23.5 million from Harriman's requests for $1.5 billion. They were politically motivated. Over half of the reductions, $12.6 million, affected programs earmarked for New York City. Others were fictional; many meant simply the postponement of payments. A few days later, the revised budget was sent to the floor of each house for debate and vote. It was passed into law (no approval by the governor being necessary) after minimal debate in each house.

Budget conflicts were not over for the year, however. A special commission (the Heald Commission) was created to study the problems of state aid to education. On February 15, it recommended a state aid formula that would have cost about $60 million more a year. Anticipating Heald's recommendations, Harriman's budget suggested an increase of $31.6 million for this purpose. In early March the governor, Budget Director Paul Appleby, and his soon-to-be successor Clark met with the Republican leaders. Heck and Mahoney, to discuss the matter. No agreement was reached, but the two sides agreed to meet again. On March 11 the Republicans quite unexpectedly publicly announced not only that they were now body and soul for the Heald plan, but also that they insisted upon a further increase in the current budget of $27 million for that purpose. Outmaneuvered and outbid by the opposition, Harriman angrily reacted by calling for an even higher expenditure to meet the Heald requirements. In the end, Appleby negotiated a $32 million increase (above the original $31.6 million) with the Republicans on March 13. [28]

On March 9 the Budget Division personnel met with the chairmen of the fiscal committees, Republican Senator Austin Erwin, and Assemblyman William MacKenzie to consider the supplemental budget. This budget is passed each year to plug holes left in the annual budget (and often to restore funds for projects eliminated for political reasons from the annual budget). The problems were not difficult to resolve, and so about $9 million were restored of the earlier reductions made by Heck and Mahoney.

One last fiscal battle had to be fought. The Republicans passed a bill reducing individual income taxes by 20 percent on the first $100 of tax assessment and 10 percent on the next $400. The maximum relief would be $60. The governor vetoed the bill on March 12. The leaders offered a compromise plan that would have saved the taxpayers a total of $40 million by a reduction of 15 percent on the first $100 and 10 percent on the next $200, to a maximum of $35. The governor objected, but the plan was passed by a party vote in each house, with the Democrats, loyal to the governor, almost unanimously voting against the measure. The session then adjourned on March 23.

During the 30-day bill period, Harriman was subject to intense pressure on the part of his budget staff to veto the bill, but on the part of local political leaders throughout the state to sign it. He first hinted at a veto, but finally succumbed to the political pressure. And despite the fact that most Democratic legislators at great political risk had loyally voted against the bill, Harriman signed it on April 6.[29]

CASE STUDY: THE 1959 ROCKEFELLER BUDGET

The first Rockefeller budget, submitted in January of 1959, was publicized as an attempt to put the finances of the state on a sound fiscal basis. To this end, the governor asked for a series of tax increases totaling $277 million. The plan soon became the target of vehement opposition on the part of legislators of the governor's own party.

Rockefeller's annual message gave no indication of the directions his budgetary policy would follow. He called for such programs as an extension of unemployment insurance and the retraining of workers displaced by automation. He suggested a major-medical insurance program for all wage earners (around which controversy still swirls) and the establishment of the following new executive agencies: an Office of Transportation, an Office of Local Government, and an agency to deal with problems of atomic energy. But about his stand on questions of the economy and the budget, he merely said in the message that those subjects call for further elucidation in several large studies that would encompass the entire range of problems.[30]

It came, therefore, as quite a surprise that his budget called for over a quarter of a billion dollars in new taxes. The governor said that he would not cut any "necessary" programs to which he had committed himself during the election campaign. The new revenues would come from increases in the cigarette and gasoline taxes, bringing in an estimated $47 million and $69.5 million, respectively, from the addition of higher brackets in the system of income taxes, from the introduction of a withholding system which would accelerate by three quarters of a year the collection of income taxes, thus making cash more readily available, and from the reduction of tax exemptions from $2,500 per couple to $1,200 and from $1,000 for an individual to $600.[31]

The legislators listened to these details of the budget at a briefing by the governor, in "stony silence."[32] On February 16, a number of upstate Republican assemblymen led by Edwyn Mason of Delaware County publicly announced their opposition to the proposal.[33] Rockefeller flew to Deaconess Hospital in Boston accompanied by Assembly Majority Leader Joseph Carlino to confer with Speaker Oswald Heck who was recovering from the amputation of a foot disabled by diabetes. A week later Heck, still gravely ill, returned to the Assembly to announce that the budget would pass despite the opposition of at least 10 Republicans. "We'll compromise and get the votes," he said.[34]

However, all attempts at compromise failed. By early March, the legislative leaders decided that to get enough votes, they had to cut the budget. The main opposition was centered in the Republican Assembly caucus. Their main objective was to prevent the adoption of the governor's proposal reducing the tax exemption to $600 per person. In view of this opposition, the leaders (not the fiscal committees) decided to lop off $40 million from the total budget so that the higher tax exemptions could be maintained.

But even with this reduction, Heck and Carlino could muster in the Assembly only 63 Republican votes for the plan, while 28 opposed any compromise. The Democrats were not inclined to help, and so other measures became necessary. From then on, the full weight of the patronage power of the governor was thrown into the battle, and key appointments to supporters of a number of recalcitrant assemblymen were immediately held up. Speaker Heck made a personal plea for support, identifying himself with the governor's cause. Finally the governor made the further concession of promising that no item cut from the budget would be restored in the supplemental budget, that stringent economies would be introduced, and that no new taxes would be asked for next year, an election year. During the negotiations, Rockefeller went on television to make the public friendlier to his tax demands. Thus, he made combined use of "the classical weapons of the modern political leader; he delayed appointments to desirable jobs; he spoke directly to his constituents on television; and he gracefully accepted some amendments to his proposals."[35] In the end, the opposition melted, and the revised budget was passed on March 12, 1959.

There was some continued bitterness in the aftermath of the fight, but the governor had come out of it a winner. He demonstrated to the legislature his staying power, establishing at the same time a national reputation as a political leader. He won out with the help of the Republican leadership in the Assembly. These men, Heck, Carlino, and Lieutenant Governor Malcolm Wilson, finally were able to help work out the solution.[36]

CASE STUDY: THE 1965 SALES TAX FIGHT

After the elections of 1964 in which the Democrats captured control of both houses of the legislature for the first time in 30 years, the victors were still battling over the new party leadership posts when Governor Rockefeller began adapting his fiscal program for 1965 to the new political situation. He knew that the Democrats had many ambitious programs to propose which would be quite costly to the taxpayer. Realizing that he would not have to stand alone in the face of taxpayer opposition, the governor committed himself to a major tax increase and believed that the best and least painful approach for the taxpayer would be a sales tax.[37]

Rockefeller then proposed a budget of $3.48 billion, with an anticipated deficit of between $300 and $500 million. His proposal for a sales tax increase at first met only minimal opposition, although The New York Times had stated that it would hurt business. Some Democratic legislators felt it was regressive, but would not commit themselves to other ways of making up for the deficit.

Accordingly, the governor asked for a doubling of the cigarette tax to 10 cents a pack, a doubling of the auto registration fees, and the imposition of a statewide 2 percent sales tax. Items subject to the sales tax would be gasoline, tobacco, alcohol, property, catered meals costing over $1, motels, hotels, and certain personal services.[38] Even though the Democrats were, at this time, still involved in their ruthless leadership fight, a few of them found time to blast the budget. Senator Samuel Greenberg of Brooklyn, later to be chairman of the Senate Finance Committee, and Assemblyman John Satriale of the Bronx, later to be chairman of the Assembly Ways and Means Committee, jointly called the proposed budget "fiscally irresponsible." State Comptroller Arthur Levitt called it "most extravagant." On January 30, the governor again went on television to defend his proposals. He stressed the need for increased expenditures in such areas as education, welfare, aid to localities, mental health, and highways. He indicated that neighboring states already had higher sales taxes than New York would have after the introduction of the 2 percent tax. Pennsylvania already had a 5 percent tax, and Connecticut a 3.5 percent tax.

Rockefeller's fight for his budget proposals was decided in his favor by one single factor: the victory in the Democratic leadership fight of that faction of the party which was supported by Mayor Robert Wagner. Anthony Travia and Joseph Zaretzki were elected leaders with the help of Republican votes in a maneuver that was engineered by the governor himself. They felt a strong obligation to repay the debt. It has even been charged that Rockefeller and Wagner made a deal which secured the needed Republican votes to the Zaretzki-Travia team in exchange for Democratic votes for Rockefeller's sales tax. Both men deny the allegation. It is true, however, that the governor did make the tax package very attractive to New York City and its men in the legislature. For example, the plan provided that while there would be a 2 percent sales tax statewide, the actual tax increase in New York City would amount only to 1 percent because the city's own sales tax would be reduced by 1 percent (from 5 percent to 4 percent) before adding the 2 percent state charge. In addition, the city's lost revenue would be restored through increased state aid financed by the stock transfer tax.

Even so, the opposition was still strong. Upstate Republicans and Democrats were up in arms against the possibility that their constituents would have to put up with a higher tax increase than the residents of the city of New York. Anti-Wagner Democrats were still angry over their loss of the leadership positions, and the more liberal among them combined this feeling of frustration with concern over the regressive effect of the sales tax. Senator Jack Bronston of Queens was the most outspoken opponent of the plan. Senator Greenberg offered an alternative plan which would have increased (instead of sales taxes) the income tax, corporation profits taxes, gasoline and liquor taxes, and the pari-mutuel tax. Senator Zaretzki said only that most of the governor's nonfiscal program would be passed.[39]

Criticism mounted steadily, and after Bronston announced his own alternative tax proposals on February 28, State Comptroller Arthur Levitt and the recently elected U.S. senator Robert Kennedy publicly attacked the sales tax. Nassau County executive Eugene Nickerson called the plan "a one-shot financial gimmickry and an act of irresponsibility that has characterized the state these last six years."[40] At a public hearing held on March 5, numerous witnesses opposed the tax.

But Mayor Wagner indicated he might support the proposal. He said on March 2 that a sales tax that did not affect the cost of food was not unduly regressive. The Temporary Committee on City Finances, a city agency, supported the tax. Gradually it became apparent that most New York City Democratic legislators would vote for the plan.

On March 17, both houses passed the cigarette tax increase by a vote of 43 to 12 in the Senate and 104 to 33 in the Assembly. Those voting in the negative were, for the most part, upstate Democrats, joined in the Assembly by the Bronx Democratic delegation.

The following week, Zaretzki acknowledged that of the 32 Democratic senators, only about half would be ready to support the sales tax at that moment and that more Republican votes would have to be found. It was, of course, unthinkable for Democratic leaders even to try to pass a Republican governor's plan for major tax increases without adequate Republican support and sharing of the responsibility. To get this support, Zaretzki indicated that the alternative to the sales tax would be a massive cut in state aid to localities and to education.[41]

Thus, the New York City Democrats supported the tax; the upstate and some downstate Democrats were opposed to it; and the Republicans were still watching. By the end of March, the Democratic leaders decided to simply sit and wait for Republican votes. Zaretzki asked for 14 Republican votes, and finally on April 2, Minority Leader Earl Brydges said there might be a chance for getting them the following week.

In the meantime, the new fiscal year had begun, and state employees were given certificates of intention to pay rather than normal salary checks. The banks honored these certificates, but the threat of payless paydays continued to hover over the scene.

Now the pressures really began to build. Business groups led by the Association of Commerce and Industry, fearing an increase in corporate taxes, suddenly swung over to support the sales tax. Local school boards and parents groups, anxious for the additional funds that would result from a sales tax, began to show interest in it. Finally, Governor Rockefeller called a press conference in which he urged statewide popular support for the plan.

Finally, the tax was brought up for a vote on April 14 in each house, and after fierce debate, it was passed by both. The vote was 82 to 67 in the Assembly, 6 votes above the minimum number of 76 needed, and 32 to 25 in the Senate. Most New York City Democrats and some upstaters and about half of the Republicans in each house voted for the measure. The tax was to be imposed on gasoline, tobacco, alcoholic beverages, certain types of personal property, and sales of real estate.

The fight against the sales tax was a unique kind of rebellion. It rather sharply divided both parties. As far as the Democratic opponents of the tax measures were concerned, their rebellion was primarily directed against their own leaders rather than the Republican governor. Most of those Democrats opposing the plan had fought against Zaretzki and Travia. They also felt that it was good politics to oppose any tax, and for the liberals among them there was the additional argument that the sales tax would hurt the poor and middle-income persons much more than it would the well-to-do.

Yet the leadership trio of Rockefeller, Zaretzki, and Travia succeeded in getting the package adopted, even though Rockefeller was dealing with an opposition party and the two leaders were brand-new in their jobs. The case supports the contention that the combined power of the governor and the leaders can generally overcome even very strong and bitter opposition.

PASSING THE GOVERNOR'S PROGRAM: HARRIMAN'S PROBLEMS

Between 1900 and 1950, Democratic candidates for governor were successful enough to maintain control of the statehouse of New York for 26 of those 50 years. Republican governors rules for 24 years. These figures show the intensity of the competition between the two major parties, throughout the state's modern history. The fact remains, however, that because of the pro-Republican apportionment formula, Democrats captured control of both houses of the legislature in only 2 of those 50 years.[42] Since 1950, Democrats succeeded in capturing control of both houses in one single year, 1965, although they managed to keep their Assembly majority from 1965 through 1968.

For Democratic governors this situation meant confrontation with a well-organized, efficiently led, and disciplined opposition party in control of the legislative decision-making apparatus and capable, at least, of obtaining important concessions from the governor in matters of legislation. Governor Averell Harriman's four-year term, 1955-58, illustrates the difficulties confronting Democratic governors who must deal with what Governor Al Smith called "the constitutionally Republican legislature."

Harriman's first approach to the task of getting his program passed was to see how much cooperation he could get from Speaker Heck and Majority Leader Mahoney. Then, should the Republican leaders rigidly insist on major changes, he, the governor, would take his campaign to the voters by publicly airing the differences.

The institutional framework for the discussion of important bills was then, and is today, "the leaders' meeting," in which only the two majority party leaders and the governor participate. Depending on the political circumstances, Minority Leaders might be brought into the negotiations. Occasionally staff is present, particularly when technical complexities are involved. But the main thing is the confrontation of the three top leaders, since it is generally their agreement or disagreement that determines the fate of the discussed legislation. Sometimes the governor meets with the two leaders separately, as Rockefeller had to do when he was faced with a split legislature between 1966 and 1968.

Harriman did try to bring the Democratic Minority Leaders to the bargaining table, but soon gave it up because he realized that in the face of the solid party discipline of the Republicans, the Democratic legislators could have little influence upon the outcome.

Harriman's efforts in these "leaders' meetings" proved a dismal failure. First of all, unlike Rockefeller, he did not call such meetings with any regularity, only when a highly controversial situation forced him to do so. Nor did he cultivate warm personal relationships with the two men. His relationship with Speaker Heck was correct and sometimes friendly, but he could never get along with Walter Mahoney. Mahoney systematically gave Harriman a bad time. Daniel Gutman, counsel to the governor, described it as "a cat and dog situation."[43] As the Associated Press described the relationships, Mahoney's strategy toward the governor was the "treat him rough school . . . . Heck has demonstrated that he is willing more often than Mahoney to reason with Harriman. He likes to get things settled even if, on occasion, he has to yield a bit more than he had planned." But Mahoney remained adamant. L. Judson Morhouse, the Republican state chairman, was somewhere in between. In the face of a third veto by Harriman of a bill on unemployment insurance, "the big three were split this way: Mahoney—send it back. The pressure is mounting. Heck—let's compromise and get this dispute settled. Morhouse—yield just a little to let the governor 'save face.'"[44]

It seems that after over a decade of almost absolute rule by Governor Dewey, the Republican leaders were quite pleased with their new independence. "With Harriman's election, the Republican legislative leaders assumed a new importance and independence;

both promptly became candidates for the 1958 gubernatorial nomination."[45] They always tried, sometimes with success, to beat Harriman to the publicity punch by announcing their own programs a day or so before the governor's scheduled announcement. In this manner, the relationship soon turned into a series of running battles, attempts by one side to outflank the other, and considerable bitterness. When, for example, Harriman vetoed a Republican bill to give the Republican attorney general, Louis Lefkowitz, the power to investigate organized crime (because the governor already had plans of his own to deal with the problem), the leaders' joint statement turned out to be an expression of partisan invective. Said Heck and Mahoney, "The veto must, in many respects, be welcome news to the underworld."[46]

Harriman characterized his relationship with the two Republicans this diplomatic way: "I got along very well with Heck. He even gave me his private phone number so we could communicate in private; not even Dewey had it. Mahoney, however, while very charming, was also very suspicious. He was willing to accept older values of political behavior, behavior that is no longer acceptable today."[47]

Bernard Ruggieri, counsel to Senator Zaretzki and, prior to that post, assistant counsel to Harriman, had this to say: "The leaders never really respected Harriman, particularly his political judgment. Heck was a nice person and remained friendly, but Mahoney didn't like Harriman and treated him very harshly, too harshly I think."[48] Milton Stewart, executive assistant to the governor, said, "Mahoney was just not the governor's cup of tea. He had a different outlook, was an upstate conservative, hard nosed, hard shelled, both for political and ideological reasons. Heck was more middle-of-the-road and a compromiser, interested in making government and the legislature work."[49]

These comments should, by no means, leave the impression that Harriman was helpless. As governor he had enormous powers to initiate programs, to determine the character of the budget, and to veto legislation. He was at the focus of public attention and was often able to present his point of view to the public effectively. But he was faced with the fierce opposition of a decisive legislative majority, and so could choose only between continuous yielding and compromise or else fervid but unproductive partisanship on his own part. This is the reason why his governorship could not match in effectiveness that of Dewey before, nor that of Rockefeller after him.

PASSING THE GOVERNOR'S PROGRAM:
ROCKEFELLER'S SUCCESS

With the election of Governor Rockefeller in 1958, the whole political picture changed. Once again, the majority leaders had a governor of their own party. The change automatically reduced the scope of their independence, but the leaders would no longer permit the restoration of the kind of absolute dominance that prevailed under Governor Dewey.

Rockefeller institutionalized the "leaders' meeting," and Malcolm Wilson, who succeeded to the governorship upon Rockefeller's resignation in late 1973, has followed suit. The meetings are held weekly, but are called more frequently during the last days of a session, or during a crisis. The leaders meet with the governor on other occasions too, but these are mostly social in nature, and little business is transacted. At first, the leaders attended the meetings alone, although the governor sometimes had his counsel and secretary or budget officials present, and, sometimes, the lieutenant governor and the attorney general. Generally, the governor's counsel prepared the agenda for the meetings, always in accord with the governor's wishes. But in 1963 Senator Mahoney attempted to restructure somewhat the relationship and had his staff attend some meetings. Then he went on to propose items for discussion at the start of some meetings. For example, there was a project to create a State Recreation Council, drafted by Senate secretary Albert Abrams with the assistance of a group of Senate interns. At a meeting of the leaders in March, Mahoney brought up the item for discussion. Rockefeller was taken aback, because the item had not been on the agenda prepared by his counsel, Sol Corbin. But he liked the idea and accepted the proposal. It was passed into law a few days later.[50]

After agreement is reached at the leaders' meetings and after a program bill is subjected to the changes required by the prospect of its passage, the bills are delivered to the leaders to be distributed for sponsorship. This is another source of leadership influence, since the sponsorship of a bill is an honor appreciated both by loyal members and insecure members from marginal districts.[51]

When difficulties arise in the way of passage, it is the leaders' business to fight for it. The governor will intercede with members of his majority party only when asked by a leader. The leader may occasionally ask the governor to talk to some recalcitrant legislator or to let the counsel or the lieutenant governor do so, if appropriate.[52] Thus, while the governor will rarely bypass the leadership of his own party, he will have no such scruples against going for opposition votes behind the back of the opposition party leadership. Whenever Rockefeller felt that he could obtain a vote or two from the Democratic side, he did not hesitate to go after them. Nor did he hesitate to let some patronage award go to a Democratic legislator who could give him a crucial vote. Rockefeller's pleasant personality was another asset in this context. According to lobbyist Victor Condello, "He is a smooth and extremely charming person who can be personally very friendly, but is tough to his enemies at the same time. Also, he always keeps his commitments, and your best asset in Albany is your word."53

In 1969, Rockefeller broke through an otherwise solid Democratic Assembly front to get the vote of Democratic assemblyman Charles Stockmeister of Rochester on a tax measure important to the governor. It was an open secret that Stockmeister had been offered an important executive position. Many felt it was in exchange for the vote, but Rockefeller insists that he appointed the man on recommendation of the Rochester Republican party. The appointment of Stockmeister as a civil service commissioner came up for confirmation by the Senate on January 27, 1970. Reform Democratic senator Manfred Ohrenstein blasted the "deal" and voted against confirmation. Senator Thomas LaVerne, a Rochester Republican, rose immediately to stress Stockmeister's "high qualifications." More significantly, two Democrats decided to criticize Ohrenstein. One, Senator Albert Lewis of Brooklyn, told him to go with his allegations of a "deal" to the grand jury. Another, Senator Edward Lentol, did not attempt to defend the deal, but he accused his reform colleague, Ohrenstein, of hypocrisy on the basis of the fact that Ohrenstein did not complain when New York City mayor Lindsay received the endorsement of reform Assemblymen Jerome Kretschmer and Benjamin Altman, both of whom were close friends of Ohrenstein, and both of whom were subsequently rewarded by mayoral appointment as heads of major departments in the city government.

The main point is, however, that since Rockefeller's election, the Republican legislative leaders were relegated to secondary positions. Thus, as far back as May 1959, the Associated Press observed the change. They recalled that under Harriman, the Republic leaders had a field day battling Harriman.

> They waged a lively, noisy propaganda war. Their ghost writers counted the day lost when there was no Heck-Mahoney blast, no jibe from Ledkowitz, no harpoon from Morhouse . . . . Since the 1959 session adjourned, Mahoney and Heck have had nothing to say. Newsmen don't ask them their opinions—and they don't volunteer any . . . . Mahoney and Heck still run the legislature, but they have been advised to stick to their legislative knitting."54

This characterization of leadership impotence is exaggerated, and Rockefeller had to discover on occasion that he still could get rough treatment from the leaders of his party. But, in the main, the leaders were compelled to yield to him the lion's share in legislative initiative and propaganda leadership.

The governor's relationship with Speaker Oswald Heck was of such short duration that few generalizations can be offered. The new chief executive gave proper respect to the veteran Assembly leader, who had served as Speaker for 22 years. Heck was already quite ill when Rockefeller took office. He returned from his hospital bed to assist in the passage of the 1959 budget. Walter Mahoney was also quite helpful in the endeavor, and during that first year, despite the bitterness of the Assembly tax revolt, Rockefeller did quite well. James Desmond, writing in The Nation, credited the governor with a very good start in the face of having to deal with a legislature led by two disappointed gubernatorial hopefuls. "That he wasn't clobbered is due, in addition to the charm which he radiates so effortlessly, to his toughness, his resilience in compromise and, above all, his patience in holding his Sunday punch until the timing is exactly right. Besides, he's very lucky."[55] Thus, he got his controversial tax program passed, along with a law restricting union racketeering, a railroad commuter act to ease local taxes collected to aid the railways, an extension of rent control, a vast middle-income housing program, the extension of emergency unemployment insurance, and a broadening of jobless pay benefits. His only failure was the defeat of his program bill to define clearly the areas of operation of savings banks and bank holding companies.[56]

From 1960 through 1964, the new Speaker, Joseph Carlino, had a close working relationship with the governor. They had a certain ideological affinity, both being middle-of-the-road politicians, slightly liberal in certain areas, both very pragmatic in their search for solutions to political and governmental problems. Carlino probably felt that his future lay with the governor, and he seems to have placed high value on personal loyalty. He was very loyal to Heck, and he transferred that loyalty to Rockefeller. There were some exceptions. During the 1964 session, suburban Republicans in the Assembly refused to support the governor's budget until he increased aid to education, a particularly critical issue in suburbia. Carlino, a suburban man himself, joined and finally led the minor revolt. The governor was forced to make concessions, and $25 million in aid to education was restored.[57] But the relationship was only rarely disturbed by such conflicts.

On the contrary, Carlino very actively participated in Rockefeller's campaign for the presidency in 1964, both in public appearances and as a strategy planner. Henry Paley, Carlino's press relations man, recalled that in the campaign Carlino went to the West Coast for the governor to enlist the collaboration of liberal and labor groups in an effort to stop the growing Goldwater boom within the Republican party. After his return, he related, at a leaders' meeting, that there was some sentiment among liberal Republicans in favor of the passage of the Civil Rights Act pending in the Congress. Rockefeller and Carlino agreed that it would be a good idea to attempt to build solid Republican support behind the bill, in order to coalesce Republican liberal sentiment which might later be mobilized behind Rockefeller's candidacy. Carlino agreed to take two hours a day out of his schedule and use some of his staff to help lobby for Republican support of the Civil Rights Bill. The campaign was only modestly successful.

Later that year at a meeting at Rockefeller's homestead at Pocantico Hills, the governor, Carlino, and Paley, among others, met with George Romney, Senator Hugh Scott, and emissaries of Henry Cabot Lodge. It was agreed that, as the key to Rockefeller's campaign, they would launch an attack on what they considered to be Goldwater's extreemist right-wing politics. Carlino drafted a liberal civil rights plank for inclusion in the platform. (He had been chairman of the Civil Rights Subcommittee of the Republican Convention Platform Committee in 1960.) At the convention, the governor had to threaten a press conference at which Carlino's civil rights plank would be publicly offered in order to obtain time for addressing the convention. That memorable address was a strong attack on extremism and on Goldwater, and the governor was wildly booed. A month after the convention, Rockefeller and Carlino reluctantly endorsed Goldwater, and Carlino and Paley attribute that endorsement, among other factors, to Carlino's defeat at the polls that fall.[58]

All in all, Carlino proved himself to be a friend and ally to the governor. This was by far not the case with Senate Majority Leader Walter Mahoney. There were reasons for Mahoney's reluctance to cooperate with the governor. The first reason was ideological. Mahoney was considerably more conservative than Rockefeller and Carlino, and the base of his strength in the Senate was the support of upstate conservatives. Other factors were the man's pride and self-assurance. He had come to prominence by taking on, in 1949, the most authoritarian of modern governors, Thomas Dewey. Thus, he certainly would not be awed by a new governor. Unlike Carlino, who was elected Speaker only months after Rockefeller was sworn in as governor and therefore still felt unsure in his position, Mahoney was Majority Leader in the Senate for five years before Rockefeller's election, and so he was entirely confident of his base of power.

As we have seen, furthermore, Mahoney succeeded in generating a high degree of institutional patriotism among the Republican senators. He felt that this inclination would make his colleagues at least suspicious of the new executive and would, under favorable conditions, prove strong enough to rally them when he saw fit to do battle with the governor. Mahoney had to portray any governor as the enemy, and he often fought with the incumbent "on behalf of his members," as he made the senators believe.[59] As Mahoney himself indicated, "There were times when some of my committee chairmen developed their own ideas on the same subjects that the governor's staff had dealt with. When they conflicted, I tried to work for an agreement. But I would always back up my chairmen."[60]

Nor should it be forgotten that in 1958, Mahoney strongly competed with Rockefeller for the gubernatorial nomination. According to Newsday, from that position Mahoney could have become the kingmaker by withdrawing and throwing his support to the ultimate winner. But he did not follow the example of Speaker Heck, also a candidate, who recognized that he couldn't win and withdrew in time to throw his committed 160 delegates to Rockefeller, thus getting credit for having created a bandwagon.[61] The likelihood is that Mahoney must have felt aggrieved that a relative newcomer to New York Republican politics could so effectively use the power of his name and money to "steal" the nomination to the highest state office. Although never publicly acknowledged, there must have been some bitterness on his part.

Time magazine touched upon this mood of the man in an analysis of the 1960 legislative session and of Rockefeller's problems with Mahoney: "Rockefeller had steamrollered upstate conservative Walter Joseph Mahoney out of the GOP gubernatorial nomination, and Senate Majority Leader Mahoney was not disposed to forgive."[62] Thus Mahoney, after giving the governor a one-session honeymoon (1959), felt free to organize the rural contingent in the Senate in opposition to Rockefeller on state-financed welfare programs, to demand unsuccessfully (due to Democratic support) a token tax cut, and, earlier than anyone else of prominence in New York State, to endorse Richard Nixon publicly for the presidency, well before Rockefeller dropped out of contention.

One of the most revealing incidents showing Mahoney's boldness in demonstrating his independence occurred in 1960. On April 1, 1960, The New York Times reported that Mahoney had rebuffed Governor Rockefeller on two very important legislative proposals. One was the Metcalf-Baker bill which would have prohibited discrimination in the sale of certain types of housing. Rockefeller had pushed very hard for the bill in the face of significant conservative Republican opposition. Speaker Carlino had used every means at his disposal to get the bill passed in his house. He succeeded in getting all but 17 Republicans to vote aye on the bill (vote was 131 to 17). It must be assumed that Carlino expected that Rockefeller would make sure that the measure would be adopted by the Senate since he, Carlino, had used most of his political credit to get conservative Republicans to vote for the measure, but Mahoney disagreed, and the Senate rejected the bill. In a second article appearing in the same edition of The New York Times, it was reported that Mahoney had defied the governor for the second time on the same day by blocking the passage of a bill that would have created 13 additional state Supreme Court judgeships for the city of New York.

The story in detail, as told to me by persons in the Senate chamber on the day both bills were defeated, is intriguing. Mahoney and Brooklyn Democratic senator Harry Gittleson (now a Supreme Court judge) had been close friends. Gittleson had occasionally given Mahoney his vote on certain legislative items. A former assemblyman recalled that Mahoney needed one Democratic vote on a bill to kill milk dating and that Gittleson had obliged.

When the bill to create new judgeships was introduced, the political leaders in the counties involved started dividing the spoils, that is, determining how many Democrats and Republicans would get the nominations and who they would be. In some instances, where necessary, candidates would receive bipartisan endorsement. Thus, in Brooklyn it was agreed that three of the new judgeships would go to Democrats chosen by the party leadership in that county, and three would go to the Republicans. Since in any election the Democrats could probably win all six posts, the agreement had to be reached for the Republican legislature to pass the bill.

This was, of course, a confidential deal, but the secret was not well kept, and several newspapers severely criticized the "horse-trading." Then both Mayor Wagner and Governor Rockefeller denounced the deal. As a result, the bill languished in the Judiciary Committees of both houses throughout the 1960 session. Mahoney considered the measure dead for that year.

However, negotiations were quickly renewed in March. A new formula for dividing up the nominations was agreed upon, and the governor and the Speaker were probably informed of these developments, since they agreed that the judgeship bill should be called up for a vote. However, whether by happenstance or by design, the bill was not acted upon in either house until the last day of the session, March 31, and then, in the chaos of the final rush to adjournment, it was passed only in the Assembly.

The story of what took place in the Senate was described to me as follows: The Senate had finished its calendar in the early morning hours of April 1. There was a lull in the action, while many bills passed in the Assembly were still being processed before they could be sent to the Senate for final action. Bernard Nadel, counsel to Democratic leader Joseph Zaretzki, was sitting next to Zaretzki across the middle aisle from Majority Leader Mahoney's seat. Nadel turned to Zaretzki during the lull and asked, "What happened to the judgeship bill?" Zaretzki said that he didn't know and suggested that

Nadel ask Mahoney about it. Nadel did inquire, but Mahoney's answer was this: "What judgeship bill? Nobody talked to me about any judgeship bill!"

Nadel reported back to Zaretzki, and so the two men walked up to the rostrum and asked Lieutenant Governor Malcolm Wilson to come to the well of the Senate (the well is the area in front of the rostrum in the center of the chamber) to clear up the mystery. A quick conference ensued, and the three men then asked Mahoney to join them. He did.

All of a sudden the entire Senate became alert to the scene, which clearly indicated that something very unusual was happening. They saw the four men in a huddle whispering back and forth, with Wilson probably telling Mahoney that the judgeship bill had been revived, that the county leaders had agreed on the details, that Carlino was amenable, and that also the governor had given his approval. To all this Mahoney responded, in a stage whisper loud enough to be heard throughout the chamber, as follows: "F___k the governor. I'm the Majority Leader of this house. No one talked to me about this bill. For all you know I may have a candidate for one of the judgeships in Brooklyn, no matter what the Brooklyn leaders decided, and I do!" One of the huddlers asked Mahoney who his candidate was. Mahoney turned toward the startled senators, noted that the only Republican senator from Brooklyn, William Conklin, was not a lawyer, and said, "My candidate is Harry Gittleson."

And consequently Mahoney had his way too. The bill had to be amended to increase the number of new Brooklyn judges from six to seven. Joseph Sharkey, the Democratic county leader of Brooklyn who had chosen three other candidates for the original nominations, was immediately told by the development over the telephone. Although not friendly with Gittleson, he was pleased to approve. John Crews, the Republican leader, when reached, was shocked to see the Republican Majority Leader stalling a judgeship bill to get a Democrat nominated. In the end, however, he reluctantly agreed.

Since amendments were needed, a new bill was drafted. However, a bill under the state constitution must sit on the legislators' desks for three days in order to qualify by "aging" before a vote can be taken. In a "message of necessity," however, the governor may certify that an emergency exists which calls for the immediate passage of a bill with the three days' waiting provision waived. In fact, the only way to get the amended bill passed in the last minutes of the session was to obtain such a message from the governor right away. Therefore, the two counsels of both Mahoney and Carlino rushed to see Rockefeller. At about 3 a.m., they found him at his desk on the second floor of the capitol building talking to a reporter from one of the New York City newspapers. He must have heard about Mahoney's pithy comments on the Senate floor because when the two counsels asked him to sign the message of necessity, his answer was even more pithy. All he said was, "F___k Walter Mahoney." He signed no message, and the judgeship bill died for that session, with Gittleson an innocent victim of clashing leadership interests.

That, however, is not the end of the story, because the second defeat of the governor followed right on the heels of the first. While many senators were permaturely congratulating Gittleson over his unexpected "nomination," Mahoney called on the Senate to resume its business. So the secretary of the Senate proceeded with calling up the Metcalf-Baker bill on discrimination in housing, and Mahoney moved that it be recommitted to committee. With the excitement on the floor over the Gittleson incident and owing to the fact that the bill had been called up only by its Assembly number (after having passed that house), no one realized the identity of the bill, and consequently, it was recommitted, literally sight unseen. There was no debate, no questions, no remarks, and in a moment's notice, one of the most controversial and important bills of the session was killed. Some observers felt that Mahoney had deliberately created an atmosphere of excitement through the Gittleson endorsement in order to make the scuttling of the Metcalf-Baker bill easier. However, a former Republican senator quotes Mahoney denying this: "The bill had nothing to do with the judgeship matter. I would have used that kind of technique if I had thought of it, but it really wasn't planned that way." In his own view, he was merely asserting the prerogatives of the Senate and the authority of its leader.

It should be added that in the same session, Mahoney also killed Rockefeller bills to "(1) combine school districts and to give them new tax powers; (2) provide tax relief for thousands of Manhattan commuters . . .; (3) encourage, by tax reductions, voluntary construction of atomic fallout shelters."[63]

In later years, until Mahoney's defeat as senator in 1964, the relationship stayed colored by the battles of 1960. Mahoney continued to be the main conservative pressure on the governor, standing alone against the two other liberal members of the top triumvirate.

When the 1965 session began, the governor recognized that, like it or not, he had to cooperate with the two new Democratic leaders. Both men felt obligated to him, and so they responded with a readiness to cooperate that went beyond all expectations. As we have seen, one good reason for this was that they felt a debt to Rockefeller for having arranged their elections. Another was that the governor's legislative program included a number of items for which the Democrats had been clamoring for years. Rockefeller's pattern of legislative initiatives has been flexible, depending on whether or

112

not he is facing some election. For example, when he ran for national office, his program reflected his interest in creating a national reputation of sober, conservative, balanced-budget government. In years prior to his reelection as governor in liberal New York, his programs have been considerably more liberal with many new plans of social improvement and much greater spending. In 1965 he was recovering from his failure to defeat Barry Goldwater, while knowing at the same time that next year he would have to run for reelection in New York. Additionally, the Democrats were hungry for an opportunity to pass as much of their legislative program as possible. What the governor chose to do was to steal their thunder by proposing most of what they wanted, in his own name, while the Democrats were still battling with one another over control of the legislature.

When, after the special election of 1965 (ordered by the federal courts to implement the Supreme Court's one-man, one-vote dictum), the Republicans regained control of the Senate, the governor had to resolve the problem of how he would handle two leaders of different parties who did not particularly like each other. One way of resolving the problem was to break precedent and meet with the two men separately.

It appears that the governor and Speaker Travia really liked each other and enjoyed dealing with each other. Said Rockefeller, "Tony was very sincere, and he kept his word. We got along rather well, considering the political differences."[64] Said Travia, "If I didn't like a bill, I said so, and the governor played ball. I never got a quid pro quo, but I did extract changes in a bill by announcing my opposition."[65] They got along well because they quite often agreed. The result was that the governor was quite successful in dealing with the Democrats over the following four years. There were many fights, but that was to be expected, and there was a great deal of cooperation as well.

Senate Majority Leader Earl Brydges was caught in the middle. He could not fight his governor since this would expose him to the charge of jeopardizing his party's position in a divided legislature. He was a conservative influence on Rockefeller, but the governor could nicely use Travia's pressures on him as an argument to convince Brydges that he must support him, the lesser liberal "evil," against the exaggerated liberal demands of the Democrats. Having been first elected Senate Majority Leader in 1965, Brydges felt insecure during his first year or two in office. There were others in the Senate interested in becoming Senate Majority Leader, and all leaders need a few sessions to build up their influence and control. Accordingly, he had reason to cooperate with Rockefeller most of the time.

CASE STUDY: THE 1966 MEDICAID FIGHT

In 1965 Congress passed and the president signed into law the National Health Act. This law, popularly known as the Medicare Law, consists of two parts. Part A deals with medical assistance to persons over 65 years of age and incorporates a series of financing schemes for that purpose. This part, Title 18, provides that the elderly would receive hospitalization paid by the federal government out of funds accumulated in the Social Security Fund. Part B provides for the payment of doctors' bills through individual contributions made monthly by participants in the program. Thus, a patient would receive 80 percent of his health costs, after he had paid the first $50 of such costs per year to his doctors, and after he began contributing $3 per month to the federal government.

The part of this law that had received far less attention was the second section, which established a new Title 19. The objective of this section, called the Medicaid Program, was to provide federal funds to states, to strengthen their medical assistance programs for persons receiving public assistance and others considered medically indigent by the states. This last phrase was not defined in the federal law, and its meaning, therefore, was left up to the states to define. Another provision required that the new federal funds be used to enlarge and enrich existing programs, instead of replacing existing state and local allocations for these purposes. The law wanted the poor to have better health care, not the states to save money.

Title 19 required that in order to receive the federal funds (from between 50 to 83 percent of the cost of enriched programs), a state would have to match funds according to certain rather involved formulas (but could charge localities a portion of the cost), and determine who would be eligible for assistance. The state would have to provide at least five basic services by July 1, 1967, in order to comply and to receive federal funds. These services were inpatient hospital services, outpatient hospital care, laboratory and X-ray care, nursing home benefits, and physicians' services. Other permissible services would be dental care, glasses, drugs, prosthetic devices, and physical therapy. The services had to be provided equally to all eligible persons and uniformly throughout the state.[66]

During 1965, few people in the state government in New York had any comprehension of the scope and potential for expanding state health services that Title 19 permitted. In that year, the Democrats controlled both houses of the legislature. A few medical professionals saw the possibilities and impressed with them the new chairman of the Senate Committee on Public Health, Seymour Thaler of Queens. When the session adjourned in July of that year, the Senate Public Health Committee received an additional appropriation of $50,000 to

114

make a study of the ramifications of the new federal law and to propose methods of implementing the program in the state. A series of public hearings were held throughout the state, and a detailed report was issued. The recommendations of the report will not be outlined here because the report had almost no impact upon the decision-making process that led to the ultimate passage of New York State's own Medicaid Law. The public hearings about the bill were sparsely attended, although the committee did its best to call attention to them. There was just no interest in the legislation in 1965.

Governor Rockefeller, however, in preparing his legislative program for 1966, a year in which he would have to seek reelection, recognized the possibility for obtaining large amounts of federal money, while at the same time expanding health services in the state. Since Title 19 required that the states wishing to participate had to submit acceptable plans that would meet federal requirements by March 31, 1966, the governor prepared a program early in that year with the help of his counsel and welfare and health officials. The report of the Senate Health Committee was ignored.

The governor submitted his first bill to the politically divided legislature (the Republicans having captured control of the Senate in the special elections held in November 1965) on March 9. The major point of the bill was that the eligibility requirements for persons allowed to participate would be set by the State Board of Social Welfare, the state organ in control of welfare agencies. Assemblyman Albert Blumenthal of Manhattan, the Democratic chairman of the Assembly Committee on Public Health, attacked the proposal, fearing that the State Board had a welfare mentality and would make the eligibility requirements too restrictive. Liberals were concerned over the fact that the program would be treated as a welfare program. They desired that it be considered as the first major step toward providing the people with comprehensive health services.[67]

The governor then announced these recommendations of the State Board: The eligibility levels would be determined not only by one's income but also by the amount of taxes one paid to the state and federal governments, his health care expenses, and his savings. In other words, a person would determine his total income and subtract from it his taxes and the health care costs that he had actually expended in a given year. If the resulting net income figures were below $2,900 for a single person, $3,500 for a couple, $4,700 for a family of four and, of course, larger amounts for larger families, then eligibility would be recognized.[68]

In the meantime, the Democrats, in control of one house of the legislature, developed rather different ideas. They wanted a far larger program that would benefit many more people. Speaker Anthony Travia now became the thorn in the governor's side, with many demands to enrich the program beyond Rockefeller's proposals. It must be emphasized that at the time, in March of 1966, the average legislator still did not sufficiently understand the complicated technical details, and even less the serious fiscal implications, of the Medicaid program. This factor worked greatly to the advantage of those who wanted a generous bill passed as soon as possible. It was only after the new law was passed and signed that it became a source of tremendous discord, particularly between upstate Republicans and city Democrats.

It was at this point that Travia met with Senator Thaler and some health experts such as Professor Frank Van Dyke of the Columbia School of Public Health, who had worked with the Senate Health Committee the year before. After these exploratory discussions, the Speaker's staff drafted a competing bill which provided for the administration of the program by the State Health Department instead of the Board of Social Welfare, and set eligibility levels much higher than the governor's proposal; a single person would be eligible with an income (after the deductions listed above) of $4,140; a couple with an income of $4,300, a family of four with an income of $6,700, and so on. Both bills, the governor's and Travia's, provided that eligible persons would receive any and all medical benefits needed for the prevention, diagnosis, correction, or cure of ailments.[69]

Travia introduced his bill via the Assembly Rules Committee which he chaired, and the Assembly passed it by the vote of 137 to 17 on March 28, an incredible vote, if matched against the vehement and growing opposition that was subsequently to develop. At the moment, however, even the 17 assemblymen who voted nay did not seem to harbor particularly strong feelings against the bill. For example, Minority Leader Perry Duryea was opposed on procedural grounds—because the bill had not been on that day's calendar but had been added to it by the Rules Committee. On the floor, he had merely this to say: "It is obvious that we are now flying headlong down the road to legislating by crisis. A vote against this bill is a vote against disorderly procedure in this house."[70]

The Senate debated the proposals the next day. In the debate, Senate Majority Leader Earl Brydges accused Travia of having acted as the tool of Democratic U.S. senator Robert F. Kennedy, whose objective was to take away from the governor the credit for the enactment of the program. Senator Thaler, speaking in favor of the Assembly bill, said, "Senator Kennedy has a very valid, a very personal, and a very legitimate interest in how this state implements federal legislation. He is to be congratulated, not scorned."[71] By the way, the influence of Senator Kennedy on this development cannot be doubted. Former Speaker Carlino said that Rockefeller, when he later made concessions to Travia on the scope of the program, was "hoodwinked by Travia and Kennedy, and had compromised without the benefit of proper staff studies on the cost of the program."[72] The governor later did acknowledge that Travia told him of Kennedy's deep interest and that, as a result, Travia might have been tougher than usual in the bargaining process.[73]

What is important is the fact that the Senate rejected the Travia version and passed the governor's bill. The two bills clashed with regard to both main points: the agency that should administer the program and the choice of eligibility levels.

With the two houses rigidly divided on the issue, the battle right away narrowed down to a leadership duel between Rockefeller and Travia. They talked a great deal in each other's offices, and on the telephone, for over a month to no avail. Both were under pressures from many directions. Travia had to countenance pressures for an even more liberal program on the part of liberal legislators like Thaler and Blumenthal, New York City government officials, and health professionals working in poor communities. Labor unions were beginning to join the fracas, as were many poverty groups. The governor, in turn, was subject to pressures from the more conservative Senate leadership, from suburban and rural government and welfare officials, and his own budget personnel concerned about the ultimate cost of the legislation. There was also some tugging and pulling on the part of the State Health and Social Services Department about the details of controlling and administering the program.

On April 27, Rockefeller submitted some minor amendments to his bill, which passed the Senate that day by a vote of 36 to 19. These slightly expanded the eligibility levels and instructed the Department of Social Services to contract with the Health Department by October 31 with regard to the required medical standards. On April 28, the governor and Travia again tried unsuccessfully to compromise their differences, and the Speaker announced he would put off a vote on the Rockefeller bill for one more day, saying, "I'm going to grant the governor one night's reprieve, so to speak, to think about it. If we can't compromise by tomorrow morning, I'm going to urge defeat of his bill."[74] Senator Brydges, upon hearing this statement, lashed back: "I think the Speaker is engaged in a cruel and cynical hoax. I think he's playing politics with a very serious subject."[75]

Travia's decision to postpone a vote came at 5:30 in the afternoon. The last time he had spoken to the governor was at noon, and since no compromise could be reached, he was about to take the unusual step of leaving the rostrum to speak on the floor against the governor's bill. It was this move he now decided to delay for a day.

On that day a compromise solution was finally agreed upon between the two leaders, reflecting substantial concessions on the governor's part. For example, for a family of four, the net income

117

yardstick was set at the level of $6,000, after the aforementioned deductions. The level was graded upward or downward, depending on size of a family. To be eligible, a person could still have $1,000 worth of cash value in his life insurance policy and $500 in savings. (Rockefeller had proposed $500 in cash value of life insurance.) The benefits included a tremendous number of services so that the measure could be called quite comprehensive. Procedures and reimbursement levels for doctors and hospitals were to be worked out by the Department of Social Welfare, and regulations for the provision of medical benefits by the State Health Department.

The bill was passed into law with only 10 votes recorded in opposition in both houses. The governor signed it the same day, April 30, and called it the greatest social program of the decade. The party leaders also praised the bill as a great social step forward, but most members still failed to comprehend how vast, expensive, and dangerously controversial the new program was to become.

The first reactions to the law came from local welfare administrators who could not understand their new responsibilities, but who immediately realized that the increased costs would play havoc with their local budgets.[76] Then, Marion B. Folsom, former U.S. secretary of Health, Education and Welfare, who two years earlier helped draft a bill in the state authorizing the State Health Department to make medical audits of the quality of care given in New York's hospitals and other medical institutions, sharply attacked the bill. Folsom said, "Income eligibility levels are too high and out of the reach of the state's resources . . . . It's just free medical care for everyone."[77] Typical of the reaction of welfare officials was the action of St. Lawrence County welfare commissioner Lee P. Finley, who suspended welfare enrollments for 30 days in the hope that by then the program could be understood. Senator William Adams, chairman of the Senate Committee on Social Services, the committee that reported out the final bill, said, "My physician and personal friend sent me a note saying he'd accept anyone who ran against me."[78]

The lawmakers were beginning to feel the mounting pressure coming from local government officials. As a result, it was decided that the Joint Legislative Committee (JLC) on Public Health, chaired by Senator Norman Lent, Republican of Nassau County, would hold hearings throughout the state, to determine the impact of the Medicaid program. Although this was, to an extent, a duplication of the similar effort made the year before, the Lent Committee started its inquiry in a radically changed atmosphere. Now the program was the law, and more and more people started to form some idea of its meaning and possible consequence. Many upstate legislators were already drafting amendments to the law. It was in this atmosphere that, in late May, after Travia had delayed appointing Assembly members to it, the JLC began a series of hearings in a number of cities, like New York, Syracuse, Rochester, Buffalo, and in two smaller counties.

At the hearings, hundreds of local government officials, legislators, medical practitioners, and, in New York City, many welfare groups testified. The result was overwhelming agreement that the cost of Medicaid would be astronomical. It was recognized that the main difficulty was the requirement imposed by the federal law, Title 19, that participating states must enrich their programs in an absolute sense. New York State had a medical indigency program on its books since 1949, which gave medical benefits to people with certain low incomes. Thus, a family of four with an income of $4,700 or less, was entitled to receive physicians' services, with the costs paid by a combined state-city fund. The same family could receive hospitalization if its net income was below $5,300. Even in New York City, where these benefits had long been in effect, the increase of the eligibility level to $6,000 for both types of services (and for expanded benefits) would still result in both considerable service enrichment and cost inflation. The problem upstate was much more serious. In that area, no locality had ever implemented any pre-Medicaid medical indigency program in spite of existing law.[79] Thus, the cost of Medicaid would be truly astronomical in communities outside New York City, since they would have to increase, literally from a starting point of zero, their local contribution (25 percent from localities, 25 percent from the state, 50 percent from the federal government) to Medicaid. In some rural areas, over 80 percent of the families earned less than $6,000. The upstate reaction was commensurate with the financial burden involved.

In the revolt against the new law, some local officials tried to blame Medicaid for budget increases which would have taken place without Medicaid; some others, in their depositions, submitted fraudulent figures to the committee. Even after the discrepencies were pointed out to them, after detailed review of records and cross-examination, these officials would still refuse to concede, and they certainly were right when they maintained that Medicaid would enormously inflate their budgets and would lead, in some cases, to mammoth local tax increases.[80]

Under the impact of the hearings, the Republican members of the JLC submitted amendments to the new law, the most important of which incorporated into it a graduated deductibility factor requiring persons eligible for Medicaid, but earning more than minimal incomes, to pay from their own pockets progressively larger portions of medical bills. Then another bill was introduced to enjoin employers from discharging an employee from the company health plan on the ground that the employee was also eligible for Medicaid. Senator Brydges himself submitted a measure to guarantee "free choice of physicians," a proposal which was soon made meaningless by the fact that several county medical societies and thousands of doctors themselves refused to accept Medicaid patients.

The medical profession itself became one of the most vocal opponents of the program, not so much because of the fear of lower rates of reimbursement by the government (the Welfare Department had set reimbursement rates at the same or even higher levels than the Blue Shield rates), but because of the suspicion that the payment of medical bills by the government might lead to government regulation of the profession.

A further complication arose on June 2, 1966, when Wilbur Cohen, secretary of the U.S. Department of Health, Education and Welfare, revealed that the Congress had appropriated only $155 million for Title 19 to be distributed among all participating states, in the face of the fact that New York's own program would require federal reimbursement in the amount of $217 million to that state alone. In view of this situation, Senator Jacob Javits introduced a bill in the U.S. Senate to permit New York to cut back on its Medicaid costs by imposing a deductible cost percentage, by introducing different eligibility standards in different parts of the state, adapted to differing costs of living, and by allowing the state to make distinctions in degrees of benefits between recipients in different social situations, like, for example, blind men over 65 years of age and healthy men of 25.

Finally, on June 21, the Senate passed a total of 11 amendments to the Medicaid Law, some of them with Democratic approval. A deductible was enacted to eliminate "abuse" of the system. Senator Thaler said that this would discourage people from seeing their doctors early enough to prevent many types of diseases. He also said that it would cost more to administer than it would save in deductions, since the deductible formula was so complicated that each patient would have to spend hours with an administrator to review his income, savings, property, life insurance, and so on to determine what percentage of a particular doctor bill he would have to pay himself. (In 1970 several upstate welfare commissioners reported off the record that they had ignored the deductible since its administration was more costly than the money saved, even though this violated the law.)

Another amendment opposed by the liberal Democrats involved the free choice of physicians provision. It was felt that this provision would disrupt the clinic services of the New York City hospital system. Other amendments were not opposed. These included withholding aid from anyone refusing to permit an investigation of his financial condition, requiring that persons eligible report any change in their financial status that would affect their eligibility, and giving the state a lien on any court award to an accident victim treated under Medicaid. All the amendments passed.[81]

Notwithstanding Senate passage, Travia let the amendments sit in the Assembly Rules Committee. Angered over the maneuver, Minority Leader Duryea on June 29 employed a little-used tactic of bringing up the amendments on the floor as riders to a bill concerned with the licensing of blood banks. Travia ruled the amendments out of order and was upheld on an appeal from the decision of the chair by a strict party vote.

However, Travia was then under considerable pressure from two sources. Upstate Democrats feared for their reelection unless they joined the Republicans in cutting back the program. Travia, not opposed to the idea of remaining Speaker, shared the concern. At the same time, Senate Republicans were withholding support from a New York City tax package which Travia wanted enacted. Thus, Travia announced on June 30 that he would let out four of the amendments. After six hours of give and take with Duryea, the two leaders agreed that one amendment should require that eligible Medicaid families with incomes above $4,500 for a family of four pay a deductible equal to 1 percent of their incomes. Another amendment agreed upon would authorize the Department of Social Welfare to go to court to recover funds obtained by a recipient fraudulently. A third would obligate applicants to report changes in income, and the fourth would prohibit recipients from transferring their property to others in order to become eligible.[82]

The deductible amendment passed 93 to 60, and the other three passed unanimously. Another amendment, introduced from the floor, was passed. It provided state reimbursement to localities that exceeded their welfare budgets because of Medicaid. On July 5, the Senate also passed the amendments with the deductible amendment by a vote of 44 to 11. The governor signed the bills, thus ending the fight for 1966.

Two years later, despite continued Democratic control of the Assembly, the legislature severely cut back the program. Congress had by then reduced the federal share by some $39 million for New York. The governor proposed a reduction in the state's contribution of about $200 million, and the Senate raised it to $300 million by reducing eligibility to a level of $5,300 for a family of four, but also by cutting out of the program all persons between the ages of 21 and 65, regardless of income, unless they were totally blind or totally disabled (these categories were left in to retain federal reimbursement under special programs) or unless they were on the welfare rolls. The Senate bill was drafted by Majority Leader Earl Brydges and had the support of almost all non-New York City senators. It was expected for some time that Travia would either reduce the size of the cutbacks or kill them completely. But the Speaker had already accepted a federal judgeship, and his imminent departure from the legislature became an open secret. When the Assembly Democrats met in conference, upstate lawmakers refused to join the Speaker and other New York City representatives in opposing the cutbacks. Travia lost control of his conference and, fearing passage of a discharge motion, he himself brought the bills up for a vote. They passed the Assembly in April of 1968, and the governor immediately signed them into law. In this manner, the Medicaid program was, for all intents and purposes, destroyed since the levels of eligibility had been reduced below the 1949 levels of the state medical indigency program.

CONCLUSIONS

The governor of New York has enormous resources that enable him to become the dominant force in the legislative process. The Constitution empowers him to recommend legislation, call special sessions, veto bills, employ the item veto on budget matters, issue messages of necessity to speed the passage of bills, and prepare and submit the state budget. He heads a large and well-organized professional staff and has access to the best brains both within and outside of the state government.

New York's governor operates within the context of very real and strong two-party competition. He is the center of public demand and expectations regarding the legislative solution of major problems and is the focus of attention for the mass media.

As a political leader, he is the chief dispenser of political reward and/or punishment. Job patronage is big business, and according to Governor Rockefeller himself, it encompasses between 10,000 and 15,000 jobs.[83] The extent to which such job patronage is employed to affect legislative decisions varies with the personal taste and style of the chief executive.[84]

The result is that the governor is authorized and required both by law and tradition to prepare a legislative program of his own conception and a budget which together delineate the agenda of important measures that the legislature has to deal with each year. Today legislators await the governor's program because they know that it is the basis of their own legislative work. They no longer resent the intrusion of his initiative on what was once their privilege. It is the governor's function to initiate programs and then consider or present alternative solutions.

This means that today there is little argument about the established fact that the governor proposes. Conflict can arise only about the question of to what extent he should dispose over the final outcome of legislative proposals. The success of the governor in getting what he wants is subject to several variables, and some of these are beyond his immediate control.

The first, of course, is the status of the political environment. If the governor is of a different party than that of the majority in both or even in one house of the legislature, then he must expect difficulty. Even if he can develop cooperative relations with the legislative leaders of the opposition party, the latter still must maintain a fighting stance against him, if only to prove their independence and their readiness to represent their own party's needs and aspirations. Governor Harriman was in constant conflict with the Republican legislature, and this was due to a large extent to the simple fact that he was a liberal Democrat. Even Governor Rockefeller, whose intervention was instrumental in electing the two Democratic leaders he preferred to deal with, often received a hard time from them.

But party division is only part of the story. Ideological considerations, which often transcend party lines, can also be a major factor. Rockefeller had more trouble with conservative Walter Mahoney than with moderate Joseph Carlino. While political leaders, in dealing with one another, are quite capable of ignoring or transcending ideological divisions in the general interest, there are always limits beyond which a political leader cannot or will not go in sacrificing or disregarding his or his party's basic principles for the purpose of accommodating a fellow leader.

Another variable of a different sort is, of course, the personality of the individuals involved—in this case the governor, the Senate Majority Leader, and the Assembly Speaker. Where there is friendship and mutual respect, the chances for minimizing conflict are better. Where there is personal dislike, distrust, and suspicion, hostility becomes more likely and grows easier and faster.

The governor and the leaders are highly rational and practical men, but in the relationships even of men of such caliber, it is not always certain in what manner they will react to some quirks or mistakes in their intercourse. The point is that the way men react to one another and the extent to which their rational interests mesh are critical factors in influencing the final outcome of legislative decisions.

Despite the variables, the overall conclusion must be that, on balance, New York's governor does very well in the role of leading lawmaker. Rarely will a major program of his be completely scuttled. Partial revisions may occur quite often, but many major program bills will be approved as proposed. In general, the governor's ability to get much of what he wants, mostly with the active help of the legislative party leaders, is impressive indeed.

In 1968 Jerome Wilson, a former Democratic state senator and later legislative correspondent for CBS-TV News, evaluated Governor

Rockefeller's relative successes in an article written for The Nation. The Rockefeller years, wrote Wilson, are years in which one first thinks of the use of power, "the easy, unself-conscious exercise of the will of one over the state's 17 million."[85] This is most evident in terms of physical construction and building in which the record "consists of things—not tone, not concept."[86] He has gotten the legislature to help him build higher education facilities for 100,000 new students, 12,000 miles of new highways, 50,000 new middle-income apartments, and a new Albany Mall project for the housing of the state government which is awesome in its grandeur and its cost.

He has gotten the legislature to approve major tax increases (in 1959 with the income tax, in 1963 with an increase in user fees, and 1965 and 1968 with the sales tax). He has gotten the legislature to go along with intricate financing schemes for his building projects, which cost the taxpayers millions more in interest payments (although Rockefeller claims that this way is cheaper than waiting and paying the price for inflation). Thus, he created in the early 1960s new agencies such as the State Housing Finance Agency and the State Dormitory Authority to float bonds for different construction projects at much higher interest rates than that of the state's normal borrowing, in order to eliminate such borrowing from the state's general budget. At that time, the governor told the country that New York was on a pay-as-you-go basis. He sold the Albany Mall project to the city of Albany, so that it would float bonds for the same purpose, although the state would then rent the buildings at a handsome profit for the city.

What is even more interesting is that he could induce the state legislature not only to accept his tax programs and fiscal maneuvers, but also to go along with his wide but well-calculated ideological shifts. In 1969 he cut back on most social services, joined in the wreckage of Medicaid, reduced the formulas of state aid to localities, and cut welfare. In 1970 he restored the cuts, provided additional funds for most social services, and promised more and more money for construction, for welfare, and all else. There is little doubt that all this was part of a permanent reelection campaign strategy.

The truly surprising feature of this picture is the willingness of the legislature to follow and sanction many of these tactically motivated changes in Rockefeller's legislative policies. The phenomenon demonstrates either the nearly irrestible weight of the powers the governor can muster or an extraordinary degree of submissiveness or sense of weakness on the part of the legislature—or both. But the power of the governor of New York is not absolute. The legislature is still a powerful lawmaking institution, with a substantial potential to affect people's lives. It may have lost a great deal of legislative initiative, but it remains the supreme critic of every proposal and the final moulder of all law. It still can, and occasionally does, kill program bills of the governor and push through legislation of its own making, and no governor, interested in providing true leadership, can afford to forget this fact.

NOTES

1. Malcolm Jewell, "State Decision-Making: The Governor Revisited," in American Governmental Institutions, Aaron Wildavsky and Nathan Polsby, eds. (Chicago: Rand McNally and Co., 1968), p. 546.

2. William Keefe, "The Functions and Powers of the State Legislature," in State Legislatures in American Politics, Alexander Heard, ed. (Englewood Cliffs, N.J.: Prentice-Hall, Inc., 1966), p. 59.

3. Jewell, op. cit., p. 547.

4. Ibid., pp. 547-548.

5. William Keefe and Morris Ogul, The American Legislative Process (Englewood Cliffs, N.J.: Prentice-Hall, Inc., 1968), p. 397.

6. A more detailed analysis of gubernatorial powers is found in Malcolm Jewell, The State Legislature: Politics and Practice (New York: Random House, 1962), chap. 5.

7. Ibid., pp. 119-124.

8. Joseph A. Schlesinger, "The Politics of the Executive," in Politics in the American States, Herbert Jacob and Kenneth Vines, eds. (Boston: Little, Brown and Company, 1965), p. 228.

9. Coleman Ransone, Jr., The Office of Governor in the United States (University: University of Alabama Press, 1956), p. 212.

10. Warren Moscow, Politics in the Empire State (New York: Alfred A. Knopf, Inc. 1948), pp. 193-194.

11. Ibid., p. 198.

12. Congressman Jonathan Bingham, former secretary to Governor Harriman, interview, December 2, 1970.

13. Daniel Gutman, former counsel to Governor Harriman, interview, January 15, 1970.

14. Governor Averell Harriman, interview, January 30, 1970.

15. Governor Nelson Rockefeller, interview, March 2, 1970.

16. Governor Malcolm Wilson (March 4, 1970), Attorney General Louis Lefkowitz (February 24, 1970), William Ronan (March 27, 1970), and Governor Rockefeller (March 2, 1970) provided the information that went into this brief summary of the governor's legislative program development.

17. William J. Keefe, "The Functions and Powers of the State Legislature," State Legislatures in American Politics, Alexander

Heard, ed. (Englewood Cliffs, N.J.: Prentice-Hall, Inc., 1966), p. 58.

18. Albert Roberts, "Concepts of Legislative Fiscal Analysis and Review," report to the New York Assembly Ways and Means Committee, November 19, 1969, p. 2.

19. Lennis Knighton, "Legislative Review of Executive Performance," report to the Joint Legislative Committee on Legislative Fiscal Analysis and Review, May 1969, quoted in Albert Roberts, op. cit., p. 3.

20. Donald Herzberg and Paul Tillett, "A Budget for New York State, 1956-57," Inter-University Case Program #69 (University: University of Alabama Press, 1962), pp. 3-4.

21. Frederick C. Mosher, "The Executive Budget: Empire State Style," Public Administration Review XII, no. 2 (1952): 83.

22. Herzberg and Tillett, op. cit., p. 9.

23. Roberts, op. cit., p. 9.

24. Ibid., p. 11.

25. The New York Times, December 22, 1955; December 29, 1955; December 31, 1955.

26. Herzberg and Tillet, op. cit., p. 25.

27. Ibid.

28. The New York Times, March 14, 1956.

29. Herzberg and Tillett, op. cit., pp. 26-29.

30. "Rockefeller Lays Out His Program," Business Week (January 10, 1959): 36.

31. "Rockefeller Taxes," New Republic 140 (February 16, 1959): 5.

32. The New York Times, February 2, 1959.

33. Ibid., February 17, 1959.

34. "Rocky's Budget Hangs on 6 Slim Votes," Newsday, February 26, 1959, p. 7.

35. "Rocky's First Test," New Republic 140 (April 13, 1959): 5.

36. Many factual items in this case study are from The New York Times, February 21, 22, 23, 1959; March 1, 2, 4, 6, 11, 1959; and Newsday, March 4, 5, 6, 11, 1959.

37. The New York Times, January 4, 1965, p. 22.

38. Ibid., January 30, 1965, p. 1.

39. Ibid., February 9, 1965, p. 30; February 11, 1965, p. 1; February 20, 1965, p. 1.

40. Ibid., March 5, 1965, p. 17.

41. Ibid., March 25, 1965, p. 1.

42. Coleman Ransone, The Office of Governor in the United States (University: University of Alabama Press, 1956), pp. 187-188.

43. Gutman, op. cit.

44. "Strategy Varies with Republican Big Three," Newsday, March 13, 1958, p. 22.

45. Clark Ahlberg and Daniel Moynihan, "Changing Governors—and Policies," Public Administration Review 20 (Autumn 1960): 197.

46. Newsday, March 18, 1958, p. 7.

47. Harriman, op. cit.

48. Bernard Ruggieri, counsel to Senate Minority Leader Joseph Zaretzki, interview, February 8, 1970.

49. Milton Stewart, former executive assistant to Governor Harriman, interview, December 30, 1969.

50. Albert Abrams, secretary, New York Senate, interview, January 21, 1970.

51. Governor Wilson, op. cit.

52. Ibid.

53. Victor Condello, counsel to the New York Association of Railroads, interview, January 16, 1970.

54. "Republican Big Four is Now a Silent Quartet," AP, Newsday, May 14, 1959, p. 7.

55. James Desmond, "Rockefeller's Fast Start," Nation 88 (April 25, 1959): 389.

56. Ibid.

57. The New York Times, March 20, 1964.

58. Henry Paley, former director of information to the Speaker, interview, December 18, 1969.

59. Senator Seymour R. Thaler, interview, December 13, 1969.

60. Former Senate Majority Leader Walter Mahoney, interview, December 18, 1969.

61. Newsday, August 21, 1958, p. 9.

62. "Rivals Revenge," Time 75 (April 11, 1960): 29.

63. Ibid.

64. Governor Rockefeller, interview, March 2, 1970.

65. Former Speaker Anthony Travia, interview, December 23, 1969.

66. The New York Times, March 20, 1966, p. 70.

67. Ibid., March 10, 1966, p. 20.

68. Ibid., March 21, 1966.

69. Ibid., March 29, 1966.

70. Ibid.

71. Ibid., March 30, 1966, p. 48.

72. Former Speaker Joseph Carlino, interview, January 12, 1970.

73. Rockefeller, op. cit.

74. The New York Times, April 29, 1966, p. 10.

75. Ibid.

76. The New York Times, May 15, 1966, p. 7.

77. Ibid., May 17, 1966, p. 49.

78. Ibid.

79. Report of Senate Committee on Public Health, 1965, p. 18.

80. Some of the instances were observed personally by the writer while he served as a staff member of the Joint Legislative Committee on Public Health.

81. The New York Times, June 22, 1966, p. 1.

82. Ibid., July 1, 1966, p. 1.

83. Rockefeller, op. cit.

84. For a detailed description of the method by which Governor Harriman distributed his job patronage, see Daniel P. Moynihan and James Q. Wilson, "Patronage in New York State, 1955-59," American Political Science Review (June 1964): 286-301.

85. Jerome L. Wilson, "The Rockefeller Decade," The Nation 206 (February 19, 1968): 235.

86. Ibid.

5

THE LEGISLATURE
AND THE COURTS

STATE COURTS AND STATE POLITICS

Many Americans share the belief that our courts are nonpolitical and that judicial decision making is simply a question of applying law, reason, and legal precedent to problems. In reality, this is not the case.

> . . . the politics of the judiciary is similar in many ways to politics elsewhere in the political system. Our investigation has shown that courts are involved in partisan activities and are responsive to interest demands; although much of what they do is routine, they are sometimes involved in political controversies of great passion; and that judges interact in patterns of conflict and consensus and are influenced by many of the same social and economic forces that move other political actors. Moreover, the organization and staffing of the courts reflect long-standing political traditions or else serve various political needs.[1]

Through the settlement of disputes touching upon public affairs, courts are intimately involved in public policy. Judicial pronouncements are made regarding the entire range of decisions taken by political institutions, the conflicts between competing interests, and the applicability of the rules, constitutional, statutory, or established by common usage, under which society will operate. The discretion of the courts is substantial indeed.

When judicial decisions involving interpretation of statutes are required, judges are forced to read exact and precise meanings into legislative acts. There are several reasons for this. The language of statutes is often imprecise. Bill drafters cannot consider all the circumstances to which a piece of legislation will apply. Occasionally, bills are poorly drafted. At other times they are left purposely ambiguous.

However, despite the fact that the power of state courts to interpret statutes and even to judge their constitutionality has been acknowledged since colonial times, judicial decisions regarding acts of legislatures have rarely affected the broad political arena. Rather, such decisions, while of crucial importance to the parties to a case, have changed the existing political arrangements in only incremental ways.

Generally speaking, court decisions regarding the constitutionality of statutes deal with technical and procedural details rather than questions of broad policy. These decisions are not unimportant in light of the fact that many state constitutions are full of detailed provisions that ought not be constitutional provisions in the first place. But broad, sweeping reversals of grand legislative designs are not typical of judicial review decision making in the states.

Most state court systems follow a similar pattern of organization. Local trial courts handle minor cases. State trial courts handle major cases on a first instance basis, and they get cases on referral from local courts. Intermediate and last resort appellate courts make final decisions in cases of major conflicts in society. Although the general pattern is approximately the same everywhere, the specific organizational and structural arrangements are quite varied from state to state.[2]

The courts deal with legislative matters or become the focus of legislative concern on several levels. The first is, of course, related to the power of the state courts to rule on the constitutionality of legislation. The courts may also be interested themselves in the introduction of certain types of legislation, and they have developed, at least in New York, a promotional or lobbying technique that can be quite effective. Finally, in a completely different vein, the court systems are sources of political patronage, and many legislators seek not only favors and jobs from the courts for their political followers but quite often appointment or election to judgeships for themselves. This chapter is concerned with the relations between the courts in New York State and the legislature and will briefly examine the character of this relationship.

THE NEW YORK COURTS AND JUDICIAL REVIEW

The court system of New York State is composed of a Court of Appeals consisting of a chief judge and six associate judges, all

elected statewide; a Supreme Court, the basic court of original jurisdiction which has an appellate division composed of five or more
judges in each of the state's four judicial departments; several special
courts to handle particular problems (such as the surrogate's court,
family courts); and finally, city and local courts such as the criminal
and civil courts in New York City and county courts and justices of
the peace elsewhere.

The judicial review powers of the Court of Appeals are specified
in Article VI, Section 3, of the state constitution, which permits appeals
from lower courts when among other instances the appellate division
of the Supreme Court has made a decision "wherein is directly involved
the construction of the Constitution of the state or of the United States,"
or when any other court of original jurisdiction has made a decision
"where the only question involved on the appeal is the validity of a
statutory provision of the state or of the United States; and on any
such appeal only the constitutional question shall be considered and
determined by the court."

Judicial review powers mean that the courts can intercede in
the policy decisions emanating from the legislature, thereby placing
the judges into situations where they can determine and/or alter
public policy for the state. Judgments regarding the constitutionality
of a statute are, however, not the only instances in which New York's
higher courts determine policy. According to Charles Breitel, chief
judge of the Court of Appeals:

> The court makes new law by every decision, and in
> many instances the legislature is asking us to fill in
> blanks. When antitrust laws are passed prohibiting "un-
> reasonable restraints of trade" with no definition in the
> law regarding what is unreasonable, or when a Family
> Court is empowered to decide cases regarding families
> without a definition of a family, we must assume that it
> was intended that we fill in the blanks.[3]

The nature of the emerging problems and the attitudes of the
judges will determine the extent of the court's willingness to "legis-
late," but the tendency for the courts in New York, as it has been on
the national level for the past 20 years, has been to get increasingly
involved in this manner. There are, however, variations with respect
to the kinds of policy questions that attract judicial scrutiny. If the
legislature is in the continuing process of revising certain types of
legislation, then the courts are likely to leave the matter alone. If
the legislature does not seek to revise and improve a body of legislation, then the courts are more likely to assume a policy-making
role. These distinctions go beyond the usual inclination to leave

inherently political questions alone.[4] The courts will, however, be strongly interested in tackling questions that directly relate to court activities such as criminal procedure or court reorganization, while they will tend to stay away from broad questions of the distribution of political power. The one major exception from the latter custom has been the question of reapportionment, but even here the courts imposed their will only after many years of unwillingness to do so.

An important factor in the matter of court involvement in political or legislative affairs is the attitude of judges toward politics and the legislature. Some observers feel that judges, born and bred within the political system, tend to shy away from interfering with that system. For example, Victor Rosenblum, professor of law and political science at Northwestern University, believes:

> In construing rules and statutes, judges who have acquired their positions through the political system would not be likely to interpret the law so as to destroy that very system unless there were no alternative. The judge, however conscientious and honorable he may be, has this pinnacle of his career as a successful player in the community's ecology of games. His power and prestige as a judge are attributable to the determinate goals and calculable strategies that ecology of games has established. If his decisions impair the operations of the game, they will, at the same time, jeopardize his own status in the community. Thus the functions of state and local judges in refereeing and resolving conflicts are likely to be performed with due regard for protecting the traditions and practices of the political system.

> Observations by Sayre and Kaufman of the New York judiciary offer further illustrations of these propositions. In their section on "Courts and Politics" (Wallace Sayre and Herbert Kaufman, Governing New York City, Russell Sage, New York, 1960), the authors stress the role of judges in determining the content and scope of the constitutional and statutory provisions that comprise the "rules of the game." They point out how, by refusing to invalidate inequalities of representation growing out of failure to redraw the lines of the old aldermanic districts, the judges buttressed the Democratic majority that benefited from the prevailing situation. They also show how judicial sanctioning of the city's power to enact rent control laws heightened the popularity of the Democratic party officials who were responsible for the measure.[5]

The Court of Appeals hears approximately 600 cases on appeal each year plus other motions from lower courts. About 50 of these raise substantial constitutional questions,[6] but only about half a dozen of the latter challenge directly the constitutionality of some act of the legislature.[7] A study of one case of this nature involving the problem of reapportionment, which requires periodic judicial review and which is of importance to the legislature, will be offered later in this chapter.

JUDICIAL LOBBYING

As mentioned before, New York courts venture into the area of encouraging the introduction of new legislation, mostly in connection with matters that are directly related to some aspect or function of the court system itself. The practice became institutionalized through the creation on April 29, 1955, of the so-called Judicial Conference.[8] The establishment of the conference itself resulted from lobbying efforts on the part of a large number of jurists, lawyers, good-government groups, and judicial administrators. The conference is formally empowered by law to make recommendations to the legislature in all matters of court reform, and it also serves as the administrative body for the unified court system in the state. As an example of its "lobbying" strength, the conference after a long fight won legislative approval for the establishment by constitutional amendment of a unified court system in 1962, the first court reorganization in a century. As a matter of fact, the conference issues an annual report outlining its legislative recommendations, the results of special studies, and data documenting its needs.

Structurally the conference is composed of an administrative board made up of the chief judge of the Court of Appeals as its chairman and the presiding justices of the four appellate divisions. The rest of the conference is composed of the Administrative Board plus four Supreme Court judges from each department (who are not assigned to the appellate divisions), one surrogate, one county judge, one judge of the family court, one judge of the civil court of New York City, and one judge of the criminal court of New York City.

The Administrative Board appoints a state administrator as its executive head. Additionally, each department has a Committee for Court Administration made up of judges and practicing attorneys. The Judicial Conference has thus become the primary administrative and regulatory organ for the state court system. In addition, it also serves as the lobbying agent for the state courts, and in this respect it is interesting to note that the chairmen and ranking minority members of the Senate and Assembly Judiciary and Codes Committees are entitled by statute to attend meetings of the conference and to make recommendations to it. Thus, there is a legal and institutionalized working relationship between the legislature and the Judicial Conference.

The conference has access to important members of the legislature not only through the meetings that the Judiciary and Codes Committee members attend, but the conference also frequently submits legislative program recommendations regarding court organization, procedures, and regulations. In an average year the conference may submit a series of a dozen or more bills to the legislature. Since a very large percentage of New York legislators are also practicing attorneys, these recommendations are likely to get greater attention than those of other agencies of government or private interest groups. Additionally, the conference may be called upon to comment on bills introduced by others. Such requests for comments might come from the legislative leaders while bills are being considered. Hundreds of requests for comments on bills are submitted to the conference each year by the governor's counsel, as determinations are being made as to whether the governor should sign or veto bills.[9]

According to Judge Breitel, this arrangement constitutes a systematically working lobbying relationship which has great impact on certain nonsubstantive kinds of legislation.

> However, while there are discussions between judges and legislators on such housekeeping matters as court operation, it is almost unheard of to discuss substantive matters. We lobby for housekeeping or procedural changes and always for more judges. But we would never enter into discussions as an institution into such questions as reapportionment, and most of us would not discuss such matters even informally.
>
> Of course, there are always individual judges who, with more or less propriety, might talk to legislators on substantive matters or even appear as witnesses at public hearings. Most of my colleagues feel that such activity is improper, and we did not approve, for example, of Judge Hofstadter's public letters on wiretapping a few years back.[10]

It must be made clear at this point that what we have designated as the "lobbying" function of the Judicial Conference has little in common with the old-fashioned, self-seeking private activity known under this term. There is no functional contact whatsoever between legislative leaders and the conference with the sole exception of the entrée for conference representatives to the Judiciary and Codes

Committees. In fact, both sides are careful to avoid embarrassing contacts. The leaders of the legislature do, of course, occasionally take an interest in proposals for the expansion and strengthening of the overburdened court system and also in the patronage aspects of the selection of new judges, but the related bargaining process is always between the legislators and the interested local party leaders, never between the leaders and judges or the Judicial Conference.

THE JUDICIARY AS A CAREER GOAL

Most of the reform rhetoric criticizing the court system in New York has centered around the need for "taking the courts out of politics." What such rhetoric implies is that the current process of judicial selection is dragging potential judges into the murky waters of political party activity, if they want to be nominated and endorsed. As The New York Times phrased it:

> How to elevate first rate legal minds to the bench
> instead of mediocrities with political connections is a
> challenge as old as the Supreme Court in the nation and
> the state. . . . In Albany . . . hack candidates can be
> nominated for the State Supreme Court in various judi-
> cial departments because reform is the last thing many
> legislators will permit to shake their political plums.[11]

Whether one agrees or disagrees with such an assessment, the essential point is that judges are elected and do need party support for their election and promotion. Many legislators, members of the institution which sets the ground rules for judicial selection, are themselves interested in attaining higher judicial positions. Thus, whenever the legislative leaders are required to guide action on bills expanding the judiciary or revising the methods of the selection of judges, they are always confronted with personal career ambitions of some of their colleagues. Sometimes the leader himself is interested in such a change.

Among the legislative leaders discussed in this study, several have won seats on the bench. Senator Walter Mahoney, after his defeat in 1964, was appointed a member of the New York State Thruway Authority until a judicial vacancy occurred, at which point he won election to the State Supreme Court in Buffalo, where he now serves. His successor as Senate Majority Leader, Joseph Zaretzki, was very much interested in 1968 in a Supreme Court nomination. How- ever, the Democratic party leadership in Manhattan (Zaretzki's home county) and in the Bronx (under great pressure from good-

government groups, The New York Times, the New York Post, and
the reform wing of the party) decided to abide by the recommendations of a nonpartisan citizens' committee of lawyers and judges.
The citizens' committee felt that Zaretzki should not be nominated
because at the age of 68 he would have only one year to serve (taking office at age 69) before he would reach the mandatory retirement age of 70.

Among Assembly Speakers, Joseph Carlino has either not been
interested or has not received a judicial nomination (and now serves
as an attorney and lobbyist), but Anthony Travia was appointed to the
Federal District Court by President Lyndon Johnson in 1968. Former
Assembly Majority Leader and Acting Speaker Moses Weinstein is
now a member of the State Supreme Court in Queens.

Most local political organizations are, of course, very much
interested in judgeships, viewing them as patronage assets. In 1968,
the legislature created 125 additional judgeships. Before the bill
was enacted, however, local political leaders in each county busily
bargained among themselves about the division of the spoils. Of
course, however, clearance by the legislative leaders was required
not only concerning the bill itself but also concerning the division of
125 new positions. Consequently, the difficult question arose of how
the parties could predetermine the division of the spoils in a situation
where the law required that all judges be elected by the people. The
solution was found in the application of the device of bipartisan or
tripartisan endorsements.

Queens County, for example, was allotted nine additional Supreme
Court judgeships, as well as other judicial positions. The local
Democratic, Republican, and Liberal party officials thereupon agreed
that the Democrats would get five; the Republicans, three; and the
Liberals, one judgeship. Each party would then endorse all judicial
candidates of the others. As a result, little option remained for the
average voter other than to cast his ballot for his party's man, unless
he wanted to vote for candidates supported by the Conservative party.
The engineer of this arrangement was Queens County Democratic
leader Moses Weinstein, who at the time was also Assembly Majority
Leader. Some people believed that Weinstein would take one of the
judgeships for himself. However, he still wanted to become Speaker,
and later that year he became Acting Speaker, after Travia became
a federal judge. In early 1969, he challenged Stanley Steingut for the
Democratic leadership of the Assembly, although the Democrats
had lost control of that house, so that Weinstein and Steingut were
competing only for the minority leadership. When Weinstein lost
that contest, he took advantage of a vacancy on the Queens County
Supreme Court, was nominated by the Democratic, Republican, and
Liberal parties to fill the vacancy, and was elected in November of
that year.

CASE STUDY: THE COURTS AND
REAPPORTIONMENT

The influence of court decisions on the New York legislature has never been more deeply felt than during the 1960s when both federal and state courts, abandoning the "political thicket" doctrine, ordered the legislature to redraw the boundary lines for political districts in a revolutionary manner. The changes meant political life or death to lawmakers and threatened to alter the composition of the legislature itself.

What is reapportionment?

Reapportionment, the act of redrawing political district boundaries, is one of the most crucial areas of concern for those who would understand state politics. An old cliche can be paraphrased as follows: "You can have the issues, let me draw the lines." The truth of this cliche is painfully apparent when one examines the reality of reapportionment politics in the United States.

Studies of voting behavior indicate that most voters go to the polls after having made conscious (though not necessarily rational) choices between candidates for high office. These candidates are generally quite visible and are perceived by the voters in a favorable or unfavorable light. Most voters, however, feel obligated, once they are confronted by a long ballot on election day to continue to vote for significantly less visible candidates running for local office. On this second level, their choices are rarely based on a perception of individual merit, ideology, or issue, but rather on the basis of party affiliation.

While many voters show considerable independence when voting for presidents, governors, senators, and mayors, very few show such independence on the local level. As a result, the level of predictability of voter performance for local offices and state legislative and congressional seats is very high. This enables mapmakers to draw district lines that maximize their own party's or faction's opportunities for maintaining legislative majorities. While the Supreme Court of the United States changed the reapportionment ground rules in 1964 by requiring that districts be, as nearly as is practicable, equal in population, the Court decision did not change the essential advantages maintained by partisan mapmakers interested in drawing district lines that would unfairly favor one political organization over another.

From the perspective of the elected legislators themselves, there is no more important issue than reapportionment. Legislative behavior is directly affected by the desire to survive politically on the part of lawmakers, and the value systems of America's legislatures accept political survival as an important component in the range of acceptable behavior. In other words, political and legislative decisions made by lawmakers that are motivated by the desire to get reelected are very easily understood and accepted in America's legislative subsystems.

The following case study of reapportionment politics in New York State serves to support the premise that mapmakers, to a large extent, determine who gets elected in the New York legislature, which party will control the majority, and therefore the kinds of policies that will be approved or rejected by that legislature.

The Supreme Court's reversal in 1962 of its own position on the justiciability of reapportionment plans triggered a revolution in American politics. New York was dramatically affected by the mandate to make the districts of popular representation more equal. The following review of events in this state may show some of the implications of the grave issue for our states in general and give an indication of the kind of impact the courts have had on the character of the New York legislature in specific.

The history and consequences of malapportionment in state legislatures and in the delineation of congressional district boundaries have been studied in great detail by a number of writers on legislative politics.[12] Many extreme examples of distorted population representation have been cited to demonstrate the magnitude of the problem. Vermont House districts in 1960 varied in population size between 35,000 and 38. In the Senate of California also in 1960, the variations ranged from 6,000,000 in one district to 14,000 in another. "The calculations by Paul T. David and Ralph Eisenberg showed that in 1960 the value of the vote (which would be 100 on the basis of one man, one vote) ranged from 76 in all counties of over half a million population taken together to 171 in all counties of under 25,000 as a group."[13] The result was overrepresentation in and control of most legislatures by rural representatives. The impact of these conditions on public policy, while difficult to measure, must have been enormous. This is true also in states where notwithstanding rural Republican control of the legislature, a Democrat had been elected governor.

What is the reapportionment story in New York? According to Harvey Mansfield:

> The New York Constitution (Article III, Sections 2-5)
> . . . puts on the legislature the duty of making decennial
> reapportionments, subject to a series of restrictions that
> are obsolete in some respects, absurdly rigid in others,
> and wide open in still others. These restrictions were
> ingeniously designed to protect upstate representatives
> against the growth of cities, and, while paying lip service
> to standards of contiguity and compactness, to preserve
> the power of county leaders generally, and to enforce on

the larger cities (by the block and town rule) a standard
of numerical equality far more stringent than obtained
elsewhere.[14]

New York's reapportionment system was written into the state
constitution in 1894. The primary objective of some of the provisions
drafted by upstate Republicans was to ensure that New York City,
which one day might have a majority of the state's population, should
never control the legislature. Thus, it was provided that every county
regardless of population should have at least one assemblyman with
the total number fixed at 150 (except for Fulton and Hamilton Counties
which share one). In regard to the Senate, the Constitution provided
that no county could have more than one-third of the seats (with New
York City counties clearly in mind), and no two counties divided by
a public waterway could have half the Senate seats (with Manhattan
and Brooklyn in mind). All Assembly districts, said the Constitution,
must be wholly within the confines of Senate districts, and no town
or county line could be broken to make up the legislative districts
unless they were wholly within that town or county. Finally, the basis
for determining population was exclusively citizen population to make
sure that noncitizens who lived in big cities (newly arrived immigrants)
would not be counted, as they must be for determining congressional
districts.[15]

In addition to all these restrictions, there was no limit placed
on the practice of gerrymandering, a practice in which New York
mapmakers have shown at least as much imagination as any others
in the country. R. W. Apple of The New York Times noted in 1964
that "reapportionment has always been an act of politics, not political
science. It has been that way at least since 1812 when Governor
Elbridge Gerry of Massachusetts added gerrymandering to the lexicon
of American politics by signing an Essex County redistricting bill
benefiting the Republicans."[16] Nowadays New York political leaders
are very reluctant to admit that the successive redistricting measures
have been more or less slanted to devolve to the political advantage
of the party which, having the majority of votes, had devised the
measure. A legislative leader a generation ago was more candid.
About the 1951 Republican gerrymander of the state's congressional
delegation, New York State Majority Leader Arthur Wicks had this to
say: "It would be hypocritical for me to deny that the bill may bring
about an increased Republican representation in Congress. Of course
that is to be expected of legislation enacted by a legislature which is
controlled by the Republicans, because the people of the state voted
more Republicans than Democrats into the legislature."[17]

Gerrymandering is possible mainly because the overwhelming
majority of voters, who consciously choose between better-known

candidates for major offices, cast their votes for candidates running
for lesser offices on the same ballot whom they do not know at all.
Consequently, this great mass of votes is cast for the most part purely
on the basis of party affiliation. This circumstance creates a very
real measure of predictability in congressional and state legislative
races. With this knowledge in hand, reapportionment mapmakers
can draw districts which increase the number of seats that their
party or faction can capture. The techniques are geared either toward
concentrating all opposition voters into a single district and thereby
removing opposition votes from several other districts in the county
or geographic area or toward breaking up a concentration of opposition
voters in such a way that a small bloc of such voters will be located
in districts in which there are larger numbers of friendly voters. In
both cases a friendly candidate has a better chance to be elected. The
process is relatively simple when population requirements do not
intrude. The equal population mandate of 1964 of the Supreme Court,
however, made the process of gerrymandering technically more
difficult. As this case study will indicate though, gerrymandering
in New York State has, by no means, become an impossible proposi-
tion.

The importance of new reapportionment statutes to the parties
in the legislature should not be underestimated. To many candidates
their provisions may mean political life or death. Consequently, the
entire legislature is deeply concerned with the manner in which the
new provisions will affect the outcome of coming elections. The
party leaders, however, are even more concerned. Those of the
latter who must themselves run for reelection in revised districts
may find their own chances at stake. In addition, they must be even
more worried over the electoral prospects of their party as a whole
and their own continuing tenure as leaders, which will depend on the
number of their colleagues who can survive the ordeal of reapportionment. Accordingly, few issues can produce a crisis atmosphere for
the leaders and the members that may compare with the anxieties
that surround all legislative reapportionment decisions.

The first statutory reapportionment of legislative districts
after the adoption of the 1894 constitutional provisions took place in
1917. It still attempted to maintain rural Republican control. Then
came the tragic years of the depression. They shattered Republican
control in the state, and in 1932 the Democrats captured control of
the Senate on the presidential coattails of Franklin Roosevelt. Two
years later Republicans continued to stay away from the polls in large
numbers, and Herbert Lehman won the governorship by a majority
of 808,000 votes, just enough to help the Democrats capture the
Assembly by a 76 to 74 margin, while retaining Senate control as
well. The Democratic majority was to last for only one session.

In 1944, another reapportionment bill, the first since 1917, was passed. The courts upheld the plan which added five new Senate seats, mostly in Republican-controlled suburban areas. The change drastically reduced the share of New York City's representation (which then had a majority of the state's population) to a mere 25 out of 56 Senate seats, and 67 out of 150 Assembly seats.[18]

Many city dwellers complained against this situation, and a few lawsuits followed, but the courts at the time still were not interested. In 1946, the United States Supreme Court refused to hear complaints related to malapportionments of electoral districts. In Colegrove versus Green, the court refused by a 4 to 3 vote to enter the "political thicket," as Justice Felix Frankfurter defined this complex of problems. Inherently political questions of this nature ought, he said, to be settled by the duly elected political institutions themselves. This, of course, gave little comfort to those unwilling to acquiesce in the continuing domination of the legislature by a disproportionately large number of rural legislators.

In 1961, attempting once again to get the ground rules changed, R. Peter Strauss, president of the New York City radio station WMCA, challenged before the federal courts the 1894 apportionment formula as unconstitutional. This petition was based on the charge that the 1894 formula violated the Fourteenth Amendment, which prohibits the denial by a state the equal protection of the law to its citizens. On January 13, 1962, the Federal District Court of New York dismissed the case.

On March 26, 1962, the Supreme Court reversed the "political thicket" doctrine of the Colegrove versus Green vase. In Baker versus Carr the court rules that apportionment cases may present valid and justiciable questions and that district courts ought to hear such cases. On August 17, 1962, yielding to the Baker versus Carr decision, the Federal District Court in Manhattan did hear arguments on the WMCA petition, but found that New York's apportionment was constitutional. The District Court was confronted with the same difficulty as all other lower federal courts faced with similar cases. The unsettled basic question was the determination of the constitutional standard under which complaints against apportionment plans should be judged. This determination was up to the United States Supreme Court which, in June 1963, finally agreed to hear the New York case and several other cases as well.

Early in February 1964, Senate Majority Leader Walter Mahoney prepared a legislative reapportionment plan that would have probably added several seats to the Republican side in both houses of the New York legislature. However, when Speaker Joseph Carlino and Governor Nelson Rockefeller opposed the idea on the grounds that the step was poor politics in an election year (particularly since the courts were then in the process of ruling on the constitutionality of the state's apportionment formula), Mahoney decided to withdraw the proposal.[19]

On February 17, 1964, the Supreme Court made two major decisions that were to affect the lines of congressional representation in New York State. In the first and more important decision, Wesberry versus Sanders, the Court ruled that Article I, Section 2, of the United States Constitution required that all congressional districts be, as nearly as possible, equal in population. Thus the principle of "one man, one vote" was pronounced for the first time as a doctrine of American jurisprudence.[20] It is interesting to note that, at the time, New York's congressional districts were generally considered to encompass fairly equal populations, since only 13 of the state's 41 districts varied by more than 10 percent from the average district size of 410,000, and the largest and smallest districts were only 14.8 percent off.[21]

The other case, Wright versus Rockefeller, challenged the layout of the seventeenth congressional district in Manhattan. In 1961, the boundaries of the district were redrawn to bring its population closer to the norm. At the same time, however, the change resulted in cutting out of the district large numbers of nonwhite residents. The district became a predominantly Republican preserve, and the Democrats brought suit. The Supreme Court ruled, however, that the districts of the area were fairly equal in size and that actual racial discrimination had not been proved. The vote was 7 to 2.[22]

On June 15, 1964, the Court handed down its most momentous decision in Reynolds versus Sims, affecting the state of Florida. Rejecting the federal analogy, the Court ruled that both houses of the Florida State legislature had to be reapportioned on the basis of the one-man, one-vote principle. The competent district court must oversee apportionment plans to determine whether they conflicted with the decision and the provisions of the equal protection clause of the Fourteenth Amendment. The Court then struck down (in several other similar cases, the same day) the existing apportionment systems in Alabama, Colorado, Maryland, Virginia, Delaware, and New York. The New York case, WMCA versus Lomenzo, was referred back to a three-man Federal District Court for the resolution of several complicating problems. The most important of these was the accomplished fact of the primary elections for the 1964 legislature which had just been held, and the repetition of which on the basis of a new reapportionment plan in the same year would have caused enormous administrative difficulties and even political repercussions. The other horn of the dilemma was even edgier. If no new primary elections were to be held, the new legislature about to take office on January 1, 1965, would be the product of a district system which the Supreme Court found unconstitutional. On this basis, the validity of the entire legislative work of the 1965 session might be challenged on constitutional grounds.[23]

While these problems were being considered by the judiciary, political leaders were busy trying to assess the political implications of the new one-man, one-vote decision. The feeling prevailed that the Republicans would be hurt, since rural areas would lose representation. The question was how big the losses would be. The Republicans derived some hope from the consideration that many Republican-dominated suburban communities had been even more underrepresented than the urban areas, and the correction of this situation by reapportionment would, to some extent, counterbalance the gains of the Democrats in urban centers and thus help minimize Republican losses. The second ameliorating factor for the Republicans was that, as the majority party in both houses of the legislature, they would be in charge of cutting out the new district lines. Thus, some measure of gerrymandering skill might help to reduce the party's losses.

The reactions of political leaders to the momentous court decisions were predictable. Mayor Wagner spoke for all Democratic leaders by hailing the rulings as a new "Magna Carta for the Democratic party." R. Peter Strauss called it a "knock-out" and was given great credit for his persistent pursuit of the case, the hiring of the winning attorneys, and spending the required $50,000 court costs. The Republicans hid their displeasure behind bland pronouncements of compliance. Speaker Carlino said that the old plan had contained some inequities "which have been a matter of concern for many of us for some time." Majority Leader Mahoney said, "The legislature would develop a new formula which would be fair and equitable for all." Governor Rockefeller said, "An apportionment plan for New York State would be developed as promptly as possible, and it will comply with the standards prescribed by the Supreme Court." It is unlikely that the latter statements truly reflected the feelings of the Republican leadership.[24]

Various Democratic groups, anxious for immediate change, began proposing plans for the quick implementation of the law. However, the power to act or to delay action was in the hands of the three top Republican leaders, and they were in no great hurry to implement a ruling unless mandated to do so that would reduce their power. They were still seeking ways and means to prevent the drastic reduction of their majorities in the upcoming 1964 elections. Speaker Carlino telegraphed his Republican assemblymen to be very circumspect in their public statements dealing with the problem. Senator John Marchi called for an immediate statewide census which would reflect the large population shifts that had occurred since 1960, mostly at the expense of the metropolitan area. The point had validity, since in 1964 there were over 1.5 million more people in the state than the

1960 census had indicated. The Democrats insisted that such arguments were simply stalling tactics, and Raymond Corbett, president of the state AFL-CIO, called for immediate action and implied union displeasure if action were to be delayed.[25]

Democratic state chairman William McKeon proposed a plan in which a special commission appointed by the governor would immediately draw up a plan for a 60-seat Senate and a 180-seat Assembly and which increased representation for urban and suburban areas. The commission would be appointed from lists of 10 names to be submitted by both major parties. The governor would choose five people from each list.

Rockefeller, however, decided to set up a special commission with a much broader mandate. The committee would study every single problem related to the central issue: The question was whether a special session should be called, whether a census should be taken, whether and how the length of legislators' terms and the number of seats should be changed, the seat of the permanent power to reapportion, the question of weighted voting (whether legislators should vote in proportion to the numbers of people they represent, thereby allowing districts with differing sizes of populations), and so on. Most Democrats felt that the special commission was created not only for the purpose of finding solutions to more or less urgent problems, but also to spend as much time as possible in its deliberations. In the meantime, the legislative leaders appointed a JLC of their own to make an independent study. Republican senator Robert McEwen of Ogdensburg was appointed chairman. Mahoney, in announcing the new JLC, declared that it was physically impossible to redistrict in 1964 and that the new legislature of 1965 ought to do the job.

Rockefeller on July 12 appointed his seven-man special committee with Dean William H. Mulligan of the Fordham Law School as chairman. The Democrats attacked the committee and its "partisan" makeup. They complained that the three Democrats on the committee were appointed without consultation with their party and that they would not represent Democratic needs.[26]

Meanwhile, R. Peter Strauss filed another petition with the Federal District Court for the purpose of obtaining a declaration that any election held under the existing apportionment system would be illegal. The purpose of the step was to require the enactment of a reapportionment statute in a special session. On July 15 the court declared with final validity that the existing system was unconstitutional. It then recessed until July 27 "to await action, if any, by the duly constituted authorities of the state of New York in the light of this declaration." The court also asked WMCA to submit a plan for the implementation of this order in case the state would fail to comply.

A characteristic background incident occurred on July 16. Representatives of WMCA and of the Democratic State Committee went to Albany to get some maps and population statistics from the JLC. They were denied access to this information. Strauss then hired a Pinkerton guard to stand outside the JLC's offices to record all persons entering and leaving the premises and to find out whether the documents had been spirited away. The guard was ordered to leave when the building closed at 5 p.m. The dispute was again ended by court intervention. Judge Sylvester Ryan, one of the three district judges, ordered that the documents be produced in court. The attorney general's office then agreed to let the plaintiffs see the documents in question and the incident ended.[27]

On July 23 the governor called on the Mulligan Committee to report to him no later than December 5, thereby effectively killing any chance of action on reapportionment for that year. The move was roundly condemned. On July 27 the three-man federal bench ordered that a new plan be enaacted by April 1, 1965, that the 1964 elections should be for a term of only one year, that the new reapportionment plan of April 1, 1965, must go into effect in a special election to be held in November of 1965, and that those elected at that time also serve only for one year. In 1966, the two-year term cycle would be reinstated.[28]

Republican assemblymen met in conference to discuss redistricting possibilities that would keep as many GOP legislators in office as possible to maintain their majority and, perhaps, appeal the ruling. Rockefeller then announced that all reapportionment plans would be considered and voted upon in a special session of the legislature he would call for December. The Democrats bitterly attacked the proposal of entrusting this important decision to a Republican-dominated lame duck session which would include men who had been defeated or retired. The Democrats at the time could not even dream of the possibility of winning in November a majority in either house. However, this is actually what was to happen, to the tremendous frustration of the Democratic party, over its failure to prevent Rockefeller's special session from taking place. State chairman McKeon did recommend that Democratic legislators refuse to attend the special session, to which Rockefeller's reply was that McKeon's proposal was a "cynical and politically motivated call for a mass violation of the law by elected officials."[29]

On November 3, 1964, Lyndon Johnson was elected president in a landslide victory over Republican Barry Goldwater. On his coattails the Democrats in New York won majorities in both legislative houses for the first time in 30 years (under the old apportionment formula), and Democrats were elected in some areas for the first time in a century. Both Mahoney and Carlino were defeated.

All the victorious Democrats could do, however, was to attack the special session passionately. On November 12, about 17 Democrats, masked as quacking ducks, greeted the governor's plane at Kennedy Airport as he returned from Spain; all in vain—the governor held out.

On November 30, the Mulligan Committee reported. It recommended that the Senate membership be increased from 58 to 65, the Assembly from 150 to 195, and the term of legislators extended to four years. It also suggested that county lines be respected wherever possible and that fractional or weighted voting be considered. The next day, Rockefeller set the date of the special session for December 15.

It should be mentioned here that the state's case before the federal courts was pleaded by the attorney general but that the Republican legislative leaders had used some of their best attorneys to assist the attorney general's staff. In some instances the leaders' staff personnel took over the handling of the case. The work on the brief opposing WMCA in the original case was conducted by Donald Zimmerman of Forest Hills, New York, an attorney on the staff of the Senate Majority Leader, Walter Mahoney.

With the date of the special session set, the Republican leaders now organized a new staff of expert mapmakers. As the legislators arrived for the special session on December 15, they discovered that there was nothing for them to do, since the reapportionment plans and the text of the final bills had not yet been prepared. The staffs worked feverishly though. Hidden on mezzanine floors of the capitol building, between the third and fourth floors, or in other inaccessible offices, mapmakers were preparing the new district lines for both Senate and Assembly, behind locked doors and in the dead of the night. While only the leaders' staff members and the technicians were supposed to be present, favored legislators and some county leaders had access to the developing results of the work and could make sure that the new district lines would satisfy their needs. Maps were spread across the floor of the large rooms, on which maps every block or apartment building was pictured. The voting pattern of each small community or housing complex was taken into account. The mapmakers then took thread and pins of many different colors and began tracing lines on the maps. When the outline of a district was completed, the total number of residents was rechecked to make sure that the new district area would conform to the population requirement. Pins and thread were, of course, often readjusted to fit the political needs of the Republican party. When a map was completed. a worker in his socks would bend down over it and read out the streets along which the thread was laid. A stenographer took down the street boundaries, and which were then incorporated into the text of the apportionment law.

After several days, the Republicans finally submitted four plans for consideration by the special session. After tumultuous debate, all four were passed. The idea was to pass Plan A, then amend it with Plan B, then amend that with Plan C, and finally cap the series of amendments with Plan D. Each plan was successively more favorable to the Republicans. The calculation of the strategists was that Plan D would become law unless the federal court struck it down, in which case Plan C would stay in force, and so forth.

In conformity with the court rulings, Plan A provided for equal districts, as did all the plans, based on citizen population (not total population) as reflected in the 1960 census. Plan B was based on voting population as indicated by the turnout not in 1964 (when Democrats poured out in masses to vote and many Republicans stayed home) but on the 1962 elections, in which Rockefeller had swamped Morgenthau. The light turnout in Democratic areas in that election would automatically reduce the population basis of the legislative representation of the districts in question, and thereby, the number of Democratic legislators. Plan C returned to citizen population as the basis of districting, but it made almost certain the reelection of all incumbents, the majority of them Republicans, by giving those candidates whose districts were smaller in population than the acceptable norm voting power modified in proportion to the number of people they represented. This plan was called "weighted voting." Thus, if each Assembly district had to contain approximately 100,000 citizens and Assemblyman X's present district held only 50,000, his district would remain intact and he would probably be reelected, but he would be allowed to cast only one-half a vote in the legislature. Thus, all incumbents could be reelected and would be encouraged to vote in the special session for the four plans. Of course, nothing was said in the bill about whether Assemblyman X would have only one-half a vote in committee too or receive one-half a salary or one-half of the normal file space, and so on. Plan D combined the provisions of Plans B and C by calling for weighted voting and district populations based on the 1962 voter turnout.

The plans were each passed in both houses on subsequent days by strict party voting, and the governor immediately signed them into law.

As the 1965 regular session opened, Democrats, now in the majority, sharply criticized the four Republican plans. R. Peter Strauss petitioned the federal court to rule all four plans unconstitutional. To his argument, Strauss added a new element. He claimed, and his evidence was convincing, that the new district lines in a number of instances violated the "compact and contiguous" provisions of the state constitution (although those terms had never been clearly defined). On January 21, however, the federal court refused to consider

Strauss's petition, saying that it was not its function to supervise the drawing of lines which might be in violation of state constitutional provisions.[30]

Five days later the court announced its decision on the four Republican redistricting plans themselves that Plans B, C, and D failed to meet the pertinent constitutional requirements but that Plan A did meet them. On February 1, the court explained its decision in a 32-page opinion. On the same day the United States Supreme Court upheld the District Court's decision requiring that a special election be held in 1965. This meant the rejection of a lawsuit which state senators John Hughes and Lawrence Rulison, both Republicans of Syracuse, had instituted against the order on the basis that they had been elected for a two-year term, which would be curtailed by the special election. By the way, the decision of the Supreme Court clearly reflected its growing preparedness to give lower courts great discretion in adjudicating apportionment issues.[31]

The Democrats, of course, refused to acquiesce on the ruling in favor of Plan A, and they decided to try a new approach. They sued in state court on the grounds that Plan A violated the state constitution through the elements of gerrymander it harbored. On March 15, State Supreme Court justice Mathew Levy agreed that Plan A violated the state constitution, but his decision was not based on the gerrymander charge but on the fact that Plan A provided for a 165 seat Assembly, while the state constitution clearly limited the number to a maximum of 150 seats.[32] (It seems that the Republican leaders had wrongly assumed that the sections of the state constitution which made the 150-man Assembly mandatory were nullified by the United States Supreme Court along with those provisions which dealt with the re-apportionment formula.)

Now faced, with the Levy decision (which they were going to appeal) and with Strauss's appeal from the Federal District Court decision, the governor and the Republican legislative leaders announced that they had hired former governor Dewey and his law firm to handle the state's defense. The Democrats, of course, strongly protested the use of public funds for such a purpose when the services of a perfectly capable attorney general were available without additional charge.[33]

Bypassing the appellate division, the Court of Appeals itself heard arguments on the Levy decision. On April 14, it upheld Levy by a 6 to 1 vote.[34] The court agreed that Plan A violated the constitutional provision requiring 150 Assembly seats and ruled that the legislature must come up with a new plan.

In the meantime, the Democratic Majority Leaders, Zaretzki and Travia, appointed a nonpartisan commission to prepare a Democratic "nonpolitical" redistricting plan, ostensibly for propaganda purposes. Now, however, seeing that Plan A had been struck down, they decided to entrust the job of drawing new district lines to a newly formed and Democratic-controlled JLC on Reapportionment, chaired by Assemblyman Louis De Salvio of Manhattan. The legislature still faced the deadline of May 1, which the federal court had extended from the original date of April 1. Many good-government groups, some reform Democrats, many Democrats who had opposed Zaretzki and Travia and who feared for their political futures, and even Mayor Wagner, joined the Republicans in condemning the abandonment of the nonpartisan commission.

The reapportionment plan of the Democrats could not be finished by the May 5 deadline. When it subsequently was made public and distributed in Albany, legislators swarmed to get copies to see what their districts would look like. The plan was definitely gerrymandered to aid New York City and suburban areas. It also would have led to the defeat of some reform Democrats and hurt others who had not stood well with the recently elected Democratic leaders. However, all this soon became totally irrelevant. While public hearings still went on debating the Democratic plan, the Federal District Court announced on May 10 that by a 2 to 1 vote it had decided that a special election must be held in November 1965 and on the basis of the Republican Plan A.[35] Since the legislature failed to meet the court-prescribed deadline, the District Court said it had no choice but to reinstate the one available plan that conformed to federal constitutional requirements. Thus Plan A, ruled violative of the state constitution, would determine the composition of the coming legislature, but only for one year. For the 1966 elections, the 1966 legislature elected in November of 1965 would have to prepare a new plan that would have to meet both federal and state requirements. Should the legislature fail to do so, said the three-man bench, the courts would step in and have the job of reapportioning done by someone else.

The Democrats thereupon tried various tactics to prevent the holding of the 1965 special election or at least to get a new hearing before the United States Supreme Court. They hired former Federal District Court judge Simon Rifkind to argue their case. After many preliminary hearings and maneuverings, the United States Supreme Court on June 1 voted 8 to 1 to reject Travia's and Zaretzki's petition to stay the lower court orders.[36] This decision put an end to all resistance and made it final that in November 1965, a special election would be held on the basis of Plan A of the Republicans. The two parties then agreed that a referendum should be held to decide whether a constitutional convention should be called, which among other things, would work out a permanent apportionment formula. The bill embodying the agreement was passed on June 15 and signed by the governor.

However, one last complication had to be ironed out. Responding to an appeal brought by Democratic senator Frank Glinski of Buffalo, the State Court of Appeals voted 4 to 3 to prohibit all preparations for the special election ordered by the federal judiciary on the grounds that Plan A violated the state constitution. Chief Judge Desmond argued that the federal court order had no final validity, and so the state court was free to make a contradictory decision. Federal Judge Waterman, who had signed the election order, insisted that the order was final and binding, whereupon Federal Judge Ryan issued on July 11, the day after the ruling of the State Court of Appeals, a temporary injunction against all state proceedings that would be in conflict with the federal court order.[37]

Thus, two courts were clashing, and behind them, two constitutions. Both courts agreed that Plan A violated the state constitution, but the federal courts considered this the lesser evil. It wanted to replace a legislature whose selection process had in the view of the United States Supreme Court violated the federal constitution. Consequently, in the end the stand of the federal judiciary prevailed. After some further legal maneuvers and appeals, the special election was held, as ordered, on November 2, 1965. In that election the Republicans recaptured the control of the Senate by a 37 to 28 margin, but the Democrats retained the Assembly 89 to 76.[38]

Before the elections the Democratic leaders appointed a six-man advisory committee on reapportionment composed of professors chosen from the state's universities. Chaired by Robert McKay, the commission announced on December 2, 1965, that it was using computers to draft a new plan in order to meet the new deadline of February 1, 1966, for the presentation of a plan to replace Plan A, as ordered by State Supreme Court and affirmed on December 9 by the appellate division.[39]

In this manner, the year 1965 ended with these results: The Democrats had missed a real chance to draw up a reapportionment plan of their own and, therefore, they lost the Senate; the federal courts asserted their dominance over the state courts and the pre-eminence of the federal over the state constitution; the Republicans had reconquered the Senate with the help of a gerrymandering rearrangement of the districts; and there was still no solution in sight for the question of how the vote of one New Yorker should be made equal with that of any other New Yorker on a permanent basis.

In early January of 1966, the McKay Commission issued its new plan intended to conform with both state and federal requirements. It turned out to be so "fair" that many Democrats roundly rejected it. Assemblyman Louis DeSalvio, chairman of the JLC on Reapportionment, said that he would lose two-thirds of his district and would probably be defeated under the McKay plan. Negro leaders

150

said that the plan would lead to the defeat of several black legislators. Even Joseph Zaretzki discovered that he would do better under the Republican plan announced on January 18 than under the McKay proposal.

The Republic plan, drafted for the most part by Donald Zimmerman, special counsel to Senator Brydges, provided for a Senate that probably would go Republican by a small margin and an Assembly that would prove a tossup in terms of which party could capture a narrow majority.[40]

Finally Travia and Brydges, the legislative leaders, announced that they would have to set up a joint bipartisan conference to iron out a compromise solution. Despite several long meetings, no compromise was reached. The impasse resulted from the fact that the negotiations on a number of district boundaries depended upon previous understandings between the local county leaders. However, the county leaders in Nassau, Erie, Monroe, and Oneida Counties could not reach agreement, and the legislative leaders were not willing to bypass these important politicos on this question. Thus, an impasse on the county level meant, of course, an impasse on the legislative level. Despite the fact that the Court of Appeals extended the deadline for the adoption of final statewide plan to February 15 and later to February 22, no agreement could materialize. The Republicans, therefore, passed their own plan (which the Democrats coined a "Zimmermandered" plan after the name of its author) in the Senate on February 9, and three days later the Democrats passed their "professor's plan" in the Assembly. Talks between the leaders continued for a while, but when no agreement seemed to be possible, Brydges charged that Travia was refusing to compromise because his "boss," United States senator Robert Kennedy, compelled him to do so. Travia became angry and the discussion ended.[41]

Finally, the State Court of Appeals decided to appoint a five-man Judicial Commission with the mandate to work out by March 14 a reapportionment plan without the participation of the legislature. The commission was headed by Orison Mardin, president-elect of the American Bar Association and a man with no political affiliation. Two former judges, Democrat Charles Froessel and Republican Bruce Bromley were appointed members along with one reapportionment expert from each party, Democrat Robert Bradey and Republican Edward Jaeckle.

The commission adopted the mode of operation of accepting district boundaries in those counties where the local party leaders had agreed on them. It then proceeded to make decisions for those counties where the local leaders could not agree and ordered the mapmakers to work out the details on the basis of the commission's approximate outlines. Very critical of this operation, Professor

Harvey Mansfield noted that the court had chosen to "arrange for, and ratify, a set of bipartisan compromises in which the regular county leaders were prepared to acquiesce."[42]

In fact, the court-imposed plan worked to the advantage of the regular party leaderships and of incumbent legislators of all factions and to the disadvantage of insurgents, upstate Democrats, Puerto Ricans, and blacks. These groups assailed the plan, but the Court of Appeals formally adopted it as the mandatory basis for the November 1966 elections. The results of that election was that the Democrats stayed in control of the Assembly and the Republicans retained control of the Senate.

For all intents and purposes, this action by the court ended the reapportionment fight over the approximate composition of the legislature of New York for the 1960s. It is true that the Constitutional Convention which met in April 1967 proposed a new redistricting formula based on certain changes in the state constitution worked out by the convention, but in a subsequent referendum the voters overwhelmingly defeated the proposed amendments and with them the suggested new formula.

Now the question arises what happened in the matter of the twin aspect of the reapportionment problem: the issue of New York's congressional districts? In 1966, David Wells, a reapportionment expert for the International Ladies' Garment Workers Union, filed suit in federal court charging that most congressional district lines in the state failed to meet the equal population mandate imposed by the Supreme Court in Wesberry versus Sanders. The Supreme Court upheld Wells's claim on two occasions, repeatedly striking down plans prepared for new congressional districts by the legislature. In 1970, again under a court order to reapportion congressional lines, the then again Republican-ruled legislature carved out new districts, claiming that they now conformed to the population requirement. Wells again brought suit, stating that lines were clearly gerrymandered. The Supreme Court in April upheld the plan though and, as requested, refused to rule on questions of gerrymandering.[43] In passing, one sidelight of the 1970 congressional reapportionment seems to deserve attention. It involved the district of the one Republican congressman from the city of New York, Seymour Halpern of Queens. Halpern had supported Mayor John Lindsay, running in the 1969 elections as a Liberal, after losing the Republican mayoral primary to Senator John Marchi, a very popular conservative legislator. Probably in order to teach Halpern a lesson, the Republicans drew a map which was sure to make Halpern the underdog in his own old district, and Halpern was forced to rush to Albany to plead with Majority Leader Brydges for some last-minute escape hatch from certain defeat. In the end, this expedient was resorted to: After the overall congressional plan was passed, a second bill amending it was pushed through for the sole purpose of revising Halpern's district. In this manner his original constituency was left more or less intact, and his chances of reelection suddenly turned bright. The primary motive of the maneuver was apparently to demonstrate to Halpern the wisdom of reestablishing in his own mind the value of party loyalty.

The Supreme Court reapportionment decisions of 1964 dramatically affected the character of American state politics. The fact that the courts got involved in this issue and in fact reversed precedent and superseded our elected decision-making bodies in this area indicates how important the process of drawing district lines is to state governmental policy.

Nevertheless, the decision by the Court, which triggered a series of controversial and important events in New York State, did not change the basic method by which district lines are redrawn. Decision-making authority over district lines remains in the hands of the majority party leaders in the New York State legislature, and while the Court decisions have imposed some restraints on the choices available to these leaders, nevertheless their near total dominance over reapportionment decisions remains. The significance of this fact cannot be overrated since the premise suggested earlier—that he who draws the lines determines legislative majorities and therefore legislative output—is as true today as it was in 1964. The issue is one of concern not only to a small group of elected officials interested in their reelection; it is of major concern to those who are deeply involved in the determination of normative standards for political behavior and for reforming our governmental institutions. Additionally, it should be of even greater significance for those citizens concerned with the kinds of laws that are passed by our state legislature since there is this direct relationship between district lines and the passage of legislative programs.

CONCLUSIONS

The relationship between the various courts in New York and the legislature is limited in terms of the kinds of contacts permitted and in terms of specific issues. The courts do have powers of judicial review and thus participate occasionally in the legislative process.

Additionally, judges do have particular interest in legislation that directly affects their profession. Legislation affecting court reorganization, creation of new judgeships or judicial staffs, or court procedures is very significant and therefore attracts judicial scrutiny. As a result, New York State judges have shown a willingness to attempt to influence the legislature on these questions, and they have therefore organized a lobby of significant influence. This Judicial Conference has great impact on questions of court reorganization, additional judges, and court procedures. It is called upon to comment on legislation originating outside of the judiciary but affecting it, both by legislators and by the governor's office. Thus, the lobbying relationship has been institutionalized, but is fairly rigidly circumscribed on the basis of functional area or subject matter.

The meaning of this arrangement for the legislative leaders is that influences upon them by the judges in the state court system are indirect at best. The leaders do not sit down to negotiate with judges as they do with the governor, lobbyists, party officials, executive officials, and the like. The involvement is distant, and propriety requires that this be the case. Despite the acknowledged involvement in of the Judicial Conference with relevant legislative committees, despite its published recommendations on certain legislative matters, and despite the general political sophistication and sensitivity of most judges, the political system, which permits many things, prohibits the kind of relationship between legislative leaders and judges that it permits between other participants in the system.

Even where the courts get involved in issues that are considered by the legislators as most critical to their careers and to the distribution of power (issues such as reapportionment), the only contact between the branches occurs in the formal court arena, where the ground rules and behavior patterns are rigidly defined by our political culture. The leaders may contribute some legal talent to the battles and certainly do plan legal strategies to obtain favorable decisions, but there is no attempt to make the kind of personal contact (from either side) that occurs when the leaders are dealing with the other participants in the legislative process.

NOTES

1. Kenneth N. Vines, "Courts as Political and Governmental Agencies" in Politics in the American States, Herbert Jacob and Kenneth N. Vines, eds. (Boston: Little, Brown and Company, 1965), p. 283.

2. For a full discussion of the structure, power, and character of state court systems, see Jacob and Vines, op. cit., chap. 7, and The Fifty States and Their Local Governments, James Fesler, ed. (New York: Alfred A. Knopf, Inc., 1967), Chaps. 12 and 13.

3. Charles Breitel, chief judge, New York State Court of Appeals, interview, March 27, 1970.

4. Ibid.

5. Fesler, op. cit., pp. 428-429.

6. Breitel, op. cit.

7. Donald Zimmerman, associate counsel to the Senate Majority Leader, interview, December 4, 1969.

8. Chapter 869, Laws of 1955.

9. See the Annual Reports of the Judicial Conference.

10. Breitel, op. cit.

11. The New York Times, editorial, March 12, 1970.

12. See Gordon Baker, The Reapportionment Revolution (New York: Random House, 1966) and Malcolm Jewell, The State Legislature (New York: Random House, 1962) for prominent examples.

13. Malcolm Jewell, "The Political Setting," in State Legislatures in American Politics, American Assembly report, Alexander Heard, ed. (Englewood Cliffs, N.J.: Prentice-Hall, Inc., 1966), p. 71.

14. Harvey Mansfield, "Modernizing the State Legislature," in Modernizing State Government: The N.Y. Constitutional Convention of 1967, Academy of Political Science, Sigmund Diamond, ed. (New York: Columbia University Press, 1967), pp. 42-43.

15. Ibid., p. 43.

16. The New York Times, December 13, 1964, Section IV, p. 10.

17. Gordon Baker, The Reapportionment Revolution (New York: Random House, 1966), p. 26.

18. Warren Moscow, Politics in the Empire State (New York: Alfred A. Knopf, Inc., 1948), p. 167.

19. The New York Times, February 5, 1964, p. 22.

20. Baker, op. cit., p. 11.

21. The New York Times, February 8, 1964, p. 1.

22. Ibid.

23. Ibid., June 16, 1964, p. 1.

24. Ibid., June 19, 1964, p. 1; June 21, 1964, p. 74.

25. Ibid., June 30, 1964, p. 1.

26. Ibid., July 15, 1964, p. 33.

27. Ibid., July 18, p. 16.

28. Ibid., July 28, p. 1.

29. Ibid., October 21, 1964, p. 34.

30. Ibid., January 22, 1965, p. 1.

31. Ibid., February 2, 1965, p. 2.

32. Ibid., March 16, 1965, p. 1.

33. Ibid., March 18, 1965, p. 1.

34. Ibid., April 15, 1965, p. 1.

35. Ibid., May 11, 1965, p. 1.

36. Ibid., June 2, 1965, p. 1.

37. Ibid., July 11, 1965, p. 1.

38. Ibid., November 4, 1965, p. 1.

39. Ibid., December 10, 1965, p. 1.

40. Ibid., January 6, 1966, p. 16; January 7, 1966, p. 10; January 19, 1966, p. 1.

41. Ibid., February 21, 22, 24, 1966, all p. 1.

42. Mansfield, op. cit., p. 44.

43. Plaintiffs memorandum submitted to Federal District Court, March 9, 1970, by David Wells, Wells v. Rockefeller et al., "66 Civil 1976," pp. 2-7.

6

THE LEGISLATURE
AND THE POLITICAL
PARTIES

POLITICAL PARTISANSHIP IN THE STATES

There seems to be a direct relationship between the degree of party cohesion in a state and the degree of legislative party cohesion. Students of American legislatures have found that the unity of legislative parties in one-party states is quite low and is significantly higher in two-party states.[1]

Therefore, the factors relevant to the continued competition between statewide political parties in two-party states would also be directly relevant to continued competition between legislative parties. Thus, according to Malcolm Jewell, there would probably be stiff competition between the two legislative parties and cohesion within each party in those states where there are large numbers of voters who support one or the other party, where the parties represent relatively homogeneous entities, where party strength lies in specific geographic areas (Democrats from the large city, Republicans from the rural and suburban areas), where voters perceive (accurately or not) certain ideological differences between the parties, where legislators share common interests and objectives with their party colleagues, and where the norms of the legislative body tend to strengthen party cohesion and find expression in the rhetoric of party loyalty or in the assertion of discipline by a strong leader or through the frequent convocation of caucuses.[2]

There is a significant difference in the intensity of party competition throughout the United States. In the South, the tradition of one-party Democratic rule is just beginning to be challenged. Similar one-party control of some northern states exists. In these circumstances, traditional partisanship is impossible. What generally replaces two-party competition is the organization of factions within the dominant party that perform many of the same functions that political parties perform elsewhere. This is true in the legislatures of these states as well as in the electoral arena.

Two states, Nevada and Minnesota, elect their lawmakers on a so-called nonpartisan basis—that is, without a party identification next to the candidate's name on the ballot. However, group rather than party caucuses are organized to operate the legislature in these states. In Minnesota a liberal and conservative caucus helps coordinate the natural competitiveness than is the hallmark of legislative decision making.

The difficulty of making detailed generalizations about the differences in party organization and cohesion from state to state is the fact that the data are sometimes imprecise and the variables are extensive and complicated. No two states have similar divisions, for example, between rural and urban interests, between the big city and the rest of the state, between ethnic and religious groups, and so on. Additionally, the most objective measure of party cohesion, the roll call, is sometimes not employed with frequency. Roll call votes are not required in Connecticut and Massachusetts on the final passage of bills. In other states where roll call votes are required, it becomes an enormous task to sift through the literally thousands of votes cast to determine which are of party consequence.

There are, however, three conclusions that can be drawn from the several studies of party behavior in the states that have been published.[3] First, real partisanship and party cohesion in a legislature can be found in the larger, primarily northern states with substantial urbanization and industrialization. Second, most legislative disputes do not involve inherent political party interests, and the overwhelming majority of bills do not result in clear party division. Third, the party divisions evident in large northern state legislatures often result from an inherent ideological or liberal-conservative split.

Where partisanship is high, it is generally reflected in the voting behavior of legislators in the case of three types of legislation. The first type is the legislative program of the governor. Whenever the chief executive commits himself to a particular bill, there is automatically a strong pressure upon legislators from his party to support the bill, and they will do so unless some sufficiently strong contrary pressure (such as constituency demand) emerges. The opposition party may likewise feel impelled to oppose the program just because of the fact that the governor wants it and may profit from it.

A second type of legislation which breeds partisanship is the bill dealing with broad social issues on which the parties disagree. Thus, questions of aid to labor or to business, increased taxes to support new social welfare programs, help to cities or to farmers all become the subject of intense partisan debate in two-party states.

Finally, there are bills that provide benefits to, or withhold them from, the parties themselves and so become the bone of sharp contention. Such measures may deal with reapportionment, the distribution of patronage, the powers granted or denied to party officials, the management of elections, and changes in legislative procedures.4

New York is a strong two-party state to which these generalizations particularly apply. In New York, there are nearly as many enrolled Republicans as there are Democrats. Although both parties endeavor to attract all elements within the voting population, in the aggregate they represent different groups of people with somewhat different social and political orientations. Thus, despite continuing fluctuations, the Democrats generally receive the support of labor, blacks, Jews, urban dwellers, low-income persons, and the like. Republicans generally represent the well-to-do businessmen, farmers, suburbanites, rural dwellers, and so on.

In the legislature, there is a further difference between the parties which is of a geographic nature: Most Democratic party legislators represent the city of New York and some upstate cities like Buffalo and Albany, with only a few elected from the suburbs. The rural and suburban areas are heavily Republican as are some upstate cities like Syracuse.

The fact that the two parties in New York represent fairly different constituencies naturally increases the stiffness of their competition, particularly in the legislature which is a decisive battleground.

This chapter will trace the effects of the party struggle upon the legislature and its leaders and upon the relationships between lawmakers and their respective state and local party organizations.

THE LEGISLATIVE PARTY IN NEW YORK

Earlier in this study, reference was made to the substantial powers of the leaders of the New York legislature, those resources that enable them to play a singularly influential role in legislative decision making. It must be noted that all the power of these leaders is derived power, and the positions they hold are essentially dependent positions. Their leadership is representative in character, and the leaders themselves are creatures of the political parties and their legislative delegations. These are men who, in exchange for their party-bestowed rank, are responsible for their actions to their party upon whose influence they and their careers depend.

In fact, whatever the functions of the Speaker of the Assembly, the Senate Majority Leader, and the Minority Leaders may perform, such as organizing their houses, negotiating with the governor or with leaders of the other party, developing legislative programs, conducting floor debates, distributing rewards, and servicing party members, all these leadership activities are pursued within the context of political party organization and partisan strategy.

The ties of the leaders with their state and local organizations are demonstrated by the fact that beyond their legislative functions, they are also prominent in general party leadership work. For example, they are often involved in the planning and conduct of general campaign schools in conjunction with their party's state committees. Both parties hold seminars for both new and incumbent candidates running for legislative and executive offices. Election techniques are discussed, of course, but so are relevant legislative issues and the overall party position on these questions. The intensive participation of most legislative leaders in these and similar general party functions strengthens their position as both party and legislative authorities.

During a campaign, the leaders provide help to individual legislative candidates of their party. Campaign literature, printing, propaganda, materials on opponents, and so on, are provided by their staffs. Occasionally funds are distributed to candidates running in marginal districts. The Republicans have been much more active in this area, but Democratic leaders have also attempted to help. In 1970, Minority Leaders Stanley Steingut and Joseph Zaretzki began sponsoring a $250 a plate fund-raising dinner to finance the legislative campaign of their party. The dinners are now regularly scheduled during each legislative campaign.

Speaker Perry Duryea, with his good looks, speaking ability, wealth, and private airplane, made many friends in the 1964 and 1966 campaigns, traveling around the state on behalf of many Republican legislative candidates. When later Duryea moved to unseat the then Republican Minority Leader George Ingalls, many showed their appreciation by voting for him.

In his unpublished doctoral dissertation, Stuart K. Witt reports, on the basis of a questionnaire which he distributed to several dozen assemblymen in 1967, the following:

> Half of the assemblymen in the sample admitted to
> having received an appreciable amount of help from their
> legislative leaders in the campaigns. Nearly all of them
> (81 percent) came from outside of New York City, and
> most (69 percent) were Republicans. Also, more of the
> members (65 percent) in their first or second years in
> the Assembly acknowledged such help than did the more
> senior members (47 percent). . . . Whereas 79 percent
> of the Republicans acknowledged appreciable help from

160

their party leadership, only 31 percent of the Democrats did.5

Apparently, the Republicans have greater resources to assist their candidates and, having been in the majority most of the time, they also can use the research and financial resources of the legislature to these ends. Witt indicates that fewer New York City candidates receive help than those running outside the city, because the districts are safer there.6 In reality, rural districts are just as safe or unsafe in a general election as are New York City districts. The fact is simply that most out-of-New-York-City districts are under Republican control, and that party is better organized and financed for the purpose of assisting its local candidates, notably the newcomers among them. The preservation of a legislative majority depends greatly upon helping newcomers whose electoral chances have not yet been tested. Most senior men, more confident of reelection and interested in seeing the advantages of the majority role of their party safeguarded, usually understand and approve of this practice.

After an election, the leaders busily organize their party ranks for the new session, devise the composition of committees, appoint chairmen where necessary, and prepare a legislative program. The latter function of leaders in the legislature is, of course, reduced in significance if the governor is of the same party and undertakes himself the preparation of his party's program for the session. Meanwhile, the leaders get acquainted with new members and use their staffs to help orient them in matters of procedure and protocol. Members travel early to Albany for these purposes and also to pre-file bills for the session.

Formally, the leaders are elected or designated for one two-year session only. If their reelection is not contested by other candidates, a conference of the legislative party is held shortly before the opening of the new session, and the leaders of the previous session are redesignated by acclamation. If there are other nominations, the party conference decides by majority vote.

During the session, the paramount obligation of the legislative leader is to work for the attainment of the party's adopted legislative goals. As soon as a firm and final party position is established, the leader, above all others, must abide by it and work for it. This imposes upon him the obligation to use every means of persuasion, pressure, threat, and actual punishment to secure rank-and-file compliance with the party goals. In this manner, the leader becomes the personification of the party's will, to which he himself is most firmly subordinated.

The general membership is, of course, adequately conditioned by custom and experience to understand that their leaders' attitudes

161

and actions are directly attuned to the service of the party's goals. They realize that the control by the leaders of the agenda, the calendar, the Rules Committee's work, the use of their appointment and patronage powers, their assistance to individual members, and the punishment of dissenters or mavericks serve the purpose of securing the victory of the party's goals, the enhancement of the party's power and prestige, and, indirectly, the improvement of the chances of the average party member to get reelected.

By satisfying the needs of the majority of his members who elected him to his high office, the leader fortifies his own position by creating within the membership the feeling that he is not only their exacting master, but also their helpful servant.

Party loyalty is, therefore, a powerful factor in the life of the legislature, both as a source of strength for the leaders and a source of confidence and assurance for the members. The party regular is a much happier and more secure fellow than the maverick. As Witt has concluded with respect to the speakership:

> The Speaker himself must operate within a margin
> of acceptability which is in part established by the mem-
> bers of his party. He must be able to deliver his party's
> votes on the floor of the Assembly; in order to secure
> those votes, he must be able to reward the members in
> one fashion or another. The willingness of the members
> to go along helps to define the limits of the Speaker's
> margin of acceptability.[7]

In terms of membership compliance with party objectives, the chief testing ground of the quality of the relationship between leaders and their party members is the party conference, the meeting of the members of a legislative party. In New York State it is the majority party conference that elects the officers of the legislature (with one major exception: in 1965 the Democratic party conferences failed to choose leaders). In the main, however, the purpose of the conference in New York State is to discuss legislation and to develop consensus on matters of party interest. Party conferences are usually called whenever the leadership feels that some problem requires collective and confidential consideration by the entire membership, or a major party split must be cured or major changes in the program must be decided upon, or just to find out the feelings of the members about some new legislative proposal.

In the course of such party discussions, a leader is quite frequently forced to change his position, amend a bill, refuse to bring a bill up to a vote, or revise program priorities as a result of the collective opinions of his colleagues. On such occasions, the legislative conference becomes the modifying will of the party itself, often after negotiations by the leaders with other important officials of the party. If opposed to such changes, a good leader who usually foresees the rising trouble probably confers with other powers within the party about how to parry the difficulty, prevent or heal dissensions, and in some way restore party unity. The Majority Leader generally has sufficient resources to succeed through the use of his wide powers and the implied threat of punishment, but much more often through his willingness to compromise.

The Minority Leader works within the same party atmosphere, albeit his authority within his own party is diminished by the fact that in the face of the rather consistent unity of the majority party, his side can have little influence on most decisions. While he, too, dispenses patronage and other favors among his members, the resources available to him are relatively meager. Like those of the majority party, the legislative conferences of the minority discuss issues and attempt to maintain or develop party unity, but even a unified minority party is only infrequently able to affect final legislative decisions.

In a two-party state like New York, therefore, partisan contention is the driving force within the legislature. Both the winning majority and the losing minority delegations in the legislature are bound by the legislative program and policy choices of their respective parties. The legislative leaders may exert considerable influence upon the determination of party objectives, but once chosen, these objectives generally bind the leaders and the members to a specific course of action.

THE LEGISLATURE AND THE STATE PARTY
ORGANIZATIONS

The first-ranking business of a statewide political party and of its local party organizations is to nominate and elect its candidates for office, including legislators. In the service of this task, each party acts as an interest group concerned with strengthening its ranks and cohesiveness, with rewarding the loyal and disciplining the unruly, and also with improving its own electoral chances by legislative means.[8] So, for example, the election law is revised periodically to fit the needs of that party organization which at the moment happens to be in power. Certain provisions of the election law aim at making the participation of third parties in political life more difficult, while others tend to restrain insurgency within the major parties. The provisions governing the filing of electoral petitions, for example, rigidly prescribe the form of the petition and the manner in which the signator must sign. The purpose is to make it difficult for insurgents to obtain enough valid signatures to get on the ballot. In such matters, the veteran law committees of county and local organizations of the major parties, familiar with all the nuances of the law and having dealt with the requirements for years, rarely make mistakes, but independent or insurgent candidates, running for the first time, often do.

Warren Moscow noted some of the legislative changes in the Election Law that have worked to the advantage of the two major parties:

> A word about the election law. Though passed by the legislature, it is actually written by the legal counsel of the two major political parties and designed by them to make smoother the functioning of their machinery within the principles of a primary system and free elections that the public has shown it wants.[9]
> Another major development was the passage of the Wilson-Pakula law by the 1947 session of the state legislature, under which a candidate was limited to entering the primary of a party in which he was enrolled and could enter another primary as a contestant for the nomination only with the consent of the county committee—that is, the organization—of the other party. . . .
> A further refinement of the law, also aimed at the then existing alliance between the Democratic and American Labor parties, provided that a man could not accept a second nomination by default. He could no longer tell the public that he wasn't responsible for whatever group chose to support him. He was required, by a section slipped quietly into the election law, to signify his acceptance, in writing, of any nomination given to him by a party of which he was not a member.[10]

The governing bodies of the state political parties are the State Committees. They are composed of elected state committeemen from each Assembly district and are chaired by state chairmen. They meet periodically to discuss and regulate party operations. But they are inordinately weak institutions. Except where the rules of county party organizations permit or prescribe that the committeemen serve as ex officio party district leaders, most committeemen are minor officials of the party or workers in local clubs who receive committee nominations as rewards. They are generally subservient to the local party leadership, and few of them attempt to act independently.

Recently the State Committees have become somewhat more important factors as a result of the statewide primary election law passed in 1968 which eliminated the convention system of choosing statewide candidates. Under that law, the State Committee of each party meets before every election for the purpose of nominating candidates for governor, lieutenant governor, attorney general, comptroller, United States senator, and judge of the Court of Appeals. The name of the person who receives the majority of the committee vote is automatically placed on the primary ballot. At the same time, however, any other candidate who receives 25 percent of the committee vote has his name placed on the ballot. Any other candidate who circulates petitions and receives 50,000 valid signatures, with at least 50 from at least three-fourths of the state's counties, would also be eligible to run. Thus, the State Committees were given a certain role to play within the nominating process.

The new rules have a substantial potential for chaos. The meeting of the Democratic State Committee at Grossinger's Hotel in the Catskill Mountains in April 1970 all but destroyed the new role of the Democratic State Committee. At that meeting, the committeemen nominated Arthur Goldberg for governor, but Eugene Nickerson, Nassau County executive, received 25 percent of the vote. Then Goldberg turned down the nomination, saying he would go the petition route to prove that he was not the candidate of the "bosses." When on the same occasion Basil Paterson, a black state senator, won the nomination for lieutenant governor, as a gesture of good sportsmanship, he released some of his committeemen to vote for his opponent, Jerome Ambro, a Suffolk County town supervisor, to allow Ambro to get 25 percent of the votes that would make him a candidate. In other races, committeemen supporting one loser would switch their votes (by dozens or hundreds) to another loser, so that the winner would have at least one opponent with 25 percent of the total vote. The unworthiness and unworkability of the system became apparent. Soon every candidate attacked the system and called for a direct open primary with candidates getting their names on the ballot through the acquisition of signatures. Goldberg promised that, if elected, a first-priority item in his program would be the passage of a direct primary law.

Governor Rockefeller, in complete control of his state committee (even to the point of ordering it to nominate Charles Goodell for U.S. senator), told this writer that he never liked the system in the first place. He said, "The primary law is going to result in chaos, and it is full of holes, but how could I veto an open primary bill. As bad as it was, I had to sign it."[11]

On paper, the state chairmen are supposed to be responsible for coordinating the activities of the party, supporting candidates, getting out the vote, raising money, and so on. In reality, the state chairman of each party is rather powerless, and if his party controls the governorship, he simply is an agent of the governor. The chairman is always caught in the middle between opposing factions and competing power blocs. The real base of party power is not the state but the county organization, but even that unit is often splintered by factionalism, particularly on the Assembly district level. The state chairman has very little influence over local organizational activity.

The former presiding judge of the State Court of Claims, Fred Young, was a former county leader and Republican state chairman. He served as state chairman under Governor Rockefeller from 1963-65. He described the state chairman's position in the following manner:

> I left the court to become state chairman to help
> Rocky get elected president. But it was a frustrating job.
> It was my function to work for the governor's programs,
> talk to people about political matters, and do his bidding.
> As chairman, I'm his man. A state chairman doesn't
> mean much with a governor in power. He is no more
> than an executive messenger, a buffer between the gover-
> nor and the county leaders. You make recommendations,
> but you have no control. If you disagree with the gover-
> nor or are against him, then you've got to get out.[12]

If a party has no real leader, such as an incumbent governor or New York City mayor or prestigious U.S. senator, then all the state chairman can do is to play the role of moderator in disputes between the local political barons, the county leaders. This was the problem of John Burns, Democratic state chairman from 1965 to 1972 and his successor Joseph Crangle of Buffalo. Burns replaced William McKeon after the latter had sided with the losers in the 1965 legislative leadership fight. Burns was a close ally of Senator Robert Kennedy and a friend of Mayor Wagner. It was their agreement that led to his election as chairman by the State Committee. He remained in the job by playing the role of peacemaker (with modest success) between the bitterly antagonistic factions of the Democratic party.

Burns's experiences in that role show what the chairman's functions really are. He presides over the State Committee, but cannot control it to any extent because each committeeman has his own local leadership to respond to or else is independent of all leadership. The chairman runs candidates' schools and holds hearings on controversial issues. He directs public fora for candidates running in primaries. He organizes fund raising affairs for the financing of the State Committee or for other party purposes. He is a spokesman for the party only on those occasions where he knows he can speak on a subject on which all factions in the party are united. He is a negotiator between factions on such matters as election law changes, judgeship legislation, and reapportionment, but his powers are too limited to affect any final decision.

On these latter questions, he will have direct contact with his party's legislative leaders, but even there his influence is based on his personal relationship with these leaders, not on his power as state chairman.

The office of the state chairman is also supposed to serve as a conduit for the distribution of patronage. In practice, however, the chairman is merely an adviser or a broker with whom the real dispensers of patronage, like the governor, New York's mayor, and the legislative leaders, may or may not work, at their pleasure.

During Burns's tenure the primary source of patronage benefits for the Democrats was the Democratic Assembly Speaker, Anthony Travia. Since 1965, the governor and the mayor of New York City, the most important sources of job patronage in the state, had been Republicans. Although Robert Kennedy was a U.S. senator, that position had, and still has, little patronage at its disposal, and Kennedy's influence on party matters depended not on patronage but on his personal prestige and the loyalty of his followers.

When Travia was elected Speaker, he refused to cooperate with State Chairman McKeon because the latter had opposed him for the speakership. However, Travia did later on work with Burns and Kennedy, and a joint patronage mechanism was organized among them. A formula was used to determine how much patronage was to be distributed to Democratic county leaders. It was based on a computation of the total sum of money available and the percentage share of the legislators representing each county in the total number of Democrats in each house of the legislature. Thus, if Buffalo elected 5 percent of the Democratic legislators in Albany, it would receive 5 percent of the total money for jobs. However, there were many exceptions to the rule. First, Travia refused to include in the joint fund the allotments to be used for legislators, committees, JLCs, and so on. Second, the Speaker insisted upon living up to his own personal commitments to those who supported him in the leadership fight. Third, there were certain long-standing patronage arrangements, such as the employment of clerical and maintenance help in the capitol itself, which went to the Democratic machine in Albany, headed by the venerable Daniel O'Connell.[13] Finally, if a leader failed or refused to tell Burns the correct amount of patronage money available to him, there was nothing the chairman could do about it. He was a very junior partner in the arrangement.

The upshot of this relative weakness of the position of the state chairman is that the legislative leaders will work with the chairman only if they so choose. Even if the chairman speaks for the governor, they will probably cooperate with him only on minor matters. On essential party issues, such as reapportionment or the nature of new judgeship legislation, they will work directly with the governor or his counsel. The state chairman is, therefore, a rather peripheral participant in the system who is often shunted aside in deliberations over party policy.

This is not to say that the leaders can afford to ignore the party apparatus, particularly on the county level. Quite the reverse is true. The leaders need the support of their legislators. These, in turn, are bound in most intimate ways to the local and county party organizations. It is on the local level that the legislative leaders and the political party organizations interact. The State Committee and the state chairman occupy a rather empty attic on top of the party structure.

THE LEADERS AND THE LOCAL PARTY ORGANIZATIONS

The legislator is not only a representative of his constituency in the legislature, he is also a representative of his local political organization. He serves as a link between the legislative leaders and the local party leaders. That link is quite important because it is the main factor that conveys a political and partisan character to the process of legislating.

The legislator's primary loyalty is to his career, his own political survival. This is acknowledged as the first priority consideration whenever professional politicians evaluate the behavior of their colleagues. Therefore, it is fully acceptable behavior for the legislator to dedicate maximum loyalty to his local political organization. That organization gave him the opportunity for a political career, nominated him, and worked for his election. He himself is a part of its structure and an adherent of its value system who readily and naturally responds to its demands.

Getting reelected requires that the legislator assemble a record that will please or prove acceptable to the majority of the voters in his district. For most legislators, the immediate problem is to keep receiving the designation of the local party club and to win in the party primary. Because most districts are apportioned in a way to maximize control by one political party and because of the prevalent apathy of voters toward local and legislative contests, the winner of the primary of the district's dominant party rarely loses in the general election.

The more closely the legislator's record in office reflects the needs and interests of his district and of its more active and vocal civic groups, the better will be his chances of reelection. Most important for him will be to meet the expectations of the local political organization itself, notably with respect to benefits which the legislature can grant, like the building of state establishments in the districts, job patronage for organization members, passage of highway and waterway measures that benefit the local community, or the granting of favors to club members and friends, favors such as contacting relevant government agencies for constituents with problems.

The legislator thus becomes a sort of lobbyist for his local political organization who makes demands on his legislative leaders, particularly with respect to legislation and patronage touching upon local interests. These demands are always presented on a partisan basis, motivated by party interests, the service of which should be common cause between legislator and leader. The leader was elected to his position of prominence by the members. In exchange, he is expected to deliver the available rewards, on a partisan basis, to his supporters.

The relationship assumes an added dimension when the local party leader himself visits the legislative leaders with requests for patronage or legislation. Some party leaders actually go to Albany to ask for the requested legislation or patronage. This is particularly the case where the local leader is a veteran politician with many contacts and a long-term working relationship with the legislative leaders. Newer, less influential party leaders are generally a little more reticent and somewhat less successful. Of course, county leaders are even more likely to assert their "prerogatives," by actually making contact with legislative leaders to ask for benefits.

There is a major difference between the parties in the degree of willingness of legislative leaders to deal directly with county leaders. The difference stems from the fact that the core of the Democratic strength is in the very large counties of New York City and in some upstate cities where the county leader can control, influence, or maintain a working partnership with a considerable number of legislators. Republican county leaders rarely control more than a few legislators. The Democratic county leaders, if effective and able to maintain the support of an entire block of legislators from their county, have muscle in dealing with legislative leaders of their party. This is even more true in those cases where the Democratic county leaders are also legislators. Thus, in the past several years, the Democratic county leaders of Brooklyn (Stanley Steingut), Queens (Moses Weinstein), and Manhattan (Frank Rossetti) were all assemblymen. Many other Democratic legislators are Assembly district leaders.

The influence of party leaders on the Democratic side is, therefore, quite significant. Joseph Crangle, the Democratic county leader
of Erie County, and subsequently Democratic state chairman, indicated
in an interview his direct interest as a leader, not only in patronage
matters, but also in questions of substantive legislation that affect
his party operations, matters like budget items that determine state
aid to Buffalo, reapportionment, and judgeships. Crangle is probably
more issue oriented than most party leaders, but he feels that his
primary role is still that of representative of his county organization.
His appointment to a staff position by Speaker Travia, and his subsequent as chief of staff to Minority Leader Stanley Steingut, greatly
increased his influence in the legislature.14

The relationship between legislative leaders and local party
leaders is, of course, a two-way street. There have been occasions
where the legislative leaders and the governor himself have gone
back to party leaders for help in convincing recalcitrant legislators
of the wisdom of bowing to the leaders' will. As Warren Moscow
described it:

> During a session they [t he Speaker and the Senate
> Majority Leader] see a lot of the county chairmen who
> drop in at Albany to secure the passage of legislation
> important back home. Maybe an important local in-
> dustry, good for a substantial campaign contribution,
> has a problem that a little bill can solve. The Speaker
> or the Majority Leader acts as a clearinghouse on
> such requests. He steers through to passage all that he
> reasonably can.
>
> A successful legislative leader knows that in a
> pinch these same county chairmen will reciprocate and
> use home town pressure to keep wandering legislators
> in line and on hand to vote the way the Speaker de-
> sires.15

It is my impression, albeit without hard evidence, that such
appeals by the legislative leaders to the party leaders do not occur
with great frequency. Most of the time the legislator shares the
interests of his local leader. If he is bucking the legislative leadership of his party, it is probably for some weighty local reason, and
his action is probably in conformity with the needs of his party
leadership at home. But such reverse pressures are still part of
the total picture. Former assemblyman William Clancy, a Queens
Democrat, noted: "Sometimes our leader would call down to various
county leaders who, in turn, would threaten some assemblymen with
loss of nomination and would send voting instructions to their men."16

There is, however, still another character trait in the makeup of this relationship, which may be even more relevant and important than the two-way traffic of hard-boiled demands for palpable benefits. It is brought about by the fact that the legislators bring certain political values with them from their local party organizations to the legislature. As Stuart Witt[17] has pointed out, the legislator has been born within the party atmosphere of the local political arena and bred on basic political values, such as strong leadership, intraparty bargaining and compromise, all of them enveloped with the strongest and highest value, that of partisanship. As he enters the arena of lawmaking, he discovers that essentially the same values prevail there as well. Instinctively he feels that he is the right man in the right place whose values he understands and appreciates. Having been thoroughly conditioned for the acceptance of these values, he is now inclined to support and reinforce them. It is no hardship for him at all to accept strong legislative leadership for he had dealt with, and profited from, strong local party leadership. He will be just as astute in following his leader in Albany as he has been playing ball with his leader at home. He will bargain and compromise just as before. He will be even more demonstrative in his partisanship, antagonizing the opposition party at least as sharply as at home. At the same time, he will use in Albany the same skills acquired in local politics of dealing with people, of cultivating personal friendships even with opponents, but certainly with the men higher up in his party, and of trading available rewards exactly as before at home. He arrives in Albany as a trained party regular and almost automatically joins his colleagues who consider conformity as the highest party value. Consequently he will strongly dislike, condemn, and help isolate the occasional party maverick in the legislature who dares to criticize "wheeling and dealing" and "unprincipled logrolling" in party life. To be publicly more virtuous than one's colleagues to be the object of scorn on the part of the overwhelming majority of lawmakers who believe that a legislative institution cannot function without compromise, the distribution of rewards and mutual "understanding and cooperation." Such values, so readily accepted and reinforced by politicians in both local and legislative arenas are, however, frowned upon by many citizens. Part of the general public's low opinion of politics is, undoubtedly, attributable to the legislators' acceptance of these "rules of the game."

CASE STUDY: THE 1965 LEADERSHIP FIGHT

No single incident can better portray the role of the party organizations as interest groups attempting to obtain benefits from the legislature than the bitter fight waged over the election of majority party leaders by the Democrats in 1965. Every influential party leader and faction outside the legislature participated in the fight since each perceived the legislature as a fertile source of political rewards that could not be ignored. The case also points up the role of the legislative party institutions, particularly the party conference as a central arena for conflict.

Traditionally, party leaders are chosen at the meetings of the party conferences in the weeks prior to the opening of a new legislative session. When a vacancy occurs in a leadership post (one subject to election by the members of a legislative party, that is), the members of the conference close the door to the meeting and hammer out a solution, presuming, of course, that more than one candidate is running. When the majority of the conference members make their choice, the lawmakers who supported the loser join with their colleagues in a united front. The actual choice of Assembly Speaker and Senate Majority Leader is made on the first day of the legislative session. Since a majority vote of all members of the House are needed, a unified majority party is required if that party's choice is to be elected to the speakership or to the office of Senate President Pro Tempore (Majority Leader).

As a matter of fact, this procedure of the losers in conference uniting behind the candidate of the winners can be formalized by a vote to make the conference into a caucus. Technically speaking, a caucus is a conference in which the vote is binding on all the members, requiring losers to support the decision of the majority.

It is rare for a party to fail to choose its leaders in the traditional manner. The 1965 leadership fight is the exception. In that year the choices of the Democratic party conferences were not finally elected. The losers in conference ultimately won with the help of Republican votes. This is a very atypical circumstance.

It must also be noted that electing party leaders with the help of opposing party votes is a rare occurrence throughout the United States. But it has occasionally happened. California is sometimes the scene of the crossing of party lines for the purpose of electing leaders. In 1961, Jesse Unruh, campaigning for the speakership of the California Assembly, demanded written pledges of support from a bipartisan majority to forestall moves to defeat him.[18] In February 1970, a total of 13 Democratic members of the California Senate joined with 10 Republicans to form a conservative bloc that succeeded in replacing a liberal Senate Majority Leader.[19]

In 1959, a bitter feud between Chicago Democrats and downstate Democrats occurred. The downstaters boycotted the caucus called to pick the Speaker of the Illinois House. They then joined with the Republican minority to elect one of their own to the speakership.[20]

The description of the 1965 fight in New York must include two important observations. First, the fight was the direct result of the landslide victory of President Lyndon Johnson over Barry Goldwater in the 1964 presidential election. Johnson's victory in every county in New York State swept into office Democratic majorities in both houses of the legislature. It was the first time Democrats had controlled both houses (or even one house) since 1935. In that year the Democrats captured majorities on the coattails of Herbet Lehman, running for governor, and as a result of the public disenchanment with Republicans due to the Depression. What is particularly significant is the fact that the 1964 victory occurred under a gerrymandered apportionment system that had been drawn by Republican mapmakers in a manner designed to perpetuate their control. The one-man, one-vote court decisions had not yet been implemented.

The second important observation involves the nature of party factionalism in the Democratic party of 1964. No political party in any state in America was so divided as was the New York State Democratic party. Four distinctive factions had been organized. The so-called regular Democrats, the party organizations in each of the four large New York City counties, were divided between those loyal to New York City mayor Robert Wagner and those who opposed him. The budding reform movement, centered at the time in Manhattan, had won some notable intraparty battles. The upstate Democrats, whose strength had been dramatically increased by a number of surprise victories in the 1964 elections (Democrats, for example, having defeated both Senate Majority Leader Walter Mahoney and Assembly Speaker Joseph Carlino), were on the verge of demanding greater recognition from the party.

Mayor Wagner was at the center of the feud. A regular Democrat for two mayoral terms, Wagner had denounced the regular county leaders during his race for a third term in 1961. Declaring himself an ally of reform, he campaigned against the so-called bosses (who had helped make him mayor in 1953 and 1957) and was joined in this effort by the reformers. Wagner's grievance was apparently aimed at the county leaders' refusal to draft him for U.S. Senate at the disastrous Democratic convention in Buffalo in 1958. It is also probable that he perceived that a two-term mayor needed some novel issue to overcome voter apathy and disdain in a race for a third term. Whatever the motives, he defeated the leaders' candidate, State Comptroller Arthur Levitt, in the primary, and Republican state attorney general Louis Lefkowitz in the general election.

Wagner had aimed his antibossism attack at Manhattan county leader Carmin DeSapio. The mayor succeeded in getting rid of DeSapio by discrediting him so badly with the public that DeSapio lost his race for the district leadership of his home district in Greenwich Village. This rendered him ineligible to be county leader.

173

Wagner also deposed the Queens leader who had opposed him and, after an interval, replaced him with Assemblyman Moses Weinstein.

Thus, by 1964, Wagner controlled the Manhattan county leadership (Councilman J. Raymond Jones, a Wagner loyalist, was the first black county leader in the country) and Queens. But two anti-Wagner leaders remained in the Bronx and Brooklyn. Charles Buckley and Stanley Steingut retained their posts despite the Wagner strategy of denying job patronage to district leaders who supported them. Buckley, a member of Congress and a committee chairman, had his own patronage sources. But Steingut, a assemblyman, did not and was under considerable pressure to resign.

Both Burkley and Steingut realized after the November 1964 election that they could dramatically enhance their power by capturing the leadership posts in the legislature. They entered into negotiations with Albany county leader Daniel O'Connell to arrange the capture of the speakership. O'Connel was induced to throw the weight of his support and that of the other upstate leaders behind the Steingut forces by being granted the power, as part of the deal, to pick the Senate Majority Leader. The arrangement was that Steingut would be the alliance's candidate in the lower house, and Albany senator Julian Erway would run for President Pro Tempore.

While the Buckley-Steingut-O'Connell forces were mobilizing, the Wagner group sat back, failing to recognize a threat. Senator Joseph Zaretzki and Assemblyman Anthony Travia, erstwhile Minority Leaders, both presumed that with tradition and Wagner on their side, they would be elected to the leadership posts without difficulty. They were to be rudely shocked.

The Assembly Democratic conference met at the DeWitt Clinton Hotel in Albany on the night of December 22, 1964, two weeks prior to the opening of the session. The Democrats had a majority of 88 to 62 with 76 votes needed to control the house and to elect a Speaker. With all 12 Bronx assemblymen, 12 of the 20 from Brooklyn, 3 from Manhattan, and 21 of 26 from outside New York City, Steingut won by a vote of 53 to 35. Travia had the support of 8 Brooklyn votes, the entire 13-member Queens delegation led by Assemblyman Weinstein, 8 Manhattan, 5 out of city, and 1 Bronx vote.[21]

Following tradition, Weinstein, leading Travia's floor fight, moved to make Steingut's designation unanimous, and the motion carried.

The Senate Democratic conference met later that evening in the same hotel. With a 33 to 25 majority, the Democrats needed 30 votes to elected a President Pro Tempore. With the Bronx, Brooklyn, and upstate delegations firm, Erway defeated Zaretzki 19 to 14. The alliance's victory seemed secure.

174

But one outspoken member of the losing side broke up the victory. When the motion to make the result unanimous was made, Senator Seymour Thaler of Queens refused to go along. One of the Senate's most powerful debaters, Thaler was asked to explain. He denounced Erway as a "Goldwater Democrat" whose reactionary record precluded his support. But Thaler pointed out that only 30 votes were needed. Without his vote, there would still be 32.

Senator Jerome Wilson of Manhattan, later to become a political correspondent for CBS television after an unsuccessful race for Congress, immediately joined Thaler. As a liberal reformer, he would not be outliberaled.

Senator Constance Baker Motley, a black woman from Manhattan, took the floor. She asked Erway to express his views on civil rights and to explain his opposition to the Metcalf-Baker law prohibiting discrimination in housing. Erway's response was crucial—and unfortunate for him.

Instead of talking practical politics to the conference, he offered platitudes. He could have explained that as an Albany senator, he had to represent the more conservative views of his constituency, but that as Majority Leader, he would certainly reflect the general views of his membership. Instead, he suggested that he was as liberal as anyone else, that his forbears had helped operate the underground railroad during the Civil War, and that he had evidence of his racial views. He then produced a Christmas card he had received from a former black maid with the word "love" over the signature. Senator Motley's attitude toward this evidence was to announce her opposition to Erway.

When Brooklyn senator William Thompson, a black, added that he, too, could not go along, the vote for Erway was recorded at 29 to 4.[22]

The four dissidents were subjected to enormous pressure, but refused to give in. Short by one vote, the conference adjourned. When Travia and Weinstein heard of the Senate results, they announced that they would not abide by the Assembly conference vote and would oppose Steingut on the floor of the Assembly.

When the legislature convened in early January of 1965 and moved to the order of business of electing officers, no candidate could obtain the necessary 76 votes in the Assembly or the needed 30 votes in the Senate. The Steingut forces dropped Erway and began to substitute candidates. Zaretski, fed up, refused to run and was replaced by Queens senator Thomas Mackell. Erway had first been replaced by black Bronx senator Ivan Warner (presumably to overcome the "conservative" label that had wrecked Erway's chances). Later on Queens senator Jack Bronston, one of the most talented lawmakers in the chamber, broke from Weinstein and Wagner to

175

join the Steingut forces as their candidate for President Pro Tempore. A furious Weinstein never forgave Bronston.

However, the lines were drawn and substantially frozen. Day after day the Assembly and Senate met. Nominations were made, votes taken, and no one elected. Each day in the Assembly, 53 Democrats would vote for Steingut, 35 for Travia, and the 62 Republicans for the leader George Ingalls. As days and weeks passed, attempted negotiations and compromises failed. Tempers flared. County leaders came to Albany to hold their troops firm. Deals were proposed but fell through. Offers were made to induce opponents to defect. All in vain.

Reporters in one instance overheard Nassau county leader John English threaten to punch Manhattan leader Jones and Jones to suggest that English try. Wagner, sitting at City Hall, sent word to his forces each day to "sit." In typical Wagner style, the strategy employed was simply to wait. Somehow it would all turn out.

Meanwhile the Republicans were having a propoganda field day. They accused the Democrats of boss control, of incompetence, of inability to govern. As the month of January drew to a close and the fight dragged on, they pointed out the obvious and painful fact that the fight meant no committees formed, no bills processed, no hearings on the budget held, and no work on the people's business begun. Republican Senate leader Earl Brydges, always ready with the pithy quotes, noted: "When the aunt of the vicar has never touched liquor, beware when she tastes the champagne." The Democrats were justifiably vilified by the Republicans and the media for their inability to settle the dispute and to govern.

One incident is instructive. In the middle of January, eight statewide Democratic leaders, including Wagner, newly elected Senator Robert Kennedy, former governor Harriman, Franklin Roosevelt, Jr., and Congressman Emanuel Celler, met to resolve the dispute. They adopted a plan calling for one final conference in each house to settle the affair. The winner would be unanimously supported. The Steingut group could not object to his solution, and Wagner was apparently trapped into accepting it.

Wagner could not oppose such a "democratic" plan in public; so he had to blow it up. The next day he denounced State Chairman William McKeon, who had sided with Steingut, as having offered bribes to pro-Wagner lawmakers in exchange for their votes. The bribes, said Wagner, were in the form of committee chairmanship appointments and extra expense allowances. There is little doubt that such offers had been made—by both sides. Wagner's public announcement of the practice was simply intended to explode the plan of the state party leaders.

He succeeded. The Republicans had more grist for their propoganda mill, and they called for an investigation of the charges by the State Investigations Commission. After a series of hearings, the commission could find no evidence to substantiate the charge. But the accusation did succeed in preventing implementation of the plan for new conferences. The New York Times deplored Wagner's stratagem and said that Wagner had often used patronage for political purposes. Said Time magazine: "Even the mayor's best friends here concede that even if the charges were true, he broke one of the inviolable laws of politics—the law that politicians, like small boys, must never, never squeal."[23]

After five weeks, the deadlock was finally broken on February 3, 1965. Before a shocked Senate, Senator John Hughes, Republican of Syracuse, who had nominated Republican Earl Brydges on 25 prior ballots, nominated Democrat Joseph Zaretski. The flabbergasted Steingut forces delayed the final vote for several hours by a number of parliamentary maneuvers. However, at the end of the debate, Zaretski was elected with 40 votes (25 Republicans and 15 Democrats) to 18 for Jack Bronston.

Later that afternoon in the Assembly, 30 Republicans joined 35 Wagner Democrats on the 27th ballot to give Travia 65 votes, still 11 short of a majority. Steingut rose during the debate and offered to meet with Travia "in search of a compromise," but he himself must have realized it was too late for that. The next day, 46 Republicans joined the 35 Travia Democrats to give him a total of 81 votes to Steingut's 56 (including 3 Republicans). The fight was over, but the bitterness was not.

The Republican move was engineered by Rockefeller. Why did they intervene? Simply to get the legislature back to work. Why did they choose the Wagner team? Their explanation was that they had worked with Zaretzki and Travia and could trust and cooperate with them. Steingut was an unknown quantity.

Steingut has a different theory. He believes that since Senator Kennedy supported the Steingut faction (with minimal enthusiasm, it being too soon for the new U.S. senator to participate in a party bloodbath), Rockefeller did not want to give a potential rival of major consequence an early victory.

A more widely accepted theory is the suggestion that Wagner and Rockefeller made a deal. In exchange for Republican votes for Zaretzki and Travia, the Wagner faction would provide votes for Rockefeller's proposed sales tax. Later in the session, the sales tax was passed with the support of almost every Wagner loyalist in the legislature. Both Rockefeller and Wagner deny a specific deal was made.[24] Said Wagner, "There was no trade concerning the sales tax. How can you deliver legislators for any major tax? They finally voted for it for the very valid reason that Rockefeller made the tax package attractive for New York City and its legislators."[25]

The leadership fight offers the best visible evidence of the attitude of party leaders toward the legislature. Its power is so significant and its resources so enormous that full-scale political war is justified to capture control, if that is possible. The control, not only over patronage but over legislative decisions that affect localities and party organizations, is so significant that the Democratic party leadership, out of power in the state legislature for 30 years, could not resist the factional pressures that led to a enormously embarrassing and costly public battle.

CONCLUSIONS

The majority of the functions of the legislative leaders are party-inspired functions. They organize their houses on a partisan basis. They reward legislators on the basis of their party loyalty and the services they render to the legislative party. They push for the enactment of a party program which emanates either from their or the governor's workshop or from a cooperative party effort between the two. They participate in or organize legislative debate on a partisan basis. They are, in fact, the leaders of, workers for, and the embodiment of the legislative parties.

Strong leadership is a natural product of the stiff two-party competition which characterizes the political life of the state of New York. Although at present fluctuations are taking place, the Democrats and Republicans still have different constituencies both in terms of geography and in terms of the character of the groups of people that support them at the polls.

Although the statewide party organizations are rather weak and ineffectual, the legislative leaders do cooperate much of the time with the state chairman, who is the nominal head of the party. Actually, the chairman is no more than an adjunct to the governor's office if he belongs to the governor's party. He is a powerless, almost a nominal party leader if he is chairman of the opposition party. The chairman has no independent base of power or resources for influencing political decisions over and above his own personal skill of persuasion and beyond the tradition that makes it "good form" for politicians to show some nominal consideration to the State Committee and the state chairman. The chairman does not even control the State Committee itself, since the committeemen are selected on the local level, and most of them are attendants of local Assembly district leaders. The legislative leaders may funnel some patronage through the state chairman, and the governor will do so. But both the governor and the leaders are entirely free to decide whether or not they will use this channel. They have the authority to choose, and the state chairman has no power to require recognition.

The local party leaders, on the level of an Assembly district and of a county alike, are important lobbyists for benefits that the legislature and the legislative leaders can provide. They are represented by elected legislators who consider it a major part of their role to secure from the leaders of the legislature the legislation and patronage desired by the local party leaders. Their support of the legislative leaders is often more or less contingent upon the success of their interventions with the leaders on behalf of such benefits.

The legislative leaders themselves call occasionally upon local party leaders for help to keep wavering legislators in line. Some of the legislators are also district or even county leaders who enhance their importance in both capacities by wearing two hats on the same heads.

However, the most important finding is that the local home-ground political training of the average legislator is the readily working and decisive factor that makes him a genuine party man in the legislature, that keeps the legislative party a working entity, and partisanship the driving force behind the legislative process. The political values, viewpoints, and practical experience which he brings with him to Albany are exactly the things he will find already in existence and operation there, precisely the ingredients that effective party operation in the legislature needs.

This is particularly true about the element of partisanship, for it is the process of bitter partisan debate, maneuvering, power pressures, and other manifestations of party conflict that creates the momentum which, in the end, brings into being the ultimate legislative product.

NOTES

1. George S. Blair, American Legislatures (New York: Harper and Row, 1967), p. 273. See also Belle Zeller, ed., American State Legislatures, American Assembly report (New York: Thomas Y. Crowell Company, 1954).

2. Malcolm Jewell, "The Political Setting," in State Legislatures in American Politics, Alexander Heard, ed. (Englewood Cliffs, N.J.: Prentice-Hall, Inc., 1966), pp. 90-92.

3. For a short bibliography on party behavior in American legislatures, see Wiiliam Keefe and Morris Ogul, The American Legislative Process (Englewood Cliffs, N.J.: Prentice-Hall, Inc., 1968), p. 315.

4. Jewell, op. cit., pp. 92-93.

5. Stuart K. Witt, "The Legislative-Local Party Linkage in New York State," unpublished doctoral dissertation, Syracuse University, 1967, pp. 111-112.

6. Ibid., p. 112.

7. Ibid., p. 127.

8. See V. O. Key, Politics, Parties and Pressure Groups, 5th ed. (New York: Thomas Y. Crowell Company, 1964), p. 196.

9. Warren Moscow, Politics in the Empire State (New York: Alfred A. Knopf, 1948), p. 57.

10. Ibid., p. 100.

11. Governor Nelson Rockefeller, interview, March 2, 1970.

12. Judge Fred A. Young, former Republican state chairman, interview, February 24, 1970.

13. Former Democratic party state chairman John Burns, interview, January 8, 1970.

14. Democratic State Chairman Joseph Crangle, interview, January 28, 1970.

15. Moscow, op. cit., p. 175.

16. Former assemblyman William Clancy, interview, January 20, 1970.

17. Witt, op. cit., pp. 246-255.

18. Time (May 5, 1961): 22.

19. The New York Times, February 15, 1970, p. 42.

20. See Thomas Littlewood, Bipartisan Coalition in Illinois (New York: McGraw-Hill, 1960).

21. Witt, op. cit., pp. 140-143.

22. Time (January 8, 1965): 17.

23. Ibid. (January 29, 1965): 22.

24. Former mayor Robert Wagner, interview, December 22, 1969 and former governor Nelson Rockefeller, interview, March 2, 1970.

25. Wagner, op. cit.

INTRODUCTION

Webster's Dictionary defines the term lobbying as follows:
"To frequent the lobby of a house of legislation for the purpose of
addressing members with the object of influencing their votes; to
solicit members for their votes in any place away from the house."

In general, it must be recognized that "lobbying" is an inseparable
and indispensable part of the democratic process of legislation. Students of politics have increasingly recognized that the understanding
of group activities aiming at changes of the law is essential to the
understanding of the legislative process itself and of political activity
in general. In 1908 Arthur F. Bentley wrote in this sense in his
pioneering work, The Process of Government.[1] In 1951, in his important study of the role of interest groups in politics, The Governmental Process,[2] David Truman substantially elaborated and brought
up to date similar basic observations. Since then, the literature on
group pressures and lobbying has become voluminous and extensive.[3]

Legislatures of all types, federal, state, municipal and local,
are targets of lobbying. Since the federal system commits to the
jurisdiction of the states for decision and regulation most social and
economic problems and since many of these problems are critically
important to a great variety of interest groups, state legislatures
are very busy focal points for group pressures.

They are also rather directly exposed to less than ethical techniques of pressure. Professor Harman Ziegler leaves unanswered
the question whether and to what extent the popular notion is correct
that corruption is a prevalent influence in our legislatures. However,
he finds that the conditions in most of our statehouses favor the emer-
gence of such influences. State legislatures are part-time institutions
and their members part-time workers, poorly paid and burdened with

181

high expenses. Many of them are newcomers, uncertain of reelection in a situation where the turnover rates are rather high. On these grounds, Ziegler believes that receptivity to influence peddling is at least potentially significant.[4]

Since, in New York, the legislative leaders direct the legislative process, it may be assumed that this role automatically places them into the center of pressures that lobbyists can apply. This chapter will examine the relationship between New York's rather sophisticated lobby groups and the legislature and its leaders.

THE PRIVATE INTEREST GROUPS IN NEW YORK STATE

Legislatures are the foci of pressures of many competing groups seeking the satisfaction of their needs and interests by the state. There are probably more than 300 different groups that are represented in Albany either by a full-time professional lobbyist or by systematic contacts maintained with legislators by group officers. In an average year, not quite 200 of these lobbyists are formally registered with the state. This is so because the law that prescribes registration applies only to those who are specifically hired to influence legislation. Only these professionals must register and list their lobbying expenditures.

Professor Ziegler's analysis of interest group influences in the states is based on the study of the pattern of conflict that often exists between major economic interests. He shows, for example, that in Maine the pattern is one of near dominance by the representatives of the power, timber, and manufacturing interests, forming an "alliance of dominant interest groups." Another state characterized by the predominance of a single interest is Montana, which is dominated by the Anaconda Mining Company. Another pattern is the conflict between two dominant groups as, for example, in Michigan where conflict between union and management in the automotive industry is decisive. Finally, there is the pattern in the large industrial states (with the exception of Michigan) with highly diversified economies in which we see what Ziegler calls the "triumph of many interests." California is given as an example.[5]

New York's pattern is comparable to California's.[6] Faced with a wide range of possible and conflicting decisions which affect a wide range of differing interests, the New York legislature is an arena in which considerable lobbying takes place. Such lobbying, in which many techniques are employed, is generally taken for granted:

In Washington a stink is occasionally raised over the fact that some lobbyist has sat in with a congressional committee and participated in the drafting of a bill. In Albany it is done all the time, and no one gets excited about it. The politically sophisticated members of the state legislature see no harm in it, and if not done sub rosa, it really isn't wrong. After all, any good lobbyist knows more about the affairs of the industry or pressure group he represents than the members of the legislature possibly can. . . .

Many a lobbyist, because of his special knowledge of a problem, has saved a legislator from looking foolish. The lobbyist's job is to make friends and influence people. He is cooperative.

In return, he receives favors, one of the principal of which is the right to eliminate from a proposed "final draft" of a measure, prior to its introduction, things that would do his client the most harm and the intended beneficiaries of the legislation the least good. . . .

Everybody takes a hand in running New York; lobbies and pressure groups of all varieties are effective in the government of the state.... .[7]

Thus, representatives of, or professional lobbyists for, a great number of groups find a welcome in Albany. These groups include labor unions, business associations, banking interests, insurance companies, veterans groups, churches, professional associations, civil service, organizations, parents' groups, farmer associations, conservation clubs, and many others. None of them dominates in the manner that Anaconda Copper influences major decisions in the Montana legislature. Some do prevail within the narrow range of their vested interests. However, this is rare because the highly partisan character of the New York legislature in most cases assures competition between two or more interest groups. An effective lobby group in New York, therefore, depends on the use of various refined techniques in the pursuit of goals.

Many New York lobbyists are members and officers of the groups they represent. This is particularly true with labor organizations. Others are attorneys who contract with one or more groups and represent their interests in a fee basis. A few are former legislators. The most notable of these is former Speaker Joseph Carlino who has represented a racetrack and a number of professional groups before the legislature.

There is a core group of veteran lobbyists who stay in Albany throughout the legislative session. Many others come to the capitol only when a particular problem arises.

It is recognized that the chief criterion of the success of a lobbyist is his ability to obtain access to the centers of decision making. As Malcolm Jewell indicates:

> The men who devote all or most of their time to
> lobbying are usually skilled and experienced in the leg
> legislative process. Lobbying, like any other business
> these days, has become a skilled profession. It is no
> longer a matter of plying legislators with food and drink
> and handing them a large denomination bill at the end of
> an evening. Today's lobbyist must understand the intri-
> cacies of the legislative process, and he must know the
> men with whom he deals. He must understand who exer-
> cises power, who is most influential on specific types
> of measures, which members are amenable to which
> types of pressure or persuasion. . . .
> Perhaps the most useful tool for understanding the
> role of the pressure group in the legislative process is
> David Truman's concept of access. Truman points out
> that "access to the legislature is of crucial importance
> at one time or another to virtually all such groups. . . .
> In some forms it provides little more than a chance to
> be heard; in others it practically assures favorable
> action. . . . The skilled lobbyist will know which point
> of access is most valuable and perhaps most vulnerable—
> the Speaker, the committee chairman, the governor's
> assistant."[8]

Once access is secured, the next problem for the lobbyist is to determine what techniques of influence he will employ. For some, the range is quite limited; for others, various approaches are available.

LOBBYING TECHNIQUES

The primary function of the lobbyist, whether a full-time professional or a part-time representative on his first and only trip to the legislature, is to convey to those he believes have power the desires of his group. This act of communication can take several forms. Some lobbyists simply visit legislators in their offices. Others attend conferences and public hearings to express their views and expectations. Others write to their elected representatives. Still others mobilize and transport large numbers of people to impress the lawmakers. Whatever the method, the business of a lobbyist for most groups is "little more than that of an agent serving to communicate the position of a group on a given issue to someone he believes will have some control over the outcome."9

The choice of the lobbying methods used is often influenced by the character of the action's purpose. Thus, lobbying for individual business firms or entire branches of industry is usually conducted in a discreet, confidential style, mostly through person-to-person contact between the lobby representative and individual lawmakers. Lobbying for large group interests, like those of a major labor or professional union, as well as the kind of lobbying for or against measures affecting some broader public interest, like divorce or abortion legislation, may spill over to the arena of broad public agitation, general publicity, and mass public participation. The techniques vary.

The League of Women Voters has been quite persuasive in communicating its wishes to the legislature. Without any political clout and without any intention to do more than persuade, the league has a legislative program which it presents year after year. Katherine Kinkead wrote a delightful case study of the league's campaign for permanent personal registration in a 1956 edition of the New Yorker. She described the organization of league chapters for a trip to Albany, at which many of the members (each assigned to belabor a certain number of legislators) so effectively stated their case that in 1955 a first-step law was enacted which allowed for local option in the matter.10

Victor Condello, currently general counsel (and lobbyist) for the New York Association of Railroads, relates that on the most crucial of issues to his group, the repeal of the full-crew law, the only weapon at his disposal was the inherent merit of his case. The full-crew law, passed at the turn of the century, prescribed the minimum number of railroad workers who had to be physically present on trains. Later, technological changes made a reduction in the number of men possible. However, the law mandated a minimum number so that the railroad companies had to go on paying the wages of unneeded men. The attempts of the railroad companies to save money by reducing the number of crewmen were met by violent opposition on the part of the railway brotherhoods which succeeded in blocking the repeal of the dated law for many years. Says Condello:

My greatest ally was Governor Rockefeller, and I won him over by simply sending him my memos on the issue. We finally won only because we were right, but it took years of fighting with the unions. And only then did we get a compromise so that two of the law's three sections have been repealed. The third one hasn't. . . . A lobbyist's expertise and knowledge are essential to him if he is going to be successful.11

Nicholas Kisburg, legislative representative for Joint Council 16 of the Teamsters Union and one of Albany's most colorful and outspoken lobbyists, describes his approach in the following manner:

You get respect because you do your homework. There's no muscle that I can use regularly. It's a question of personal ties. I have some legislators who I got close to, first by giving them ideas and using my knowledge. Now we are friends and I can ask them favors. A couple are committee chairmen and that's helpful. I gave one senator my child allowance bill, which is a new concept for New York State, and he's gotten a lot of play with it. We think we'll eventually pass it. Others may spend money and entertain, but I think they're crazy. Can you change someone's vote for a dinner?

We had a bill that would permit dentists to list their fees in union papers where they were under contract with unions. This violates the education law which prohibits professional advertising. We passed it in 1965, but it was vetoed. The next year I persuaded Travia and Lefkowitz [attorney general] to support it. Also one senator had a friend on the Board of Regents and he was my buddy. So we finally got the regents to write a memo saying they wouldn't oppose it, and in 1966 we passed it and the governor signed it.[12]

Kisburg emphasized the importance of the relationship between lobbyist and legislator. He provides legislative ideas and even draft legislation itself to friendly lawmakers. He also freely shares his expertise with them in a wide area of subjects, ranging from labor problems to welfare. Greatly interested in statistical analysis, Kisburg has done extensive research on many subjects, often unrelated to his specific legislative interests. Thus, he often serves as a source of information and of ideas for some of the legislators.

Former senator Basil Paterson, the Democratic candidate for lieutenant governor in 1970, and formerly president of the New York branch of the National Association for the Advancement of Colored People (NAACP), notes that black groups have given up systematic lobbying in Albany because they feel that the position of being "an Albany insider doesn't help."[13] Most of the lobbying on behalf of black people is done, says Paterson, by their legislators. Occasionally a legislator can arrange for some emissaries from the black community to talk with party and legislative leaders. David Spencer and Rhody McCoy, important leaders in the two black demonstration school districts in New York City (Spencer was chairman of the IS 201 School

Board, and McCoy was unit administrator for the Oceanhill-Browns-
ville district), could spend an hour and a half with Senate Majority
Leader Earl Brydges because Paterson maintained good relations
with the Senate leader. But, as Paterson feels, the kind of professional
lobbying that depends on artificially sowing and reaping contacts and
friendships just doesn't work for black interest groups.

All lobbyists recognize the exalted place in the legislative process
of the party leaders. But access to them is more difficult because
their time is more precious than it is to the average lawmaker. They
can influence such a great diversity of bills that there is a constant
clamor and swarming by groups to get to see them. Some succeed;
others get to see only the leaders' counsels. It is fair to say that the
leaders usually try to do what lobby groups want if those groups have
observed the amenities of the legislative system, have not displayed
hostility to the leaders, and are not opposed by some stronger groups
in the matter at issue. In the latter case, the leaders must either
choose between the opposing interests or else seek a compromise
solution. Much of the time of the leaders is spent in such discussions,
the burden of which they accept as an integral part of their legislative
function.

The overwhelming majority of interest groups are limited in
terms of lobbying techniques by their lack of resources to do more
than seek out legislators to plead their cases. This is true for private
economic interests concerned with special treatment through changes
in the law as it is true for so-called good-government groups whose
concern is with the "public interest" as they perceive it. The techniques available to interest groups depend less on their needs, outlook,
or ideology than it does on their political resources.

For example, a group has a better chance of influencing action
if, in addition to the merits of its case, it is composed of a large
number of people who are united behind their group's programs and
will respond to its leadership. Such response might mean a willingness to vote for legislators solely on the basis of their reaction to
the group's legislative needs. Few large organizations can command
that kind of unity, however.

An interest group with sufficient money to lodge a lobbying
campaign will increase its effectiveness. Such lobbying effort might
consist of a media campaign to drum up public support. It might include a willingness to provide funds and workers for elected officials
who support the group's goals. It might, on a less ambitious scale,
simply be aimed at a supporting the activities of the paid professional
lobbyist. Thus, there is a relationship in many instances between
money and lobbying success.

Of course, the employment of resources without skilled leadership may lead to considerable waste and lack of success. This latter

intangible factor has sometimes been an effective substitute where numbers and financial resources are lacking.

A recent example of the systematic use of political resources was the campaign of the United Federation of Teachers (UFT) in the fight over school decentralization in the city of New York. A relatively new organization, the UFT has won great power in the education subsystem in New York City. As a result of its victory in the decentralization struggle in 1967 and 1968, the union is probably the dominant force in that subsystem today.

According to Alice Marsh, UFT legislative representative, "The decentralization fight broke down the old ivory tower behavior of teachers. We now know how to repay debts, and we have organized accordingly."[14]

The union has rather complex democratic decision-making procedures. But, as is the case with most interest groups, the UFT is controlled from the top.[15] President Albert Shanker has to deal with an executive board of 51 officers and a large Delegate Assembly to ratify policy. A two-thirds vote is necessary for the organization to take a political position for or against candidates. However, Mrs. Marsh said that she could not remember a proposal by Shanker that had not been approved, although some have been modified.[16]

Today the UFT is in a position to organize its teachers and their families and friends into a strong nucleus for political action. The union newspaper can build up or hurt candidates. Demonstrations are easily organized, and hundreds of articulate union members can be sent to Albany to affect legislation. This weapon was successfully used in the case of the Marchi bill that set up a system of elected local school boards in New York City.

The UFT has worked hard against legislators who were conspicuous in their opposition to the wishes of the federation. Former assemblyman Jerome Kretchmer, and advocate of community control of the schools, was a particular target, and UFT members went into his district to agitate for his opponent. The union has a legislative fund and contributes to country dinners and other party functions.

In this manner, the UFT employs a wide range of pressure tactics far beyond the means of persuasion based on the merits of an issue. In the decentralization battle, the union was able to arouse the passions of the great majority of middle-class parents in the city. It was able to intimidate very high public officials on all levels. Today certain legislators themselves ask Mrs. Marsh for UFT bills to sponsor, and the union gets a great deal of satisfaction to its demands in the area of pension legislation, union rules, and other matters of consequence to the operation of the school system.

Few interest groups, however, can really deliver on a threat to defeat a candidate. Even the UFT has not been very successful in this respect. In general, groups with large memberships usually cannot decisively influence the votes of their members. In our middle-class society, even union members have developed independent interests, sentiments, and loyalties which affect their voting behavior. But well-heeled groups can help defeat an undesirable office seeker by providing campaign funds, manpower, and other free services to his preferred opponent. For example, on a minor scale, several New York unions do printing of brochures and posters for candidates they support. Some provide cars equipped with loudspeakers and even manpower to ring doorbells. The threat of withdrawal of services of this nature is a clear and present danger to a candidate. In one instance several unions vowed to defeat Speaker Travia in his home district in Brooklyn because, in April 1967, he permitted the passage of the Taylor Law which labor vehemently opposed.[17] Travia was appointed to a federal judgeship before the threat of the unions could be implemented. Generally, however, no such threat is needed. The group supports those candidates who are known to be committed to support their general program.

Campaign contributions can be an important link between politicians and certain lobby groups—although relatively few groups do contribute very substantially. Whether through a direct contribution or the purchase of a table at a legislator's fund raising dinner, or by subscription to an advertisement in a fund raising ad journal, the gift builds a tie between the legislator and the giver, with at least a slight hint at reciprocity implied. Since such contributions are legal, crude direct bribery is unnecessary and probably rarely resorted to. There is, of course, no way to determine the extent of the incidence of direct bribery, but people normally do not take unnecessary risks. Why should a legislator who, for example, is an attorney get involved in a direct and naked payoff when he can simply and legally accept a retainer from the interested lobby group for his law firm?

If, therefore, the present study is expected to attempt an answer to the question of whether there are some legislators who are beholden to specific interest groups to the extent that they act under the influence of personal lucre, the answer must be in the affirmative. Fortunately, the practice is probably not as widespread as the man in the street believes. In this respect, the situation is certainly better than it was, let us say, a generation or two ago. Both the politician and the self-seeking interest group know only too well how deeply public opinion is aroused today against the existing abuses of the public interest to risk exposure and condemnation for involvement in some shady deal. Legislators are probably less willing to risk their careers for what are relatively small rewards. This is particularly true for those whose ambitions extend beyond the legislature to future careers in Congress, the courts, or other high office. On the other hand, unethical behavior on the part of legislators and lobbyists still exists. However, a distinction between illegal activity and unethical behavior must be made. It certainly is made by those in the legislature who wish to directly profit from their position of influence without violating any law and who therefore encourage lobbyists to legally pay them off through campaign contributions donated to repay favors given, or through law retainers or other "legal" techniques.

GOVERNMENTAL LOBBYING:
THE STATE AGENCIES

Administrative agencies are just as concerned with the destiny of legislative proposals of interest to them as are private interest groups. The term "administrative agency" refers here not to those executive officials and agencies who work directly on the governor's legislative programs, but rather to administrative units which, while subject to ultimate supervision by the chief executive, have their own legislative needs. Their performance mandates emanate from the legislature, and their methods of operation are very often altered by legislation. Almost every agency in New York State therefore keeps close tabs on pending and newly proposed bills and, within limits set by the governor's counsel, it will send its counsel or chief bureaucrats to the lawmakers to pressure for or against the proposed changes.

Thus, there is a continuous give-and-take relationship between agency personnel, on the one hand, and legislative committees and individual legislators, on the other. Some agency lobbyists are more aggressive than others, but most of them try to maintain a more or less decorous distance and a relationship based solely on considerations of professional needs and interests.

The concept of legislative oversight, which is becoming so increasingly important with respect to the authority of congressional committees and subcommittees,[18] does not play the same significant role in New York. In Albany there are no such closely knit and permanent power alliances between legislative committees and executive agencies as exist in Washington. Important among the reasons for this is the fact that the legislature is a part-time operation. Most of its members do not have the time, interest, or inclination to develop the kind of uninterrupted day-to-day relationships with the administrative side that has so long prevailed in the Congress. The turnover rate is high, meaning that many men who have acquired some measure of specialized expertise leave the legislature before they can establish themselves as strong men vis-a-vis the corresponding executive agency. One interesting illustration of this situation is the case of Senator Norman Lent of Nassau who, as chairman of the JLC on Public

190

Health from 1966 through 1970, developed a measure of expertise in a variety of health matters. His committee was very effective in studying and preparing legislation on such matters as Medicaid, abortion, health insurance, medical experiments, and human transplants. When in 1970 Lent announced that he would leave the Senate to run for Congress, the Republican party leaders, Senator Earl Brydges and Speaker Perry Duryea, abolished the committee altogether because there was no Republican with sufficient qualifications to handle the JLC adequately. In this decision the leaders were probably influenced by the apprehension that the JLC would be dominated by two veteran Democrats who were highly specialized in health matters.

There are, of course, exceptions to a generalization of this nature. Some legislators and committee chairman do develop close and sometimes intimate relationships with administrative personnel working in their areas of interest. But for the most part, the joint concern is with new legislation or revisions to existing legislation. There is very little systematic oversight of the general operation of agencies. The basic assumption of legislators, leaders included, appears to be that the agencies are doing what they are supposed to do. If trouble occurs or a scandal breaks, then the legislature may get involved.

Interviews with agency personnel interested in influencing legislative decisions indicate that government lobbyists use some of the same techniques that private lobbyists use. Primary among these is the development of long-term personal contacts and relationships which afford the government lobbyist access to key legislators, notably the leaders, and once access is established, a chance to argue the merits of a particular viewpoint.

One of the more aggressive and successful agency lobbyists is Dr. Andrew Fleck, currently first deputy commissioner of the State Health Department. Fleck is both a licensed physician and an attorney. He joined the Health Department in 1958 as an associate commissioner for Community Health Services. In five years he was made second deputy commissioner in charge of representing the department in its dealings with other executive agencies and departments and of coordinating joint boards and commissions such as the Health and Hospital Council and the Water Pollution Control Board. He was, in fact, a sort of departmental ambassador inside the executive branch.

"However, I soon discovered that these boards were not the most significant points of decision. There were institutionalized negotiations and many private discussions, but real power rested with the legislature and the governor's staff. So that's where I began to concentrate."[19] It was Fleck's job to think up a list of desirable legislative possibilities in the summer and have his staff review the technical

191

problems of each. He cleared the objectives (not yet actual drafts of bills) with the commissioner, Hollis Ingraham. Once overall approval was obtained from the commissioner, Fleck was pretty much on his own to set priorities and to lobby for the bills.

Some observations by Fleck regarding his role:

> My operation is apparently unique. Douglas [Governor Rockefeller's counsel] sent out a memo one year calling on departmental counsels to be more active in terms of legislative activity. He then told me that the memo didn't apply to me since I was too active already.
>
> Departmental lobbying depends on one's own view of one's mission. We are consumer protection oriented at the top of the Health Department, but lower-level health officials are much more specialized in terms of their interests, and concern with professional special- ties can sometimes conflict with general policy. We've had to deal, therefore, with some of these officials.
>
> I'm quite willing to work with private lobbies to trade packages. I've worked very hard getting close to Charles Tobin of Catholic Charities since we seemed in the past to be on opposite sides. We've got a good understanding now on most things and are close regarding objectives.[20]

The secret of Fleck's operation and of all effective lobbyists' is the cultivation of personal friendships through the years, securing access and an ear willing to listen. If access is combined with pro- fessional competence, then the lobbyist is in business, provided there are no insurmountable ideological or political obstacles in the way of granting his wishes.

In addition to his ability to influence people and his professional competence, Fleck benefits also from the fact that the agency he represents is considered nonpolitical in basic character, distinct from other executive agencies which are rather deeply involved in the allocation of patronage among supporters of the governor.

Most such departments and agencies are considered by party leaders, the governor, and the Civil Service Commission primarily as sources of patronage, and their work is less highly regarded. As Daniel Moynihan and James Q. Wilson point out in their study of executive patronage during the Harriman administration:

> In all this [political appointments], the Civil Service Commission and its staff were willing participants so long as no great violence was done to the general

principles of "fitness." Nine departments were subject to this kind of political interference, the most important of which were Public Works, Taxation and Finance, Correction, and Conservation. The others were Agriculture and Markets, Labor, State, the Division of Veterans Affairs, and the Rent Control Commission. Other departments were emphatically not subjected to such intervention, including Education, Health, Social Welfare, Mental Hygiene, and the State Police, even though the administration was often under considerable pressure from party leaders to relax the restrictions. . . .

Generally speaking, party intrusion into a department is most likely to cause an adverse popular reaction when the department is the province of a well-organized profession which is able and willing to resist intrusion publicly on the ground that it violates "professional standards." Educators, doctors, psychiatrists, social workers, and public health officers effectively control their departments, and these departments, in turn, are perceived by voters as being agencies in which "neutral competence" and "expertise" ought to prevail.[21]

Administrators of agencies used as vehicles for political patronage may, when they attempt to influence legislative decisions, suffer from the perception by legislators that they are political animals rather than suppliers of needed technical expertise. For example, when Edward J. McLaughlin, appointed in 1955 as director of veterans affairs by Governor Harriman, had business in the legislature and attempted to lobby for legislation, he was markedly less successful than Fleck, not only because he was a Democrat dealing with a Republican majority, but mainly because he was a political appointee.

McLaughlin, active in Queens County politics as well as in veterans affairs, had his name submitted to Harriman for appointment by his own district leader. It had been decided by Harriman's office that the veterans' job should go to a Queens Democrat. After obtaining approval by his county leader, McLaughlin was interviewed by Carmine DeSapio. He was also endorsed by George Backer, a leader of the Liberal party. Finally, he was interviewed and approved by Milton Stewart, Harriman's patronage dispenser, and by the governor himself. But the whole process took months before the appointment was made.

McLaughlin is a quiet, precise man, an experienced attorney with an analytic mind. He is very personable and rarely shows anger. Yet in his few dealings with important legislators, he was unsuccessful in winning their confidence and support. One reason probably was the political nature of his appointment.

193

In 1956 McLaughlin was told by Stewart that the State Veterans Counseling Service was to be phased out in accordance with an agreement between the Dewey administration and Austin Erwin, chairman of the Senate Finance Committee. The Counseling Service provided advice to veterans on their rights and benefits. But the Republicans felt that the service duplicated the efforts of local veterans counseling services and of private veterans groups. McLaughlin took the position that he was not bound by such an agreement and asked Stewart not to honor it. Stewart compromised by suggesting that at least vacancies on the staff of the service should no longer be filled, but McLaughlin told him that he had already begun interviewing candidates for four vacancies. Stewart agreed that the four positions should be filled, but further hiring should be stopped.[22]

It was then that Senator Erwin, a very crusty Republican veteran, called McLaughlin into his office. "He said to me, 'You have hired too many counselors. Don't hire any more.' When I suggested he look into my report on the necessity of continuing the Counseling Service, he told me to get the hell out of his office."[23]

McLaughlin's very limited success in the role of agency lobbyist was typical for the standing of most of his colleagues appointed by Governor Harriman. It is clear that the dislike the Republican leadership felt for the governor was transferred to his political appointees almost automatically.

But apart from partisan feelings, the main factors that determine the relative degree of success of an agency lobbyist are still these: the political or nonpolitical nature of his role within the administration, his personal reputation as an administrator and expert in his field, and, of course, his ability to get along well with people.

In addition to the lobbyists for "political" departments and their specialist counterparts working for agencies with more professional reputations, there is still another category of lobbyists. These are men who represent the so-called independent agency. These are called independent only because they are structurally beyond the control of the governor. For example, the state comptroller and attorney general are elected officials and thus potentially independent.

The incumbent attorney general, Louis Lefkowitz, was elected in 1957. He or his attorneys intercede with the legislative process either by opinions on the constitutionality of legislation, the political advisability of others, or else by the submission of his own legislative proposals, mostly on matters pertaining within his own jurisdiction.

Lefkowitz describes his responsibilities as follows:

I submit to the governor a memo on every bill that passes, regarding its legality and constitutionality, plus

an opinion regarding the bill's substance and policy
significance. Of course, nothing is binding, as the governor gets memos from all over. Additionally, I have my
own legislative program regarding items over which the
attorney general has jurisdiction or which is of interest
to my office. We'll submit bills regarding civil rights,
the criminal code, consumer protection, pollution, in-
vestment policy, theaters, cooperatives, trusts, and so
on.[24]

The attorney general's program, which is submitted separately
from the governor's, averages between 30 and 45 bills a year. They
result from his own views and experiences, staff recommendations,
points made by judges in court, or the discovery of deficiencies in
some law. His techniques of lobbying are comparable with those of
other departments. But after long years of collaboration and shared
experience, Lefkowitz has so ready and easy access to the majority
party leaders and to the governor as to be free of any worry about
lobbying styles. He simply calls up the competent leader or legislator and explains what he wants. Unless there is some strong reason
for questioning his suggestion, he will promptly get satisfaction because the general assumption is, particularly on technical matters,
that the attorney general is a tested authority in his field, whose
proposals merit confidence and serious consideration. This is an
easy stance to work from.[25]

GOVERNMENTAL LOBBYING:
THE LOCAL GOVERNMENTS

A most important category of lobby is that of the local governments whose demands on the state for financial and other assistance
and for home rule powers have been mushrooming year after year.
On occasion, these governments have formed alliances for the purpose of applying combined pressure on both the governor and the
legislature for the passage of legislation for the satisfaction of their
growing needs. The larger localities such as the city of New York
have their own personal lobbying operations, and local political leaders
became quite active in the pursuit of government benefits expected
from Albany. As Warren Moscow has noted:

The State Conference of Mayors and the Association
of Towns for years had tremendous influence in Albany
with the members of the legislature—an influence easily
understood, since the legislators come from localities

195

and return to them at the end of the session. What the
local government wants is important to them, even if
they are no longer directly on the payroll.[26]

Malcolm Jewell comments, "City and county officials in a
legislator's district get attention not only because they may be politically powerful but also because the legislator respects their knowledge of local affairs and is trying to serve the needs of local governmental units in his district."[27]

The governor is the chief target for lobbying activity by local
governments, especially the large cities. Since most large city mayors
are Democrats and since most of the time the legislative leaders
have been Republicans, the mayors have aimed their pressure at the
more vulnerable chief executive. The governors are considered more
vulnerable because they must campaign for reelection with big city
(and particularly New York City) support. The Republican leaders
have no such problems.

But the decisive reason for the fact that big city pressures are
concentrated upon the governor as the target is of a clearly financial
nature. As we have seen, the author of New York State's annual budget
proposals is the governor himself. In recent years, the provisions
and appropriations of the state budget for the rapidly growing needs
of the larger cities, particularly of New York City itself, have been
found more and more inadequate and wanting. It is, therefore, natural
and inevitable that year after year the mayor of New York should
publicly accuse the governor of the state of New York in person of
having callously shortchanged the struggling city. Similar charges
are often made by mayors of other large cities. The governor's most
frequent answer to these complaints has been the countercharge of
financial irresponsibility and mismanagement on the part of the city
leaders.

New York City has maintained an elaborate lobbying operation
for decades. Mayor Robert Wagner, who served in that post from
1953 through 1965, set up a relatively large lobbying operation with
a chief legislative representative and a staff of attorneys and research
aides. Among his lobbyists were Victor Condello, who later continued
his lobbying activities in the service of the Association of Railroads,
and Bernard Ruggierri, later counsel to Senate Minority Leader
Joseph Zaretzki.

Wagner was often personally involved in fights over legislation,
and much of his time was spent dealing with Albany:

I was fortunate in having been an assemblymen
from 1938 through 1941. Therefore I knew Heck and
Mahoney and MacKenzie [chairman of the Assembly Ways

and Means Committee]. Knowing these men meant that I had access, although it never meant I could get my bills passed. But at least I got to talk to them and they heard my side. . . .

Rockefeller liked to get a list of New York City bills by December 1 of each year. I would get a program together through discussions with my staff people and the Democratic leaders. Then I met regularly with the Democratic leaders, at my initiative. I met with the governor periodically, but it wasn't on a systematic basis. . . .

Dewey originally had a different system. He started to tell me whom I could bring to Albany. He said, "your predecessors all had to call my secretary Mr. Bixley (I think was his name) in order to get me!" I told him that I will either deal with him or with the newspapers. For the one year we were both in office, I dealt directly with him. . . .

I was, of course, very close to Averell Harriman. We campaigned for each other, and he made promises to help the city. But he couldn't keep those promises. I remember he promised to restore the part of the pari-mutuel tax that used to come to New York but that Dewey had taken away. But as governor, Harriman forgot about it. Actually, I did better with Rockefeller than Harriman, since Averell had much more serious problems with the legislature.

Every year, I went to Albany to testify before the Finance Committees. I'd make my pitch. MacKenzie would say, "Nice presentation, Bob"; he'd offer me a drink and then show me the bills that had already been drafted. My performance was pro forma.[28]

Wagner's successor as mayor of New York City, John V. Lindsay, expanded the size and scope of his legislative representative's office in Albany. Among his appointees to the post were two men with wide legislative experience. One, Anthony Savarese, currently a criminal court judge in Queens County, was a former Republican assemblyman. He served as the city's lobbyist from 1967 to 1969.

Savarese had an office staff that included four attorneys and several clerical people who worked out of both the New York and Albany offices. The city has, for decades, maintained a suite of offices in Albany for its lobbying operations. During Savarese's tenure, the city program totaled an average of 200 bills a year, most

of which dealt with questions of state aid and local finance. According
to Savarese, Mayor Lindsay was personally involved in the treatment
of all major controversial questions of budgetary legislation that
affected the city. But he had other pet bills to press for, as, for example, the fourth platoon law (permitting the police commissioner to
create a fourth platoon during peak crime hours) on which "he wouldn't
let us let up; he had to beat the PBA" (Policemen's Benevolent Association).29

Like Mayor Wagner, Lindsay and his representative Savarese
had tremendous political difficulty in getting legislation passed in
Albany. All the key positions of decision making were occupied by
men who were either anti-Lindsay or anti-New York City. For example, reports Savarese, the Rockefeller-Lindsay feud badly hurt
the chances for the passage of many important bills. "No specific
bill was lost because of the Rocky-Lindsay fights, but the atmosphere
was lousy, and it frankly made it very tough for me to go to the legislative leaders."30

Additionally, "whatever the city got was because Marchi okayed
it. He was regarded highly by the Senate leadership in connection
with New York City legislation and was considered the key man whose
recommendations the leaders consistently accepted."31 Senator John
Marchi of Staten Island was chairman of the Senate Committee on the
Affairs of the City of New York. "When he became a candidate for
mayor against Lindsay, our access to him was lost."32

Another example of legislative influence upon city interests is
the following case: "Thaler was the key man on the Hospital Corporation Bill, and until he approved of it, we couldn't pass it."33 The bill
provided for the creation of a new public benefit corporation to administer New York City's Municipal Hospitals in order to control and
reduce administrative red tape. Senator Thaler, a Democrat and
ranking minority member of the Senate Public Health Committee,
refused to give his assent to the bill until the city agreed to assure
the corporation a minimal level of financial support. The city was
very hesitant to appropriate more substantial funds to a corporation
that was meant to operate outside of its budgetary control structure.
The Republicans, notably Public Health Committee chairman Norman
Lent, had a close working relationship with Thaler. Additionally,
Lent was not about to debate Thaler on the Senate floor to defend a
Lindsay proposal, since few Republican legislators felt particularly
friendly toward the Mayor. The city ultimately gave in, and the bill
was passed with the amendment desired by Thaler.

It is, therefore, interesting that after Savarese's appointment
to the criminal court bench in 1969, Lindsay decided to appoint in
his place a protege of Senator Thaler. Richard Brown was appointed
legislative representative for the city by Lindsay after the possible

choices were discussed with the legislative leaders. Brown, a Democrat, served as associate counsel to Assembly Speaker Anthony Travia, and then to Assembly Democratic Minority Leader, Stanley Steingut. It was from Steingut's staff that Brown was recruited by Lindsay (with Steingut's blessing). Originally, however, Brown came to Albany in the capacity of a legislative assistant to Thaler. When Travia won the speakership in 1965, Thaler recommended Brown to him for promotion. Before that, Brown served as president of Thaler's local political club in Forest Hills, Queens.

Thus Brown, as the mayor's lobbyist in Albany, brought to his job the wide experience of a Democratic legislative expert. In 1970 he was placed in charge of a considerably expanded joint representation in Albany of the state's six major cities, an idea initiated by Lindsay in 1969. The "Big Six" mayors worked together, discussed strategy, and submitted joint proposals for increased state aid to urban areas. During the 1970 legislative session, they were quite successful in persuading Governor Rockefeller to grant much larger appropriations of state aid to the cities than anyone could have anticipated. The systematic pressures coming from the group, taking the form of persistent public appeals, had great impact on the governor, mainly because in his 1970 campaign for reelection, he had to defend his record on city problems before the masses of urban voters.[34]

The organization of the Big Six meetings and the drafting of the mayoral lobby's legislative program were Brown's responsibility. The mayor's initiative has added consistency and strength to this type of lobbying by local governments.

CONCLUSIONS

Lobbying is a highly informal, unregulated, freewheeling but, at the same time, integral and indispensable part of the legislative process. It might even be suggested that, ranking behind elections and the referendum, it is still one of the key channels of popular self-government. But it is a channel through which a great and unwieldy mass of demands inundates the legislature and pressures its leaders. This is particularly true in New York, the busiest, culturally and socially most complex, state of the Union.

It is, of course, the legislature itself that decides what laws should or should not be enacted. But the first impulse and the initiative for, as well as the driving impetus behind, any legislative idea or proposal may come from anywhere. Such initiatives come from countless sources within and outside the government on behalf of an unpredictable variety of public needs and private interests, ranging from lofty stirrings for public improvement to unabashed claims for personal gain. This means that the halls of the legislature are usually crowded with all kinds and types of people, even state officials interceding on behalf of the executive with the legislative branch, representatives of the most massive urban interests in the world, and of the smallest individual needs.

The success of lobbying depends on quite a few variables. The proposal must, of course, make sense, and its objective must be, at least formally, legitimate. The position and strength of the lobbying group (membership, money, influence) can make quite a difference, as can the personal ability and know-how of its representative. The degree of receptivity of key legislators to the proposal is a very important factor, as well as the degree of their interest in giving satisfaction to the sponsoring group.

The primary approach of lobbying is the use of convincing argument on the merits of the proposal. But a key to success seems to be the enlistment of the support of the top leaders of the majority party through effective argument and effective approach. This is sometimes a difficult and delicate enterprise as most leaders feel that they must maintain at least the image of a higher degree of "unapproachability" than the average legislator. But, generally speaking, there are always ways to enlist the interests of a leader in a legislative idea of significance. The techniques may widely differ, but it is fair to assume that lobbying for some private business interest will be rather personal and discreet in style, while the pressure for some important public cause is likely to be public and loud.

Lobbying may be a nuisance to lawmakers, but it is here to stay as a needed connecting link between the legislature and the public. Some lobbying is certainly suspect, and sometimes manifestly dishonest, but the practice as a whole works on behalf of the public interest. Most of our important social, political, and economic improvements would probably never have come about without vigorous, often desperate, lobbying activity.

NOTES

1. Arthur F. Bentley, The Process of Government, rev. ed. (Bloomington, Ind.: Principia Press, 1949).

2. David Truman, The Governmental Process (New York: Alfred A. Knopf, Inc., 1951).

3. For a review of the literature on group activity as well as the development of a theory of group politics, see Earl Latham, "The Group Basis of Politics: Notes for a Theory," American Political Science Review XLVI (June 1952): 376-397.

4. Harmon Ziegler, "Interest Groups in the States," in Politics in the American States, Herbert Jacob and Kenneth Vines, eds. (Boston: Little, Brown and Company, 1965), p. 104.

5. Ibid., pp. 117-125.

6. An important early study of lobby group activity in New York State is Belle Zeller, Pressure Politics in New York (Englewood Cliffs, N.J.: Prentice-Hall, 1937).

7. Warren Moscow, Politics in the Empire State (New York: Alfred A. Knopf, Inc., 1948), pp. 200-201.

8. Malcom Jewell, The State Legislature (New York: Random House, 1962), pp. 72-73.

9. Ziegler, op. cit., p. 135.

10. Katherine T. Kinkead, "A Reporter at Large," New Yorker 32 (May 5, 1956): 118ff.

11. Victor Condello, general counsel, New York Association of Railroads, interview, January 16, 1970.

12. Nicholas Kisburg, legislative representative, Teamsters Union Joint Council 16, interview, December 10, 1969.

13. Senator Basil Paterson, interview, December 8, 1969.

14. Alice Marsh, legislative representative, United Federation of Teachers, interview, January 14, 1970.

15. Emmette Redford, David Truman, Alan Westin, and Robert Wood, Politics and Government in the United States (New York: Harcourt, Brace and World, 1968), pp. 121-125.

16. Marsh, op. cit.

17. The Taylor Law replaced the Condon Wadlin Act which prohibited strikes by public employees and mandated punishments on workers who struck. The Taylor Law shifted punishment from the worker to his union while continuing the prohibition against public employee strikes.

18. See, for example, Joseph P. Harris, Congressional Control of Administration (Washington D.C.: Brookings Institution, 1964).

19. Dr. Andrew Fleck, first deputy commissioner, New York State Department of Health, interview, March 2, 1970.

20. Fleck, op. cit.

21. Daniel P. Moynihan and James Q. Wilson, "Patronage in New York State, 1955-59," American Political Science Review LVIII, no. 2 (June 1964). 296.

22. Edward J. McLaughlin, former New York State director of veterans affairs, interview, December 1, 1969.

23. Ibid.

24. Attorney General Louis Lefkowitz, interview, February 24, 1970.

25. Ibid.

26. Moscow, op. cit., p. 202.

27. Jewell, op. cit., p. 71.

28. Robert F. Wagner, former mayor of New York City, interview, December 22, 1969.

29. Judge Anthony Savarese, former assemblyman and former legislative representative for the city of New York, interview, February 18, 1970.

30. Ibid.

31. Ibid.

32. Ibid.

33. Ibid.

34. See, for example, The New York Post, December 22, 1969, an article with the headline: "Lindsay Warns Rocky: Help the Cities or Else."

8

This study has attempted to examine the nature of power in the New York legislature. Before conclusions can be reached, a brief summary of findings may be helpful.

Power inside the Assembly and Senate is very much centralized in the hands of the Assembly Speaker and Senate Majority Leader. These "legislative leaders" are elected by the members of their respective legislative parties. Together, with the governor, they can generally control or significantly influence most legislative decisions.

The powers granted to the Speaker of the Assembly and the Majority Leader of the Senate are more than sufficient to make them real leaders of their respective houses of the legislature. They control assignments of members to committees, appoint chairmen, allocate funds, appoint special committees, control procedural decisions, and occupy themselves the chairmanships of their respective Rules Committees, which in turn are invested with formidable powers to control the selection and the flow of legislation. This array of formal powers is an effective basis for any elected leader to accomplish domination over the legislative process, if he so chooses. However, the majority party leaders' dominance depends not only on the sum total of formal powers at their disposal but also on the atmosphere in which such powers may be exercised. This atmosphere is composed of certain factors that can substantially alter, both positively and negatively, the scope of the leader's potential to dominate. One of these major factors is the leader's own view of the manner in which he should use the formal powers available to him, with single-handed rigidity or in a more decentralized and collaborative style. The countervailing atmospheric factor of great significance is composed of the generally prevailing expectations of the membership with regard to leadership behavior. In New York most members expect their leaders to lead, to act purposefully, and to employ their powers effectively in the service of the legislative party's interest. These expectations exert a positive influence upon the ability of the majority party leader to affect the outcome of the legislative program of his party. Another factor affecting the leader's role in the legislature is the way in which he fosters goodwill among his colleagues by providing for them various kinds of benefits in which they or their constitutents are interested.

However successful a majority party leader may be in the control of his own house, the ultimate effectiveness of his leadership depends on the quality of his working relationship with other important participants in the legislative process. One of these, the leader of the other house, is his equal with whom a cooperative association must be developed in the common interest. If the two leaders represent different parties, such association is more difficult to achieve. Ideological differences may disturb the relationship even if the two men belong to the same party, and sometimes even personal rivalry between them may interfere.

The two major variables that affect the relationship between leaders of the majority party and the minority party in a particular house are the size of the majority and the extent to which the minority leader is prepared to sacrifice potential advantages of patronage or of the passage of legislation favored by him for the sake of confronting the majority party with a united opposition. This latter option disappears, however, where the minority is too weak numerically, even if unified, to affect the results of legislation.

The chief rival of the legislative leaders, though, is the governor himself, because he is equipped with great powers to influence the legislature. Both a combination of constitutional and statutory powers and general public expectation make it incumbent upon the governor to present to the legislature each year its agenda of major legislation. This role of the governor as chief lawmaker is now so fully institutionalized that not only does he prepare and submit the executive budget but also a comprehensive program of legislation dealing with the major problems that in his view require solutions by law. The leaders do not usually participate in the preparation of this important program. In fact, the governor today simply expects that the leaders, if they are members of his party, will use their influence to support the program, and they generally do. There are, of course, circumstances in which the leaders feel that they must stand up to the chief executive, and there are even times when a group of legislators stand up to both the governor and the leaders. These are infrequent occurrences, however.

Certain other participants in the legislative system also affect legislative decisions, but to a lesser degree than the legislators, their leaders, and the governor. Some of these participants are influential only in a limited range of legislative matters or are only peripherally involved in the process.

The judges of the state courts, for example, are part of the formal legislative process only insofar as they have the power of judicial review and decide to employ that power. There are also matters in which judges are directly interested such as legislation dealing with court reorganization and procedures. Occasionally they lobby for legislation of this nature. Since these concerns have been acknowledged as legitimate, judicial lobbying has become institutionalized by the creation of a Judicial Conference which serves not only as the central administrative body of the court system but also as its chief lobbying organ. In a much more personal way, some legislators and particularly their leaders have displayed interest in the courts as a place where they may end their careers. Since the legislature sets the ground rules for court operations and can periodically increase the number of judicial positions, this kind of legislation has become very important to quite a few lawmakers.

Additionally, the political party organizations outside of the legislature may be interested in legislation that affects their operations and chances of success. This is true not only for the state committees but also for the local and county organizations. Of course, within the legislature the general influence of partisanship and party loyalty finds expression not only in the behavior of legislators but also in the organization of each house, the election of leaders and other officers, and the composition of the committee system itself.

An essential element in the process of legislation is the numerous interest groups, both private and public, which systematically attempt to exert influence upon decisions of the legislature. Using a variety of techniques to gain access to and gain the support of lawmakers for their needs and desires, these groups and their lobbying representatives are an integral part of the entire process. While private lobbies have been the object of more public scrutiny and of increasing critical concern on account of the occasional use by some of them of ethically questionable tactics, the increasingly important role played by governmental lobbying, both state and local, should by no means be overlooked. Since the legislature has authority over the general framework of operations of administrative agencies and over the determination of much of the financial means available to local governments, these agencies and localities strive more and more frequently to influence and to pressure the legislature for the satisfaction of their needs.

THE LEADERS AND LEGISLATION

Having considered all these various influences, what conclusions may we reach with respect to the place of the governor, the Assembly Speaker, and the Senate Majority leader in the legislative system, and what is their impact on the legislative product of that system? This central question may be subdivided into a series of very pragmatic ancillary questions: Can a leader arbitrarily impose his will upon his house? Can he arbitrarily kill a bill wanted by the majority of his legislative party? In his leadership capacity, is he an instrument in the hands of his membership, or is he, and to what extent, in control of the membership? Is he an agent of the governor or an equal partner, capable of standing up, if need be, to the great constitutional and political power of the chief executive? To what extent is he dependent on, or independent from, the demands of the political leadership of the general organization of his party?

The best approach to answering these questions is to examine the impact of the leaders on certain specific categories of legislation, selected not on the basis of subject matter, but according to the original source of the sponsorship of the legislation.

Three different categories of bills enter consideration. The first includes proposals that originate from individual lawmakers themselves, either at their own initiative or at that of constituents or lobbyists. These are the so-called private or local bills which usually affect special and/or local interests.

The second category includes those bills that are considered to be of major consequence and are, therefore, rather controversial and that also have not been introduced by the governor or by the legislative leaders, but by some individual legislator or group of legislators or else by the minority party in the legislature. Most of these bills result from initiatives and agitation on the part of interest groups and larger segments of the population.

The third category of bills are those that emanate from the governor himself and constitute his official legislative program. Some of these, too, can be controversial; some others may represent large new programs initiated by the chief executive; and others may be quite free from controversy. The criterion differentiating the three categories from one another is simply the source of its origin.

LOCAL OR PRIVATE BILLS

It seems correct to define bills belonging to this category as items of legislation that are of limited public interest but of definite importance to individual lawmakers who depend on their passage as a means of building a record. They include bills that benefit local party organizations, local communities, other local interest groups, or even leading citizens in the home district.

It is generally recognized that on such matters, the Speaker and the Senate Majority Leader have "life-and-death" power. This is a phrase that is commonly employed by legislators when asked to assess the influence of the leaders on the fortunes of these bills. According to former assemblyman William Clancy, commenting about Speaker Heck, "Heck had life-and-death control over practically all legislation in which the members were personally interested."[1] Former Senate Majority Leader Walter Mahoney stated, "On lesser bills the leader has life-and-death control, and this fact gives him leverage in attempting to influence men to cooperate on more important bills."[2]

We have discussed in some detail the power resources available to the leaders. Perhaps the most important among these resources is their ability to permit or to deny passage of such private or local bills introduced by their colleagues. Most of these bills end up in the Rules Committees in each house. As we have seen, the Rules Committees are completely dominated by their chairmen, the legislative leaders. Speaker Travia stated that he had never lost a vote in the Rules Committee.[3] Former Speaker Joseph Carlino noted, "Rules controlled all local bills."[4] William Keefe and Morris Ogul have very aptly described, in general, the Speaker's influence over the lot of private and local bills as a vital element within the totality of their power to make their members follow their wishes in the treatment of major legislation:

> In summary, the Speaker's influence in the states
> is compounded by numerous elements. In the first place,
> he is the guardian of party fortunes and policies. Second,
> he is charged with many official duties, nearly all of
> which hold implications for the party interest. Thus
> typically, he appoints the members of standing, special,
> and conference committees; he chairs the Rules Com-
> mittee; he refers bills to committee; he presides over
> house sessions, decides points of order, recognizes mem-
> bers, and puts questions to a vote; he has it within his
> power to assist a member with a "pet" bill or to sand-
> bag it; he can ease the way for new members or ignore
> them; he can advance the legislative careers of members
> or throw roadblocks before them. All of these preroga-
> tives contribute to a network of influence.[5]

The lesson from all of this for all members (of both parties) is simply that the prospects of their private bills depend on cooperation with the party leadership. In a study of state and local governments in New York, a unit of the State Education Department formulated the following stern assessment of the leaders' power over private bills:

> What is more, the leaders, by control of the legislative procedure, hold life-and-death power over the bills that members introduce. A false step, an unsuccessful revolt, and the pet projects of the rebels would die in committee. To the average legislator such a fate would be political death, for he depends on cooperation for the passage of private or local bills that are vital to his constituency.[6]

CONTROVERSIAL BILLS THAT ARE NOT INITIATED BY THE GOVERNOR OR THE LEADERS

While the numerically overwhelming majority of bills processed by the New York legislature are local or private bills with limited interest to the general public, year after year a number of bills are introduced in the legislature which may propose new approaches to the solution of major problems of general interest or affect the concerns of large groups of the population in a highly controversial manner. Some of these emerge as a part of the governor's own program. Others originate from sponsoring sources other than the governor and the legislative leaders.

The governor and the leaders are often confronted with popular demands for reform legislation, hotly pursued by large sectors of the public, and opposed with equal heat by other sectors of the population. It is very often in the political interest of the governor and the leaders to evade involvement in such controversies altogether, or at least to delay involvement in them as long as possible. Such tactics, however, do not always make the problems disappear. On the contrary, the longer the delay, the stronger the clamor tends to grow, the more interest groups line up for and against the proposal, and an atmosphere develops in which some legislator or group of legislators, or the minority party itself, finds the situation ripe for the introduction of some legislative solution of the contested issue, and the governor and the legislature are forced to deal with the problem.

Examples of such bills are quite numerous. Some of them have been presented in this study. The common characteristics of such bills are their highly controversial nature, their impact on differing public interests, and the fact that the governor and the legislative leaders have tried to evade involvement in the conflict. Another important feature distinguishing these proposals from the category of private and local bills is the fact that the leaders have no absolute "life-or-death" control over their passage or rejection. The leaders are still in a position to exert strong influence over the outcome, but their influence is no longer totally decisive, since in these cases many legislators feel free to choose between party loyalty and the demands of their own constituencies, and even to follow their own personal ideological or sometimes religious preferences. Placed between the anvil of loyalty to the leadership and the hammer of prevailing constituency demands, many a legislator may rather incur the leader's ill will than lose his chances of reelection. Leadership control is similarly limited in the case of bills that deal with fundamental religious and moral questions. Many legislators believe that problems of this nature transcend party interests and political loyalties.

The following examples of this category of bills will show that while the Speaker and the Senate Majority Leader exerted strong influence upon the treatment of such bills, they could not necessarily control the outcome.

The issue of abortion reform was thrust upon the legislature by the persistence of a group of legislators led by Democratic assemblyman Albert Blumenthal. While it is true that at first Speaker Travia referred the bill to the Codes Committee in 1967 and tried to have it kept there "pigeonholed," the next year he was forced by public pressure to present the bill to the floor for a vote where it was defeated. In 1970, the dramatic attempt to defeat this legislation by presenting it in a form deemed so excessively liberal as to preclude its acceptability to most legislators resulted from the single-handed decision of one man, Senate Majority Leader Earl Brydges. Instead of finishing off the issue once and for all, the attempt boomeranged since a majority of legislators were inclined to yield to public pressure or to their own consciences to the extent of voting for the new bill which, in effect, repealed all restrictions on the practice of abortions. Once the bill reached the floor of the Senate, Brydges no longer had control over the outcome. No amount of leadership influence and pressure could persuade practicing Catholic legislators to vote for the bill, nor dissuade more liberal lawmakers, many of whom had publicly fought for changes in the old law for years, from voting against the bill. When the Senate passed the repealing act by five votes, Brydges wept openly on the Senate floor. In his turn, Speaker Duryea was forced both by the Senate action and the insistence of the liberal wing of his house to let the bill come up for a vote on the floor twice in a row until the minimum number of 76 affirmative votes was obtained.

The controversy that surrounded the course of the passage of a bill liberalizing the state's divorce law in 1966 was less dramatic. Here again, two leaders of the Catholic faith, Brydges and Travia, felt compelled by the pressure created by two Democratic legislators, Senator Jerome Wilson and Assemblyman Percy Sutton, to revise the existing law. In this case, however, the leaders found it wiser to steal the thunder of Sutton and Wilson by seemingly ignoring their recommendations (resulting from long-term committee hearings) and producing their own "leaders' bill" which, in fact, was to accomplish much of what the two Democrats proposed. This carefully considered step was taken only after detailed negotiations with representatives of the archdiocese of New York had ironed out many of the problems involved.[7]

The reapportionment legislation mandated by the federal courts reflects another type of pressure that restricts leadership options. In 1964, 1965, and 1966, the legislative leaders still freely controlled the drafting and passage of redistricting bills in their own houses, but they were obligated by judicial mandate to redraw the lines on the basis of the standard of equal district populations. They were also obligated to comply with fixed deadlines. When Governor Rockefeller called the legislature into special session in 1964 to enable the lame-duck Republican-controlled legislature to redistrict under the one-man, one-vote order before the Democrats took control of both houses, the leaders had to devise certain new techniques to satisfy the needs of quite a number of legislators to get enough Republican votes to pass the proposed bills. To improve the chances of lawmakers whose districts would be eliminated by reapportionment to return to the legislature, the concept of weighted voting was introduced. Only by this device would be leaders expect to obtain the votes of the members of their own party whose districts were being eliminated. The leaders recognized that no man would place party loyalty over his own political survival.

During the 1964 session, under pressure from most of the state's media of public information and good-government groups, the legislature passed a Code of Ethics for lawmakers. The climate of anger and disgust created by newspaper revelations of abuses became insistent enough to convince the leaders of the necessity to enact some statute regulating legislative ethics. That the final result fell short of public expectations and that the overwhelming majority of lawmakers actually voted for whatever restrictions the leaders wanted to impose on their behavior may be contrued as an indication of the leaders' strength. In reality, however, this entire development demonstrates a basically different fact: It shows that the legislative leadership must and does meet at least halfway the demands of an aroused public opinion.

There are other examples substantiating the same point. The leaders were limited in their options when it came to the enactment of new judgeship bills (such as the legislation creating 125 new judiciary positions in 1968). In this matter, they had to yield to the traditional stand taken by the leaders of the general party organizations and many legislators that in each county the regular party leaders should have the right to participate in negotiations designating candidates for judgeships and in the processes that would ensure that the candidates chosen in those negotiations would actually be elected. (The use of bipartisan and tripartisan endorsements originates from this development.) In 1964, agreement was reached to create a Temporary State Commission to revise the Penal Code. Subsequently, a revised Penal Code was drafted and submitted to the legislature. Regardless of their own views, the leaders knew that no amount of leadership pressure could have induced a majority of lawmakers to vote, for example, in favor of a commission suggestion to legalize adultery, sodomy, and homosexual acts committed in private by consenting adults. The majority of lawmakers felt such a change to be either wrong or unpopular.

It is clear that in relation to this second category of controversial legislation sponsored by others than the governor and the two Majority Leaders, the latter still may exert strong influence but no unquestioned, decisive control. Many legislators independently determine their positions on such issues on ideological or religious grounds, as a result of some personal commitment or in most cases in consideration of the views and preferences prevailing among the voters in their home districts.

THE LEGISLATIVE PROGRAM OF THE GOVERNOR

The third category of legislation consists of bills that emanate from the office of the chief executive of the state. As the highest-ranking official elected on a statewide basis, the governor is mandated by the Constitution to produce the annual budget of the state. The public at large looks to him for the solution of most major problems. Accordingly, the governor submits each year a comprehensive program of bills including proposals for the solution of those problems of the day that he considers most important and urgent. While some further controversial and significant legislation is processed by the legislature, in the sponsorship of which the governor is not directly involved, the majority of important bills dealing with such problems originate with him.

211

This also means that in the face of the governor's program, the two legislative leaders give up their mantle of leadership to the extent that year after year they accept that program as the approximate guideline for the work of the legislature, while at the same time they retain their right to react to the program with whatever modifying advice they may deem necessary. However, if the leaders belong to the party of the governor, they recognize as an aspect of their office to serve as the governor's agents vis-a-vis the legislature, committed to work for the passage of the executive budget and program. Of course, there may be exceptions, and occasional rebellions against the budget or some program bill do occur. More often than not, however, such rebellions are launched not by the leaders themselves but in defiance of them by groups of dissatisfied lawmakers. Cases of public opposition by the leaders to important proposals of the governor of their own party occur relatively seldom. It is true that in his day Walter Mahoney did scuttle some Rockefeller proposals, notably the fair housing legislation of 1960. This action however, constituted an exceptional occurrence. Generally, revolts are triggered by groups of legislators who find it difficult to go along with a particular piece of legislation. If a major group of legislators shares the same feeling of opposition, they usually find themselves opposed not only by the governor but also by his leaders, as in the case of the Rockefeller budget of 1959 and of the sales tax fight of 1965. Even when Speaker Carlino decided to join a minor rebellion of suburban Republican assemblymen to force an increase in the allocations for assistance to local school districts, he did so reluctantly and only after the opposition had seriously coalesced and only because he himself felt vulnerable to voter disenchantment as a representative of a suburban community.

Despite occasional rebellions, the governors of New York have had, during the period covered by this study, a highly satisfactory batting average in terms of the passage of their proposed budgets and legislative programs. The decisive power resources available to the chief executive explain this gubernatorial success both vis-a-vis the legislature in general, and the legislative leaders in particular. The governor is the political leader of his state party as a whole. In the area of legislation, he has the veto power and, on money bills, the item veto. He controls a vast complement of patronage which enables him to use the stick-and-carrot method to retain the loyalty of party officials outside the legislature, who in turn can, on the governor's behest, bring pressure on some vacillating legislators. Patronage resources also permit him to make arrangements even with leaders of the opposition party outside the legislature to hold their legislators in line in exchange for patronage. The governor is the most visible political leader in the state, and he has daily access to the press.

Thus, he can easily mobilize public opinion through its exposure to his "campaigns" for his objectives and translate their reactions to such objectives into voting choices at the polls. Thus, the governor usually can have his way, as we have seen in connection with such measures as the tax increases of 1959 and 1965, the Medicaid program, the fallout shelter program, steeply increased aid to education, the fair housing legislation, the creation of the Urban Development Corporation, the financing schemes for capitol construction under such agencies as the State Dormitory Authority, the building at enormous expense of the Albany Mall, and the allocation of public assistance to parochial and private school children. While Governor Harriman had greater difficulties with his legislative proposals than Governor Rockefeller, it was only a difference of degree caused by the fact that he was faced with a strongly partisan Republican majority in both houses of the legislature.

In general, therefore, the leaders oppose the governor only when the proposed program is, in their judgment, totally unacceptable or when forced to do so by a strong bloc of the legislators to whom they owe their election. Additionally, they do not really have the time or the specialized expertise to scrutinize with sufficient critical sophistication the many program proposals of the governor, since their time and energies are rather fully taken up by the tasks of running their respective houses, appointing and supervising the network of committees, dealing with a multitude of local and private bills, distributing patronage, and devising the strategies and tactics of resolving unexpected controversies that periodically occur within and outside the ranks of their party.

The meaning of all this is that the two Majority Leaders of the New York legislature are relegated to a secondary and ancillary position behind the governor in the matter of initiating the substance of the official legislative program of each session. This does not diminish the great significance of their specific power and influence over the destinies of legislation. First, they are very influential in the area of recommending changes in gubernatorial proposals before the proposals are brought into the open, if they themselves are not satisfied. At the same time, the leaders systematically gauge the reactions of their membership and then determine what changes should be urged to make passage more likely. No governor ever submits his program formally and publicly without first consulting the leaders and taking their views into consideration. It is after all this is done that the point is reached where the power and influence of the Majority Leaders are fully employed in the service of their task of making sure that the ideas of the legislative program are translated into the meaningful reality of the law.

The record shows clearly that the legislative leaders take the existing distribution of roles for granted. They all recognize that in this state it is the function of the governor to propose and their function to react and then to carry into effect. No leader has ever hinted at any time at the possibility of changing the relationship. No leader in the past 15 years has ever proposed a comprehensive legislative program to rival with and supplant the total program of the chief executive. Occasionally some proposals are tentatively developed by leaders, but in the main only for public relations purposes or to show to the governor himself that alternatives are available which he ought to consider before submitting his own final program. On other occasions such leadership-developed programs are merely intended to supplant some single items in the governor's program. Such attempts occur either on the part of the party in opposition or on that of some leader who is already feuding with the governor. These small gestures of this kind do not have even symptomatic significance in the face of the established fact that in the state of New York the governor is the recognized master planner of major legislation. From the important point of view of the usefulness and popularity of legislative programs, this role of the governor's has certain built-in potential advantages. Unlike the two Majority Leaders of the legislature, the governor is elected by all the people and exposed to the aspirations of all the people—upstate, downstate, urban, and rural. This situation enables him better than any other official to react to popular demands. The result is that the governor can, and most of the time does, adapt his legislative measures to the prevailing balance of popular expectations, according to his perception of need.

THE NEW YORK LEGISLATIVE SYSTEM: AN ASSESSMENT

Probably the most meaningful basis for the assessment of the merits of the New York State legislature would be a review of those findings that throw some light upon the question of the general responsiveness to public needs of legislative activity in Albany.

To clear the deck for such a review, it seems advisable to take at least a fleeting glance at those observations of our study that seem to indicate that the legislature in its daily practice often serves interests that are not identifiable with the interests and responsive to the needs of the public at large. We have seen how eagerly the leaders serve their members' private interests and ambitions and how seriously the membership insists upon such leadership services. We have seen that in the life of the legislature, a continuous pattern of negotiation and bargaining goes on, trading votes against patronage and passing bills that often serve only private interests. We have seen the heavy impact of lobbying. We have also seen that not very long ago constituency views and demands sometimes played a subordinate role in the decision-making processes of the legislature. We have seen that occasionally the leaders stretch their powers beyond defined limits. Above all else, we have seen that the governor and the majority party leaders "dominate" the legislative process. Is it not appropriate to ask, therefore, in whose interest do these powerful politicians "dominate" the lawmaking system and, through it, the governance of one of the two largest and most important American states?

Most of the majority party leaders have come from conservative, nonurban districts. As such, in their individual capacities, they have not been paragons of social progress and partisans of major "liberal" programs, whatever the clamor of urban residents. However, as soon as such programs were presented by the governor, these conservatives generally fought for their enactment.

Admittedly, one can be easily dissatisfied with the record of some particular legislative session or with the quality of some particular enactment. On balance, however, the record of this legislature since 1954 has borne the mark of undeniable general responsiveness to many public needs and of meaningful accomplishment in the application of creative solutions to a variety of serious problems. If we compare this record with the accomplishments of most other state legislatures, the value of the legislative work in Albany becomes clear.

A generation ago, Warren Moscow of The New York Times felt convinced that ". . . one cannot examine the work of the legislature over a period of years without concluding that it has been more responsive to public needs and public opinion than most legislative bodies including Congress."[8] Recently former legislator and lobbyist, Judge Anthony Savarese, stated to this writer: "Generally speaking, New York's legislative product is very good, and probably better than all the other states with the possible exception of California."[9]

Malcom Jewell in his landmark study The State Legislature stated, "If this book has a theme, it is that the best means of making the state legislature responsible to the voters is a viable two-party system."[10] If Jewell is correct, then New York with its intensive partisanship and strong centralized party leadership in the legislature is as responsive and responsible to the public as any state in the nation.

What will the future bring? We can only guess that in the prevailing restless atmosphere, the contest between the two parties will become ever keener and sharper, with growing responsiveness to the needs and demands of the voters, who are increasingly concerned with governmental decisions and responses. This may well mean that the parties will increasingly try to outbid each other in the development of competing legislative measures aimed at appealing to the majority of voters.

It is, therefore, certain that the individual legislator will be confronted with some measure of increasing competition within his district, with greater insecurity for the prospects of the incumbent and with the growing need to respond more readily to constituency demands. This development, accompanied by improving techniques of dissemination of news regarding legislative activities, will make such activity more and more visible and of growing interest to the public, and thus public pressures will be more keenly felt by the legislators. The inevitable result will be a commensurate diminution of the leaders' influence which can be fully effective only in a vacuum into which no counterpressures can penetrate. There can be little doubt that the tasks of the legislative leaders will become more complicated and difficult.

It is true, of course, that the average lawmaker will persevere as before in the pursuit of his local and private bills, of his advancement in the legislative hierarchy or in other career opportunities, and of attainable patronage benefits. It is also true that all the related tools of power and influence are going to remain intact at the leader's disposal. He will continue to use these instrumentalities of power for the enforcement of his authority over the legislative process as before, but he will undoubtedly encounter greater resistance on the part of his increasingly constituency-influenced and publicity-conscious membership.

The probable consequence will be that the two Majority Leaders may from now on more and more depend on the support of direct intervention by the governor with reluctant or recalcitrant members of the legislative party to attain compliance with the party program (provided, of course, that they all belong to the same party). If so, the predominance of the governor over the total performance of the legislature will become even greater and more pervasive than before. It may be justified to look with grave apprehension upon such further aggrandizement of one man's already preponderant influence over decisions that may affect the lives of millions. Other opinions, though, welcome the prospect of even stronger central executive leadership, even to the detriment of the position of the leaders of the legislature. For example, Dr. William Ronan, the closest adviser of Governor Rockefeller before he became chairman of the Metropolitan Transit Authority, has this to say:

> New York's success as a vanguard state in legislative matters is due to its strong executive and legislative leadership. You need strong, responsive leadership.

216

Over the past several decades, New York has had great
leaders in both branches of government.

On the other hand, it does not make sense to have
legislative leaders challenging executive initiatives. We
have a tradition of strong executives, ever since Hughes
and Al Smith. Not only does this challenging make no
sense, I don't think it is really feasible. The legislative
program today is too much for the legislative leaders
to review, and much more so to initiate. A great deal
does originate with the legislature, but the legislature is
not capable of continuing leadership in this field. It is my
feeling that the legislature is more comfortable when it
is not making great decisions. The attitude should be to
react to initiatives and to respond to events as they
occur.[11]

Thus, the realities of the situation are these: First, the
governor of New York is, as matters stand today, the primary initiator
of legislation in the state. Second, this authority of the governor's
is anchored in the Constitution and sanctioned by unquestioning public
acceptance or acquiescence and, therefore, not likely to be exposed
to the possibility of modification in the near future. Third, the
governor of New York is, as we have already seen, the one most
powerful state official who is fully and most directly exposed to the
wants and wishes of the population as a whole and who is, by dint of
his political interests, most inclined or compelled to respond to those
wants and wishes positively and creatively. Finally, if our expectations in this respect are correct, there is the prospect of significantly
greater responsiveness of legislators and of the legislature as a whole
to the needs and demands of the public. As far as the future position
of the legislative leaders is concerned, the likelihood, therefore, is
that their importance is destined to decline in relation to the influence
of the governor and his willingness and ability to take the lead in
responding to public demands and in the face of the relatively more
independent attitudes of the membership that probably will result
from the expanded interest in political activity on the part of voters
whose concern has been dramatically increased by the turmoil of the
times.

In sum, therefore, it is this writer's belief that while the pressures for action and response to the urban and suburban problems of
the 1970s and 1980s will be enormous, the responding institutions in
New York State are sufficiently viable to respond. This judgment
takes into account the participation of the federal government through
the multibillion dollar revenue-sharing program commenced in 1972.

Failure to respond will not be the result of any particular institutional defect in the legislature or the governorship, although substantial reforms, particularly for the former, are needed. Rather, they will be the result of the lack of foresight and comprehension of the leaders New Yorkers choose as their governor and lawmakers pick as their leaders.

Change and responsiveness will certainly come more slowly than the victims of urban and suburban blight will demand, but the state's institutions are becoming increasingly visible and therefore subject to increased public pressure. This fact, when combined with the great powers inherent in the governorship and the legislature, is the cause for some measure of optimism.

REFORMING THE LEGISLATURE

The legislature has the potential for substantially ameliorating many of the ills that plague the people of New York State. Reaching potential, however, requires not only the judicious recruitment and selection of qualified people with sufficient vision, comprehension, and skills to positions of high office but also the constant reforming of governmental institutions empowered to effectuate change.

The New York legislature has accomplished some modernization in its own operation. Reduction of the number of committees in the Assembly, the increased visibility of committee activities, the incorporation of modern management techniques in the administration of both houses, and the professionalization of staff have rendered the legislature capable of keeping up with the enormously increasing need for organizing, deciphering, comprehending, and using vast amounts of technical information.

But modernization itself is not reform. Modernization means administrative improvement. Reform means a change in power. The former adds to the ability of those in power to accomplish their ends. The latter may threaten their position. The reform of one man, one vote substantially reformed the general unrepresentativeness of the legislature and shifted the balance of power in the state to the elected representatives of the suburbs. But this reform was imposed from without, and legislative leadership reaction was aimed at minimizing the "damage" to the leadership that the reform threatened.

Any set of reforms must have some clear purpose in mind. A number of constitutional changes over the past several decades have served to increase the power of the governor in legislative matters. Most people concerned with reform supported these developments, for they recognized that the governor has a statewide constituency and therefore a statewide outlook. His response is, therefore, more likely to reflect general population needs.

218

Reformer attitudes regarding the centralization of power in the majority party leaders are somewhat more ambivalent. Ideally, the efficient operation of a legislative body requires centralization of power. Congressional critics point out that the Congress' frequent inability to act is the result of the massive dispersion of power and influence among individual committee chairmen, state delegations, ideological groupings, and so on. Party leaders in Congress are without the formal powers that are of such significance for the party leaders in New York.

But the ability to get things done and to do them efficiently is only part of a normative picture. A priority consideration must be the output of the legislative process, the kinds of laws that are passed. Considerations of output must reflect the needs of different constituencies. Thus, to suggest that strong centralized leadership is desirable in a legislature is not enough for those who speak for an urban constituency or for the poor, who are unrepresented in a leadership system. The ideal may be worthy of support by academicians searching for appropriate models but not for the losers of political battles. If one's ally is in power in the New York legislature, then strong tralized leadership is highly desirable. If one's opponent is in power, then decentralized structures are preferred to, hopefully, minimize the damage that may be forthcoming.

Such a stance may be criticized as cynical, but it is the only realistic viewpoint for those actively competing for power and searching for solutions to major problems. Any serious suggestions for reform must reflect the general policy bias of those making the suggestions. Likewise, anyone evaluating reforms must comprehend underlying motives, the source of the suggestions, the perception of need on the part of the suggestor, and those constituent groups for which the prospective reformer speaks.

As a political scientist and as a lawmaker representing an urban constituency in the city with the largest urban problems in the world, it is this writer's bias that the state government has been far from responsive to such problems as poverty and its concomitant crime, drugs, economic stagnation, racial conflict, public education, public health, and the provision of a wide range of essential services. The institutions of the governorship and legislature have the inherent strength and resources to respond effectively to a number of problems, but have often lacked the will to do so. Our leaders since 1954 have perceived that their political strength was based outside urban New York and therefore gave priority consideration to the rural and suburban communities with which they identified. In this case, strong centralized leadership was an impediment to the passage of legislative programs whose impact could have substantially helped urban dwellers.

219

The following suggestions for reform of the New York legislature reflect this underlying bias. A strong governor is vital to urban interests. The legislature should maintain centralized leadership, but a leadership whose power can be implemented in a fashion supportive of continued executive initiatives but not strong enough to resist such initiatives. The leadership's power should not be so all encompassing as to be able to ignore the concentrated clamor for legislation addressed at solving the problems of urban blight. Waiting with bated breath for the occasional capture of leadership posts by those representing urban areas is not enough.

Reforms should aim at increasing dramatically the visibility of legislative activity and providing individual lawmakers the opportunities for dealing with the problems of their own constituents. Visibility and greater individual lawmaker effectiveness will be substantial pressures on legislative leaders to respond to larger needs.

Thus, the reforms suggested have three general aims: to increase the ability of the legislature to deal with executive initiatives without reducing gubernatorial power in this area, to increase the visibility of the lawmaking process thus subjecting the powers-that-be to maximum public scrutiny, and to increase the individual lawmaker's ability to effectively perform his representative function.[12]

Permit Legislature to Compete with the Executive

1. Full-time legislature is necessary since problems do not stop in June or July of each calendar year. The legislature should meet full time, possibly on a two- or three-day-a-week schedule, to be available to respond to problems as they occur.

2. There should be a division of session into functional segments because whether full or part time, the legislative session should be divided rationally to permit the legislature to deal with its varied functions: an opening period for introduction of bills and consideration of executive appointments, a period for evaluation and action on the executive budget, a period of committee consideration of legislation, a period for final action on bills (this latter sequence of committee action and final floor action could be continually rotated throughout the session).

3. There should be a legislative call for a special session. Currently, only the governor can call a special session and set its agenda. This power should be shared with the Assembly Speaker and Senate Majority Leader although it would be obviated by a full-time legislature.

4. Create a legislative office in Washington, D.C. A permanent staff in the nation's capital would provide the legislature with invaluable

information on the federal government's intentions for the states — grants, regulations, and so on, which so dramatically affect state action.

5. Create an office to review the operation of the executive branch, or expand the existing Legislative Commission on Expenditure Review to play a meaningful role in overseeing the operation of executive agencies, both in terms of how they spend their money and in terms of how they implement the law.

6. Eliminate the joint legislative committees, which operate between sessions to research legislative problems. Their functions should be granted to permanent, full-time standing committees so that the standing committees can develop maximum expertise in specified areas.

7. Extend the life of standing committees in the Assembly where they go out of business weeks before the end of the session and are replaced by the Rules Committee.

8. Permit legislature to waive the three-day aging of bills rule by a two-thirds vote of each house rather than have to wait for governor to sign message of necessity. The determination of the need to waive the rule should be a legislative decision.

Increase Visibility of the Legislature

9. Permit televising and radio transmission of debates and hearings to increase public awareness of legislative activities. Visibility directly affects legislative decisions.

10. Require open committee meetings to permit press and public to view proceedings. In certain circumstances a majority vote of the committee membership would permit executive or closed committee sessions.

11. Publish a journal of all legislative activities on the order of the congressional record, including floor action, committee deliberations, all activities.

12. Provide immediate roll call tallies to any interested party as soon as they can be xeroxed. Thus, press, members, lobbyists, and public can have the vote on any bill immediately available.

13. Require many more public hearings on legislative issues as well as time-saving joint hearings by Assembly and Senate committees sharing jurisdiction on legislation.

14. Create permanent judicial commission on reapportionment with appropriate staff to draw new lines when required after a census or by court order, thus eliminating the self-serving system of legislators drawing their own district lines.

Maximize Individual Lawmaker Effectiveness

15. Increase legislative salaries so that full-time service can be expected and a full-time legislature created.

16. Provide adequate staff to members because professionalization and expansion of staff have helped the leadership elite. Individual members get very little staff assistance and that for the session only, in many cases.

17. Establish home district offices so that members can meet with and service their constituents. This means home district staff as well.

18. Provide four-year term so that turnover is not as great and so that members can concentrate on legislative tasks rather than reelection.

19. Create local community ombudsmen to relieve legislators of the tasks of solving nonlegislative constituent problems; at the very least provide legislator with sufficient staff in home district to perform this time-consuming function.

Miscellaneous

20. Restore electronic voting machines and require that a vote on a bill be cast within a short time period to dramatically increase the speed and efficiency of roll calls and reduce the ability of the majority party leaders to manipulate the vote.

21. Publish uniform rules and specify backup rules (such as Roberts Rules of Order) to cover gaps in each house's rules.

Since the governor and the legislature of New York State are granted a wide range of substantial powers and operate in a framework of public expectation that supports the positive search for solutions, these institutions have sufficient strength and viability to attack many of our social ills. Modernization and reform can enhance their performance and provide them with the tools to address these many problems. Nevertheless, the particular skills, attitudes, ideologies, ambitions, and integrity of the men and women elected to legislative and executive office are the key variables in the determination as to whether these institutions will, in fact, be responsive to public need. In a democracy, public officials do respond to public pressure when it is loud and clear. Their future ambitions depend on their responsiveness. To a large extent, the failure of institutions of government is often the result of the failure of leaders to perceive the public mood and to anticipate solutions. All too often, political leaders wait, sometimes too long, for public opinion to coalesce before acting.

By the time a response is forthcoming, a problem has become a crisis. Good intentions are not enough. The willingness to gamble, to study potential problems and suggest dramatic and far-reaching changes to problems before they get out of hand before public frustration is maximized is the key to successful leadership. The problem lies in the recruitment process because it boils down to voters electing people who have the personal attributes required to anticipate problems in this way and the talent to make the gamble work. That's a tough job for a voter, but his failure to make the successful effort, his willingness to accept old patterns of choosing candidates and to accept mediocre people in important positions are going to cost him a great deal.

Reforming institutions are essential in preparing the tools of government to perform effectively. But the tools are only as effective as the people who use them.

NOTES

1. Former assemblyman William Clancy, interview, January 20, 1970.

2. Former Senate Majority Leader Walter Mahoney, interview, December 18, 1969.

3. Former Speaker Anthony Travia, interview, December 23, 1969.

4. Former Speaker Joseph Carlino, interview, January 12, 1970.

5. William Keefe and Morris Ogul, The American Legislative Process (Englewood Cliffs, N.J.: Prentice-Hall, Inc., 1968), p. 270.

6. State University of New York, State Education Department, Bureau of Secondary Curriculum Development, New York State and Local Government (Albany: State University of New York, 1959), p. 129.

7. Richard Reeves, "The Other Half of State Government—Travia," The New York Times Magazine, April 2, 1967, p. 85.

8. Warren Moscow, Politics in the Empire State (New York: Alfred A. Knopf, Inc., 1948), p. 184.

9. Judge Anthony Savarese, former assemblyman and former legislative representative for the city of New York, interview, February 18, 1970.

10. Malcolm Jewell, The State Legislature (New York: Random House, 1962), p. 6.

11. Dr. William Ronan, former secretary to Governor Nelson Rockefeller, interview, March 27, 1970.

12. For a good discussion of legislative reform, see Keefe and Ogul, op. cit., pp 480-499, and Citizens Conference on State Legislatures, The Sometime Governments (New York: Bantam Books, 1971).

BIBLIOGRAPHY

BOOKS AND DOCUMENTS

Advisory Commission on Intergovernmental Relations. Apportionment of State Legislatures. Washington, D.C.: U.S. Government Printing Office, 1962.

Baker, Gordon. The Reapportionment Revolution. New York: Random House, 1966.

_____. Rural Versus Urban Political Power. New York: Random House, 1955.

Barber, James D. The Lawmakers: Recruitment and Adaptation to Legislative Life. New Haven, Conn.: Yale University Press, 1965.

Beck, Joseph A. The California Legislature. Sacramento, Calif.: State Printing Office, 1957.

Bentley, Arthur. The Process of Government. rev. ed. Bloomington, Ind.: Principia Press, 1949.

Blair, George S. American Legislatures: Structure and Process. New York: Harper and Row, 1967.

Boyd, William J. D. Patterns of Apportionment. New York: National Municipal League, 1962.

Breckenridge, A. C. One House for Two: Nebraska's Unicameral Legislature. Washington D.C.: Public Affairs Press, 1957.

Buchanan, William. Legislative Partisanship: The Deviant Case of California. Berkeley and Los Angeles: University of California Press, 1963.

Caldwell, Lynton. The Government and Administration of New York. New York: Thomas Y. Crowell Company, 1954.

Clerk's Manual. Albany: The New York Legislature, annual, 1954-69.

224

Colvin, David L. The Bicameral Principle in the New York Legislature. Privately printed, 1913.

Council of State Governments. American Legislatures: Structures and Procedures. Chicago: Council of State Governments, 1959.

_____. Legal Services for State Legislatures. Chicago: Council of State Governments, 1960.

_____. The Offices of Legislative Clerks and Secretaries in the States. Chicago: Council of State Governments, 1957.

David, Paul T., and Ralph Eisenberg. Devaluation of the Urban and Suburban Vote. Bureau of Public Administration. Charlottesville: University of Virginia Press, 1961.

DeGrazia, Alfred. Apportionment and Representative Government. New York: Praeger Publishers, 1963.

Diamond, Sigmund, ed. Modernizing State Government: The New York Constitutional Convention of 1967. (Academy of Political Science.) New York: Columbia University Press, 1967.

Editor and Publisher Yearbook, 1962, 1963.

Ellis, David M., James Frost, Harold Syrett, and Harry A. Carmen. A Short History of New York State. Ithaca, N.Y.: Cornell University Press, 1957.

Fesler, James. The 50 States and Their Local Governments. New York: Alfred A. Knopf, Inc., 1967.

Fordham, Jefferson. The State Legislative Institution. Philadelphia: University of Pennsylvania Press, 1959.

Harriman, Governor Averell. "Public Papers." Albany, 1955-58.

Hartman, Myron, ed. The New York Red Book. Albany, N.Y.: Williams Press, annual, 1954-69.

Heard, Alexander, ed. State Legislatures in American Politics. (American Assembly.) Englewood Cliffs, N.J.: Prentice-Hall, 1966.

Herzberg, Donald G., and Paul Tillett. A Budget for New York State, 1956-57. (Inter-University Case Program, no. 69.) University: University of Alabama Press, 1962.

Jacob, Herbert. Justice in America. Boston: Little, Brown and Company, 1965.

Jacob, Herbert and Kenneth Vines. Politics in the American States. Boston: Little, Brown and Company, 1965.

Jewell, Malcolm, ed. The Politics of Reapportionment. New York: Atherton Press, 1962.

_____. The State Legislature: Politics and Practice. New York: Random House, 1962.

Jewell, Malcolm, and Samuel C. Patterson. The Legislative Process in the United States. 2nd ed. New York: Random House, 1973.

Keefe, William J., and Morris S. Ogul. The American Legislative Process. Englewood Cliffs, N.J.: Prentice-Hall, 1968.

Key, V. O. American State Politics. New York: Alfred A. Knopf, Inc., 1957.

_____. Politics, Parties and Pressure Groups. New York: Thomas Y. Crowell Company, 1964.

_____. Southern Politics in State and Nation. New York: Alfred A. Knopf, Inc., 1949.

Lipson, Leslie. The American Governor from Figurehead to Leader. Chicago: University of Chicago Press, 1939.

Littlewood, Thomas. Bipartisan Coalition in Illinois. New York: McGraw-Hill, 1960.

Lockard, Duane. New England State Politics. Princeton, N.J.: Princeton University Press, 1959.

Manual for the Use of the Legislature. (secretary of state.) Albany: New York Legislature, annual.

McKay, Robert. Reapportionment and the Federal Analogy. New York: National Municipal League, 1962.

Moscow, Warren. Politics in the Empire State. New York: Alfred A. Knopf, Inc., 1948.

Munger, Frank. American State Politics: Readings for Comparative Analysis. New York: Thomas Y. Crowell Company, 1966.

National Legislative Conference. American State Legislature in Mid-Twentieth Century. Chicago: The National Legislative Conference, 1960.

Ransone, Coleman B., Jr. The Office of Governor in the United States. University: University of Alabama Press, 1956.

Redford, Emmett, David Truman, Alan Westin, and Robert Wood. Politics and Government in the United States. New York: Harcourt, Brace and World, 1968.

Roberts, Albert. "Concepts of Legislative Fiscal Analysis and Review." Report of the New York Assembly Committee on Ways and Means, 1969.

Rockefeller, Governor Nelson. "Public Papers," annual, 1958-69.

Schlesinger, Joseph A. How They Became Governor. East Lansing: Michigan State University Press, 1957.

Siffin, William J. The Legislative Council in the American States. Bloomington, Ind.: Indiana University Press, 1959.

Sorauf, Frank. Party and Representation. New York: Atherton Press, Inc., 1963.

Steiner, Gilbert Y., and Samuel K. Gove. Legislative Politics in Illinois. Urbana: University of Illinois Press, 1960.

Straetz, Ralph A., and Frank J. Munger. New York Politics. New York: New York University Press, 1960.

Truman, David. The Governmental Process. New York: Alfred A. Knopf, Inc., 1951.

Wahlke, John C., and Hans Eulau. Legislative Behavior. Glencoe, Ill.: Free Press, 1959.

Wahlke, John C., Hans Eulau, William Buchanan, and Leroy C. Ferguson. The Legislative System: Explorations in Legislative Behavior. New York: John Wiley and Sons, Inc., 1962.

Walker, Harvey. The Legislative Process. New York: Ronald Press, 1948.

Wildavsky, Aaron, and Nelson Polsby, eds. American Governmental Institutions. Chicago: Rand McNally and Co., 1968.

Witt, Stuart K. "The Legislative-Local Party Linkage in New York State." Unpublished Ph.D. dissertation, Syracuse University, 1967.

_____. "Reorganization of a State Legislative Committee System." Report to the New York Assembly, August 1969.

Zeller, Belle, ed. American State Legislatures. Report of the Committee on American Legislatures of the American Political Science Association. New York: Thomas Y. Crowell Company, 1954.

_____. Pressure Politics in New York. Englewood Cliffs, N.J.: Prentice-Hall, Inc., 1937.

PERIODICALS AND JOURNALS

Ahlberg, Clark, and Daniel Moynihan. "Changing Governors and Policies." Public Administration Review 20 (Autumn 1960): 195-204.

Albany Knickerbocker News, 1963-69.

Albany Times Union, 1964-69.

"Alimony for Men? NY Bill." Newsweek 71 (January 8, 1968): 58.

"Antistrike Law Upheld But. . . ." U.S. News and World Report 63 (December 25, 1967): 67.

"As New York Goes." Business Week (April 3, 1954): 122-123.

Bendiner, Robert, "Provincial Politics of the Empire State." Reporter 22 (May 12, 1960): 21-23.

Bickel, A. M. "Case of New York: Apportionment." New Republic 151 (December 26, 1964): 11.

"Bicker over Liquor." Newsweek 60 (December 10, 1962): 60.

"Bonus for Rocky." Time 79 (March 2, 1962): 21.

Buffalo Courier Express, 1964.

"Business as Usual (Reapportionment: Nothing New)." Newsweek 65 (April 26, 1973): 30 ff.

"Can New State Law End Public Worker Strikes?" Business Week (April 8, 1967): 98.

"Choking Off Community Schools." New Republic 161 (July 19, 1969): 16-18.

"Coming of Age (Mahoney): National Review 15 (July 16, 1963): 10.

"Crimes for the Times: N.Y. Penal Code Revised." Time 83 (March 27, 1964): 36.

"Cutting the Bonds of Acrimony (Divorce)." Life 60 (February 11, 1966): 4.

"DeSapio Gives Ave a Beating." Life 45 (September 8, 1958): 30-31.

Desmond, James. "Rockefeller's Fast Start." Nation 188 (April 25, 1959): 359-360.

Dunkirk Observor, August 1963.

"Effects of the Election: Issues That Matter." New Republic 131 (November 15, 1954): 10-11.

Egan, Leo. "Can Rocky Save GOP?" Reporter 19 (October 30, 1958): 9-11.

_____. "Governor and Mayor in Collision." The New York Times Magazine (May 20, 1962): 34.

_____. "Harriman Becomes the Governor." The New York Times Magazine (July 3, 1955): 12-13.

Elfin, Michael, "Rites of Spring in Albany." Reporter 24 (April 27, 1961): 28-29.

"End of the Line for Governor Dewey." New Republic 129 (November 30, 1953): 4.

"Enforcing One Injunction at Least—UFT." Time 90 (October 13, 1967): 58.

"From Behind Bars." Newsweek 42 (October 19, 1953): 39.

"Governor and Booze." Life 56 (April 10, 1964): 2.

"Great Society: Rocky Style." U.S. News and World Report 58 (January 18, 1965): 20.

Greenfield, Meg. "A + B + C + D = NY^2, New York Reapportionment." Reporter 33 (December 2, 1965): 32-35.

Hacker, Andrew. "Message on the State of the State." The New York Times Magazine (July 22, 1962): 15. See reply by Senator Walter J. Mahoney, The New York Times Magazine (August 19, 1962): 6ff.

"Headless in Albany: Split in Democratic Ranks." Newsweek 65 (January 25, 1965): 26.

Hechinger, Fred. "Teenage Problem: Drinking Age." The New York Times Magazine (September 30, 1962): 15ff.

"Honest Ave Should Have Laid Off Waterfront." Saturday Evening Post 228 (March 17, 1956): 10.

"Hospital Insurance for All: A New Plan." U.S. News and World Report 58 (April 26, 1965): 89-90.

"How to Run Things from Jail." U.S. News and World Report 35 (October 30, 1953): 46-48.

"Keeper of the Keys: Influencing New York Senators." Newsweek 63 (March 2, 1964): 21-22.

"Long Night in Manhattan." Time 64 (November 15, 1954): 32.

"Look No Hands: Dems New Order." Newsweek 65 (January 4, 1965): 14.

"Lulu of a Fight." Time 85 (January 29, 1965): 21-22.

Mazo, Earl. "Give 'em Hell Harriman." New Republic 134 (May 28, 1956): 7.

Moscow, Warren. "End of a GOP Era: Has Dewey Had Enough?" Nation 179 (July 26, 1954): 89-92.

Mosher, Frederick. "The Executive Budget, Empire State Style." Public Administration Review XII, no. 2 (1952): 79-80.

"Move to Ban Busing." U.S. News and World Report 66 (April 7, 1969): 12.

Moynihan, Daniel, and James Q. Wilson. "Patronage in New York State, 1955-59." American Political Science Review LVIII, no. 2 (June 1964): 296.

"Mr. Rockefeller's Program." Commonweal 69 (February 20, 1959): 534.

Newburgh News, August 1963.

Newsday, 1958-69.

The New York Herald Tribune, 1961-63.

The New York Post, 1969.

"New York Reforms Divorce Law." Time 87 (May 6, 1966): 75.

The New York Times, 1954-69.

"New York Tries to Kick the Habit (Narcotics)." Ebony 24 (September 1969): 29-32ff.

"Official Ethics." Business Week (April 24, 1954): 32.

Otten, Alan, and Charles Seib. "Rocky's Triple Threat Brain Trust." Harpers 227 (July 1963): 74-79.

Poughkeepsie Journal, August 1963.

"Protest to Budget Cuts." New Yorker 45 (April 26, 1969): 35-37.

Reeves, Richard. "The Other Half of State Government—Travia."
The New York Times Magazine (April 2, 1967): 24-25ff.

"Reporter at Large: PPR Bill." New Yorker 32 (May 5, 1956):
118ff.

"Revolt Squashed Wicks Resignation." Time 64 (November 1, 1954):
17.

"Rivals Revenge." Time 75 (April 11, 1960): 29.

"Rockefeller's First Test." New Republic 140 (April 13, 1959): 5-6.

"Rockefeller Lays Out His Program." Business Week (January 10,
1959): 3.

"Rockefeller Taxes." New Republic 140 (February 16, 1959): 5.

"Rocky Crisis (Finance)." Time 92 (December 20, 1968): 20.

"Rocky's Future—Liquor Scandals." U.S. News and World Report
54 (April 29, 1963): 20.

"Rush to Juarez." Time 90 (September 1, 1967): 64.

"Sadness in Juarez." Newsweek 70 (September 4, 1967): 31-32.

"Scandal's Rocky Road." Newsweek 61 (January 21, 1963): 31-32.

Schenectady Gazette, November 1963.

"Shared Time (Schools)." America 117 (August 5, 1967): 127.

"Someone Will Pick Up the Pieces." Time 85, (January 8, 1965): 17.

"Speaker Stumbles." Time 79 (February 16, 1962): 22-23.

"Strike Against the Law." America 107 (December 15, 1962): 1241.

"Substitute for Condon-Wadlin." America 116 (April 15, 1967): 547-
548.

Tyler, Gus, and David Wells. "Camel Bites Dachsund." New Republic
145 (November 27, 1961): 9-10.

Utica Daily Press, August 1963.

Utica Observor Dispatch, August 1963.

"Victory's Losers—Leadership Fight." Newsweek 65 (February 15, 1965): 23.

"Wagner-Rocky Feud Highlights Scandals." Architectural Forum 114 (March 1961): 7.

Walker, Jack L. "The Diffusion of Innovations Among the American States." American Political Science Review LXIII (September 1969): 880ff.

Weaver, Warren. "Political Evolution of Rocky." The New York Times Magazine (February 16, 1964): 11ff.

"What a Union Can Do When It Uses Its Power (Condon-Wadlin)." U.S. News and World Report 60 (January 17, 1966): 84-86.

"Whiskey and Water." Newsweek 63 (April 27, 1964): 29-30.

Wilson, Jerome. "City Schools and Albany Politics." Nation 207 (December 16, 1968): 648-650.

_____. "The Rockefeller Decade." Nation 206 (February 19, 1968): 235.

Zion, Sidney. "Rocky the Cop." Ramparts 6 (June 16, 1968): 22-25.

INTERVIEWS

Abrams, Albert J., secretary, New York Senate.

Berman, Samuel I., former assemblyman (Democrat of Brooklyn).

Bingham, Congressman Jonathan, former secretary to Governor Harriman.

Bisceglia, Philip J., counsel to the Speaker of the Assembly.

Blumenthal, Assemblyman Albert (Democrat of Manhattan).

Breitel, Chief Judge Charles, of the New York Court of Appeals.

Brown, Richard, former legislative representative for the city of New York, former counsel to the Speaker of the Assembly and associate counsel to the Assembly Minority Leader.

Burns, John, former chairman of the New York Democratic State Committee.

Carlino, Joseph, former Speaker of the Assembly (Republican of Nassau.)

Clancy, William, former assemblyman (Democrat of Queens).

Cohen, Joel, former associate counsel to the Senate Minority Leader, former associate counsel to the Speaker.

Condello, Victor, general counsel, New York State Association of Railroads, former legislative representative for the city of New York.

Crangle, Joseph, New York Democratic state chairman and Erie County Democratic chairman.

Dominick, former senator D. Clinton (Republican of Rockland County).

Fleck, Dr. Andrew, first deputy commissioner, New York State Health Department.

Gold, Senator Emanuel (Democrat of Queens), former counsel to the Majority Leader of the Assembly.

Gutman, Daniel, former counsel to Governor Harriman.

Harriman, former governor Averell.

Henderson, Assemblyman Charles (Republican of Steuben County).

Kingston, Assemblyman John (Republican of Nassau County), Assembly Majority Leader.

Kisburg, Nicholas, legislative director for Teamsters Joint Council 16.

LaVerne, Senator Thomas (Republican of Rochester).

Lefkowitz, Attorney General Louis.

Lithgow, William, budget analyst for the Assembly Ways and Means Committee.

Mahoney, Supreme Court Justice Walter, former Senate Majority Leader.

Marchi, Senator John (Republican of Staten Island).

Marsh, Alice, legislative representative of the United Federation of Teachers.

Martin, June, director of Assembly Central Staff.

McLaughlin, Edward J., former director, New York State Division of Veterans Affairs.

McNamara, James, former assemblyman (Republican of Manhattan).

Paley, Henry, former director of information for Speaker Carlino.

Paterson, former senator Basil (Democrat of Manhattan), vice-chairman, Democratic National Committee.

Rockefeller, former governor Nelson.

Roman, Samuel, former assemblyman (Republican of Manhattan).

Ronan, Dr. William, former secretary to Governor Rockefeller.

Roth, Richard, director of information for the New York Senate.

Ruggieri, Bernard, counsel to the Senate Minority Leader, former legislative representative for the city of New York, former associate counsel to Governor Harriman.

Savarese, Judge Anthony, former assemblyman (Republican of Queens County), former legislative representative for the city of New York.

Shamulka, William, counsel to Senator Warren Anderson, chairman of the Senate Finance Committee.

Steingut, Assemblyman Stanley, Assembly Minority Leader (Democrat of Brooklyn).

Stewart, Milton, former executive assistant to Governor Harriman.

Thaler, former senator Seymour (Democrat of Queens County).

Travia, Federal District Court Judge Anthony, former Speaker of the Assembly.

Wagner, Robert F., former mayor of the city of New York.

Welsh, Mark, former associate counsel to Senate Majority Leader Earl Brydges, former counsel to Senate Majority Leader Walter Mahoney.

Wilson, Governor Malcolm.

Young, former Court of Claims judge Fred A., former Republican state chairman.

Zimmerman, Donald, special counsel to the Senate Majority Leader.

Ethics, Code of, 210
Eulau, Heinz, 26-27
Expenditure Review, Legislative
    Commission on, 221

Federal District Court of New
    York, 141, 142, 144, 148,
    149
Federation of Jewish Philan-
    thropies, 88-89
Ferguson, LeRoy, 26-27
Fifth Avenue Bus Line, 67
Fink, Stanley, 55
Finletter, Thomas K., 88
Finley, Lee P., 118
Fisher, Harold, 15
Fleck, Dr. Andrew, 191-92
Florida, 12, 142
Flynn, John, 32
Folsom, Marion B., 118
Fordham Law School, 144
Fourteenth Amendment, 141, 142
Frankfurter, Justice Felix, 141
Froessel, Charles, 151

Gerry, Elbridge, 139
gerrymandering, 139-40, 143,
    148, 149, 150, 152, 173
Gittleson, Harry, 110, 111, 112
Glinski, Frank, 150
Goldberg, Arthur, 165
Goldwater, Barry, 37, 107, 108,
    113, 145, 173
Goodell, Charles, 165
Governing New York City, 132
Governmental Process, The, 181
governor, 81-125, 206; case
    studies, New York situations,
    95-122; constitutional powers
    in New York, 85-87, 91-92,
    122, 217; legislative pro-
    grams developed by, 88-90,
    102-24, 204, 211, 214, 217;
    patronage dispenser, 83-84,
    122, 167, 193-94, 212; as

policy maker, 82, 85, 122,
    123-24, 217; predominance
    of, 84-85, 212, 216, 217;
    and responsibility for budget,
    90-102, 122, 196, 204, 211;
    special sessions called by,
    83, 85-86; as target for lob-
    bying, 196; veto power of,
    82-84, 86, 91, 92, 212
Gray, Jesse, 46
Greenberg, Samuel, 100
Gunning, Rosemary, 52
Gutman, Daniel, 88, 103

Halpern, Seymour, 152-53
Harriman, Governor Averell,
    33, 36, 66, 71, 72, 88, 89,
    93, 95-97, 102-04, 106, 123,
    176, 192, 193, 194, 197, 213
Hausbeck, Albert, 19, 28
Heald Commission, 96-97
Health, Education and Welfare,
    U.S. Department of, 120
Health and Hospital Council, 191
Health Department, (N.Y.)
    State, 116, 117, 118, 191-92,
    193; Community Health Ser-
    vices, 191
Heck, Oswald, 11, 42-45, 51,
    52, 59, 66, 70, 71, 72, 75,
    95, 96, 97, 98, 99, 103-04,
    106, 107, 109, 196, 207
Henderson, Charles, 28, 43
Hofstadter, Judge, 134
Hospital Corporation Bill, 198
Housing Finance Agency, (N.Y.)
    State, 124
Hughes, Charles Evans, 217
Hughes, John, 36, 37, 38, 148,
    177
Hurd, ----, 90

Illinois, 172
Ingalls, George, 52, 160, 176
Ingraham, Hollis, 192

239

governors, 85-122, 124-25, 204, 212-13; lobbying in, 182-92; modernization in, 218; partisan competition in, 159-63; and party organizations, 163-79, 205; power relationships, internal, 65-76, 204; professional staff services in, 57-60, 61, 222; and reapportionment controversy, 137-53; reform program for, 218-23; rules of, 6-9, 13, 18, 21, 23, 55, 60; Rules Committees, 21-22, 23, 70, 73, 74, 75, 203; Senate leadership, 32-42; standing committees, 12-17, 21, 70, 73, 221; statutory committees, 18; voting methods in, 9, 222

Lehman, Herbert, 140, 173
Lent, Norman, 118, 190-91, 198
Lent Committee, 118-20, 190-91
Lentol, Edward, 37, 106
Levitt, Comptroller Arthur, 100, 101, 173
Levy, Justice Mathew, 148
Lewis, Albert, 106
Lieutenant governor, 7, 8
Lifset, Harvey, 14, 15, 71
Lindsay, Mayor John V., 50, 51, 106, 152, 197, 198-99
Lithgow, William, 59
lobbying, 181-82, 199-200; judicial, 133-35, 153-54, 205; by local governments, 195-99, 205; by New York City, 196-99; in New York State Legislature, 182-99, 205; by private interests, 182-90, 205; by state administrative agencies, 190-95, 205; techniques of, 184-90, 191-94
Lodge, Henry Cabot, 108
LoPresto, John, 55
Lowden, Frank O., 82
Lulus, 20, 74

McCoy, Rhody, 39, 186-87
McEwen, Robert, 144
McGinnies, Speaker, 45
McKay, Robert, 150
McKay Commission, 150-51
Mackell, Thomas, 175
MacKenzie, William, 97, 196, 197
McKeon, William, 144, 145, 166, 167, 176
McLaughlin, Edward J., 193-94
McNamara, Robert S., 48
Mahoney, Francis, 69
Mahoney, Walter, 16, 29, 32-37, 38-39, 40, 41, 51, 52, 58, 66-67, 69, 75, 95, 96, 97, 103-04, 105, 106, 107, 108-12, 123, 135, 141, 142, 143, 144, 145, 146, 173, 196, 207, 212
Maine, 182
Majority Leader, Assembly, 7, 8, 20, 23, 74, 163
Majority Leader, Senate, 7-8, 9-10, 12, 13, 18, 19, 20, 21, 23, 60, 73, 74, 95, 159-60, 163, 172, 203, 206, 216, 220; controversial bills, uncertain control over randomly initiated, 208-11, private bills, life-and-death power over, 207-08; second to governor in initiating legislation, 213
Mansfield, Professor Harvey, 138-39, 151-52
Marchi, John, 29, 143, 152, 188, 198
Mardin, Orison, 151
Marsh, Alice, 188
Martin, Mrs. June, 59, 60
Maryland, 142
Mason, Edwyn, 54-55, 98
Massachusetts, 158
Mayors, State Conference of, 195

Medicaid, 40-41, 51-52, 53, 61, 114-22, 124, 191, 213

Medicare Law. See National Health Act

Mental Hygiene, (N.Y. State) Department of, 193

Metcalf-Baker law, 43, 109, 112, 175

Metropolitan Transit Authority, 216

Michigan, 182

Minnesota, 158

Minority Leader, Assembly, 20, 22-23, 74, 159-60, 163

Minority Leader, Senate, 8, 20, 22-23, 74, 159-60, 163

Montana, 182, 183

Morgenthau, Henry, Jr., 147

Morhouse, L. Judson, 103, 106

Moscow, Warren, 87-88, 164, 170, 195-96, 215

Mosher, Professor Frederick, 93-94

Motley, Constance Baker, 175

Moynihan, Daniel, 192-93

Mulligan, Dean William H., 144

Mulligan Committee, 144, 145, 146

Nadel, Bernard, 110-11

Nation, The, 107, 124

National Association for the Advancement of Colored People (NAACP), 186

National Guard, New York State, 43, 45

National Health Act, 114

Nebraska, 12

Nevada, 158

New Hampshire, 9

New Jersey, 26

New Mexico, 12

New York, City University of, 46, 55

New York Post, 15, 136

New York Telephone Company, 66

New York Times, The, 10, 15, 32, 50, 99, 109, 110, 135, 136, 139, 177, 215

New York University School of Public Administration, 89

New Yorker, 185

Newsday, 109

Nickerson, Eugene, 101, 165

Nixon, Richard M., 109

North Carolina, 82

Northwestern University, 132

O'Connell, Daniel, 71, 167, 174

Ogul, Morris, 4, 82, 207

Ohio, 26

Ohrenstein, Manfred, 14, 40, 68, 106

ombudsmen, 222

Paley, Henry (Hank), 46, 47, 48, 107, 108

parties, New York political, 163-79; Democratic leadership fight (1965), 171-78; leadership, acceptance of, 171, 179; local allegiance of legislators, 168-70, 179; State Chairmen, 164, 165-68, 178-79; State Committees, 164-68, 178, 205

party conferences, 162-63, 172

party leaders, elected, 3

Paterson, Basil, 39, 165, 186, 187

patronage, 83-84, 122, 167, 192-94

Penal Code, Temporary State Commission to Revise, 211

Pennsylvania, 21

PM, 45

Policemen's Benevolent Association, 198

power relationships, internal

242

243

ALAN G. HEVESI is an Assistant Professor of Political Science at Queens College, City University of New York. Additionally, he is a member of the New York State Assembly, having been elected for the first time in 1971. From 1963 to 1971, he served in a number of staff positions in the New York State Senate and has, therefore, been an active participant in and student of the New York State legislature since 1963.

Dr. Hevesi received his B.A. from Queens College and his Ph.D. in Political Science from Columbia University. He is the co-editor of The Politics of Urban Education (Praeger, 1969) and the author of several articles on legislative politics.

EDUCATIONAL POLICY-MAKING AND THE
STATE LEGISLATURE: The New York Experience
Mike M. Milstein and
Robert E. Jennings

POLITICAL CLUBS IN NEW YORK
Blanche Davis Blank and
Norman M. Adler

REVENUE SHARING: Legal and Policy Analysis
Otto G. Stoltz

STATE LEGISLATIVE INNOVATION: Case
Studies of Washington, Ohio, Florida, Illinois,
Wisconsin and California
edited by James A.
Robinson

STATE LEGISLATURES: An Evaluation of Their
Effectiveness
The Citizens Conference
on State Legislatures

SUPERCITY/HOMETOWN, U. S. A.: Prospects
for Two-Tier Government
League of Women
Voters Education Fund